BACK TO THE STUDIO

Other books by Peter Meares

Legends of Australian Sport (2003)
Wallaby Legends (2005)
Treading Water – The life story of Tracey Wickham (2009)

BACK TO THE STUDIO

The inside stories from Australia's best-known sports commentators

Peter Meares

FOREWORD BY PETER FITZSIMONS

ABC Books

The ABC 'Wave' device is a trademark of the Australian Broadcasting Corporation and is used under licence by HarperCollins*Publishers* Australia.

First published as *All Piss and Wind* in 2008
by ABC Books for the Australian Broadcasting Corporation.
This updated and retitled edition published 2011
by HarperCollins*Publishers* Australia Pty Limited
ABN 36 009 913 517
harpercollins.com.au

Copyright © Peter Meares 2008, 2011

The right of Peter Meares to be identified as the author of this work has been asserted by him in accordance with the *Copyright Amendment (Moral Rights) Act 2000*.

This work is copyright. Apart from any use as permitted under the *Copyright Act 1968*, no part may be reproduced, copied, scanned, stored in a retrieval system, recorded, or transmitted, in any form or by any means, without the prior written permission of the publisher.

HarperCollins*Publishers*
Level 13, 201 Elizabeth Street, Sydney NSW 2000, Australia
31 View Road, Glenfield, Auckland 0627, New Zealand
A 53, Sector 57, Noida, UP, India
77–85 Fulham Palace Road, London W6 8JB, United Kingdom
2 Bloor Street East, 20th floor, Toronto, Ontario M4W 1A8, Canada
10 East 53rd Street, New York NY 10022, USA

National Library of Australia Cataloguing-in-Publication entry

Meares, Peter
  Back to the studio : the inside stories from Australia's best-known sports commentators / Peter Meares.
  2nd ed.
  ISBN: 978 0 7333 3023 0 (pbk.)
  Includes index.
  Sportscasters–Australia.
  Sports journalism–Australia.
070.4497960994

Cover design by: Priscilla Nielsen
Cover illustration by: Boo Bailey
Typeset in Bembo 11/16pt

*To Bill and Barbara Brown who showed me
that you're never too old to laugh*

Agnew: 'Well, what high drama we have here, Kerry. What will he do?

O'Keeffe: 'He'll go for it.'

Agnew: 'But he could come back tomorrow and wait for a loose one down the leg side ...'

O'Keeffe: 'Stuff tomorrow, Aggers. Tomorrow is for silver medallists. We're Australians. *Poms* come back tomorrow. Australians only want the gold and we want it now. He'll go for it.'

Two seconds later, Dawson dances in again, flights his spinning orb towards Waugh ... pitching just outside the off-stump ... while the crowd hangs in suspended animation ... as it lands and snarls up ... as Waugh moves ... onto his back foot ... and CRACKS it ... straightintothefence!

Loved it. Love O'Keeffe. Quite like Agnew. Love this book!

Peter FitzSimons

PREFACE

My first sports commentary on ABC Radio in Queensland was of a Rugby League match in Toowoomba in 1971. It was a game between Toowoomba and Ipswich in the Bulimba Cup, a triangular tournament that also included Brisbane, and I was terrified.

The problem was that I had just come up to Brisbane to join the Sports Department from Sydney, via Hobart. The

Ready for anything. Peter Meares, budding ABC commentator, departs on his first international trip, the Edmonton Commonwealth Games, 1978

main reason I got the job was because I had said that I had called Rugby League, which was stretching the truth a bit. Actually, all I had done was record my commentary on Easts (now Sydney City Roosters) games, sitting on the hill at the old Sydney Sports Ground.

On the way up the range to Toowoomba, my co-commentator Cyril Connell, sensing that I was a complete novice, gave me some invaluable advice. 'Go to the dressing-rooms and have a look at the players. There are lots of things that you can use to identify them apart from their numbers. Then write down their surnames and numbers on a manila folder and concentrate on the players who are most involved in the play, like the halves, the hooker and the full-back. Don't worry about the other names — it doesn't matter if you get them wrong — you're only on radio.'

So I dutifully knocked on the door of the Toowoomba dressing-room and a slim, dark-haired youngster answered. His name was Wayne Bennett. Little did I know then how many times our paths would cross over the next 35 years!

After checking out both teams I settled down behind a card table on the sideline, our makeshift commentary box, alongside six other tables. In the early 1970s, League was the only game in town in Queensland, and almost every radio station covered it. I began to call the match and, after a while, forgot my nerves. Bearing Cyril's advice in mind, I concentrated on the star players and, if I was struggling for a name, I only had to listen to the other callers and I would have it.

Toowoomba were attacking and I was getting really animated: 'Rose gets it away to Cowley and here's Bennett, chiming into the line from full-back. He's flying for the corner, but a great covering tackle from Johnny White takes him into touch …' WHOOSH!

I had been elbowed in the ribs by my scorer, Brian, a burly former Ipswich prop. On air 'live' I couldn't say anything, but I glared at him meaningfully. A few minutes later, when we crossed back to Eagle Farm for the next race description, I asked what on earth he was doing.

'Just keep your mind on the job.'

Before I had the chance to ask what he meant, we were back on air. Now it was the turn of Ipswich and they were hammering away at the Toowoomba line, looking for the first try of the game. I lifted my tempo, screaming out my commentary when — WHOOSH — another elbow, knocked the breath out of me. When we went to the next race I really turned on Brian: 'What the hell are you doing? This is my livelihood you know — if I stuff this up, I'm on the next plane back to Hobart. What's the problem?'

He said nothing, but simply turned my manila folder upside down and said: 'Toowoomba are in blue — Ipswich are in green!'

Fortunately there hadn't been a score, so disaster had been averted. Cyril had been too much of a gentleman to correct me. When I fronted the boss on Monday, he asked how my first call went. 'Great — when's the next game?'

Sports commentary on radio in Australia began in 1924 with our national sport, cricket. Bill Smallicombe, from commercial station 5CL, broadcast the Third Test between Australia and England at the Adelaide Oval. It was an incredible feat, as it was a timeless Test and lasted seven days. Bill described every ball, all by himself. As few had radio receivers, Bill's commentary was broadcast on loudspeakers all around the city of Adelaide. It was a huge success.

Everyone remembers the name of the first man to climb Everest and the first men to fly a plane, but who remembers Bill? Sports commentators are the forgotten men and women of sport, yet they provide a service which has become an integral part of the fabric of Australian life.

Football came next — the 1925 VFL Australian Rules semi-final between Geelong and Melbourne from the Melbourne Cricket Ground on a commercial station, 3AR. A.N. Bishop and former Geelong player Wally 'Jumbo' Sharland were the commentators. The station also gave race results and reports on progress in the Melbourne to Warrnambool cycle classic.

Two weeks later, the ABC began broadcasting football on station 3LO, with coverage by Mel Morris and Rod McGregor of the Grand Final between Geelong and Collingwood (which the Cats won by ten points).

In July 1932, Prime Minister Joseph Lyons inaugurated the national Australian Broadcasting Commission network, with twelve stations across the country. Among the first programs was 'Racing Notes with W.A. Ferry', which included commentary on the race meeting at Randwick, juxtaposed with 'Morning Devotions', British Wireless News and 'The Children's Session with Bobby Bluegum'. They were humble beginnings.

Sport was a national obsession and the ABC realised it.

Under general manager, Sir Charles Moses, a former first grade Rugby player, cricket broadcasts became a regular part of programming in the 1930s. Former Test players Monty Noble and Vic Richardson were the first regular commentators and were soon joined by Hal Hooker and a young Alan McGilvray.

Before the advent of television in 1956, radio sports commentary was extremely popular and there were regular 'live' descriptions of football, cricket, tennis and racing. I can still recall listening to the ABC call of the epic 1953 Davis Cup Challenge Round, in which the young Lew Hoad and Ken Rosewall upset the experienced Americans, Vic Seixas and Tony Trabert. I was listening to my transistor radio at the council swimming pool in my home town of Forbes, and soon I had a crowd of about twenty people gathered around me, also listening to Doug Heywood and Alf Chave. From that moment I wanted to be a sports commentator.

I played a lot of sport as a boy and, when I went to Sydney University, played in the First XI cricket team. I had visions of becoming a Test star and wanted to try my luck in the Lancashire League. However, my father insisted I further my education, so I enrolled in arts/law. I played every sport I could and had a wonderful time — perhaps too good a time. The demands of law proved to be beyond me and I failed first year, so I lost my Commonwealth Scholarship. Dad was going broke on the land and I had vowed to support myself after school, so I picked up a job as a groundsman at Sydney University Oval. It dovetailed nicely with my sport and studies. By day I would prepare the pitch on which I would bowl the following weekend and by night I finished off my arts degree.

One day I was picking up rubbish on the banks of the oval amongst the papers I noticed an ad for a specialist trainee in the Sports Department of the ABC, but I wasn't sure what the application process was, so I tore it out and stuffed it in my wallet. A few days later I was at a friend's place for dinner, celebrating my BA, but wondering what I would do with my life. Copious amounts of wine were consumed, so I was holding forth on the selection of the Australian cricket team on the upcoming 1968 Ashes tour. When my hosts cleared the table I was left with a charming fellow who asked what I intended to do with my degree. When I mumbled something about joining Qantas as a trainee pilot, he said: 'You would be much better suited to something involving sport, and we've got a job in our Sports Department. I'm sure they would be interested in you.'

I dug into my wallet and produced the crumpled ad, saying: 'Oh, you mean this job?'

'Ah, you are interested,' he said, 'that's great. I'm Arthur Wyndham, and I'm program manager for 2BL. I'll have a word with Bernie Kerr, the Head of Sport, and we'll see what we can do.'

A week later I was working at the ABC. Such is the fickle finger of fate or perhaps it was just luck, but it's been my passion for over 40 years now. As someone famous once said: 'Luck is when preparation meets opportunity.'

The business of becoming a broadcaster was not as easy as I had imagined, though. In those days, my central western NSW accent was considered too broad for the ABC. I was born at Forbes in the wheat belt of NSW, 250 kilometres west of Sydney, and had the typical 'bushie' accent of farmers in the area. So, once a week, I would have a session with Gordon Scott, one of the 'old school' British-style broadcasters who worked with me on my lazy speech patterns. For example, a cricket script might read: 'The cricket score from the SCG — NSW 2 for 223 in their first innings.' When I read it aloud Gordon said my words came out as 'criget', 'undred' and 'twenny', so I had to practise, practise, practise. I would do scores of practice tapes and try to get one of the senior commentators to listen to them — commentators such as Bert Oliver or the late John O'Reilly — who sadly passed away while this book was being published. 'Nugget' May used to say: 'When you've done a thousand come back and see me.'

In those days all trainees went through the same system, so they developed a certain ABC style. That's why Drew Morphett, Gordon Bray, Tim Lane, Jim Maxwell, Dennis Cometti, Alan Marks, Roger Wills, Peter Gee and the late Wally Foreman all sounded the same. We all learned from the greatest of them all, Norman 'Nugget' May.

'Nugget' began with the ABC just after television was introduced to Australia in 1956. He was the first full-time TV sports commentator, so he made the rules. Those rules were handed down to trainees who, in turn, passed them on and they still apply today. I still have my 'Training Course Reference Papers' which include, on yellowing, roneoed sheets, 'Television Commentary Techniques' as written by Norman May. Among the highlighted headings are

Enthusiasm, Pitch of Excitement, Anticipation and Talking to Picture, the integral aspects of the art.

At my audition for the position as a specialist trainee with the Sports Department, Norman stopped me mid-way through reading a sports news script, asking: 'Why are you speaking like that?'

'Because all you ABC blokes speak with a plum in your mouth,' I replied. 'I was trying to sound like James Dibble.' (He was a prominent ABC newsreader of the time, with impeccable diction.)

'Not in *sport* you don't. Just imagine we meet in the pub after you've been to the match and I haven't. You're telling me all about it, clearly, concisely and enthusiastically — and above all, in your own natural voice. Remember, radio is an intimate medium and you're normally talking to an audience of just one person, not a town hall gathering.' It was the best advice I ever had in broadcasting.

At that training course we were lucky to have some wonderful mentors — apart from Norman May, there was Jim Fitzmaurice, a marvellous commentator from Perth, who encouraged us to widen our vocabulary, and Paul Murphy, a savvy current affairs reporter, who taught us the art of interviewing. I can still recall the two basic edicts Paul passed on. First, never ask a question to which you don't know the answer (or, in other words, do your research). And second, the interview is about him, not you, so keep your questions brief.

It's interesting to note some of the names of training course members way back in 1969: Andrew Olle, Michael Bailey, Bob Maynard and John Sexton. Andrew became one of the country's outstanding current affairs reporters, Michael is still one of Australia's most experienced weathermen, Bob is a leading broadcaster with ABC Classic FM and John is one of Australia's foremost film producers.

Scores of future household names passed through that ABC Training School. Another TV training course I attended included people like Gordon Bray, Drew Morphett, Geoff McMullen ('Sixty Minutes'), Alan Humphries (TV weatherman) and Jim Maxwell. And what fun we had!

After lectures finished we usually gathered at a favourite watering-hole in William Street, the Gladstone Hotel, near the Training School in Kings Cross. There we rubbed shoulders with sports personalities like former Wallabies Cyril Towers, Trevor Allan and Ken Catchpole, Rugby League star Dick Thornett, actors Rod Mullinar and Tony Bonner, and ABC legends Alan McGilvray, race-caller Geoff Mahoney, Margaret Throsby and radio producer Alan Marks. There were trivia contests, lively debates and much merriment, with trainees like myself regularly dispatched to the nearby TAB to place bets.

In those days the ABC had the telecast rights to most major sports, including Olympic Games, Davis Cup tennis, Rugby League, Rugby Union and cricket, so we rookies were fortunate enough to call a variety of major sporting events. On weekdays we would present a fifteen-minute radio sports round-up each evening called 'Sporting Highlights', as well as the occasional film story for News. Before the days of ENG or video cameras everything was shot on film, so it had to be in the lab by 2.00 pm in order to edit and present it on air at 7.00 pm. Every weekend we would cover sport, either at a TV OB (outside broadcast) or on radio 'live' from the ground. One was supposed to be familiar with the sport, so if you didn't know the rules, you learned them. Then you always sat next to an expert, a former international or famous player, who would preview and review the action. We never gave our opinions — those were reserved for the expert analysts. We simply stuck to describing the action, which meant knowing the players instantly by sight, and giving the score.

When I moved to Hobart in 1970 after two years as a trainee in Sydney I got my big break. Although I had very little experience in broadcasting, limited to the occasional studio program on radio, in Tasmania I was involved in three television shows in my first week. On a current affairs show called 'Lineup' I did voxpops (spot interviews) with the public, asking questions on topical issues, such as daylight saving. Then there was a rock show called 'Scene' with Ric Patterson, where I interviewed dancing couples on their thoughts about the music on the show. And finally, I was thrust into the hot seat for a show on Australian Rules, called 'On the Ball'. This was the toughest gig, as I had never played or even watched much Aussie Rules. Nevertheless, with the sympathetic support of the panel, local footy legends Vern Rae, 'Nunky' Ayers and Peter Marquis, I managed to get away with it. In fact, after a couple of weeks, my boss Don Closs even threw me onto the Monday night footy show, 'Who Won and Why?' It was simply a matter of asking the same naïve questions a viewer at home might ask and never trying to sound like an expert.

My first TV interview was with world squash champion Geoff Hunt. I wore my brand new three-piece suit and had a list of questions ready. I had just taken up playing squash so I was genuinely interested, but I grew more and more nervous when my make-up and hair were done. It grew worse, until I simply lost my voice. I was terrified so, as a last resort, ran up and down the park outside the studios. It worked, but when I did the interview, perched on a stool next to Hunt, I kept going far too long. I had been told 'ten minutes' by the director, but had no idea how long I was going and had never seen a floor manager's signals before — so I just kept going and going. We had got to the stage of discussing what Geoff ate for breakfast when the floor manager just yelled: 'That's enough. Wind it up.' I had gone nearly twenty minutes and was bawled out by the director but at least I had broken the ice. Interviewing was later to become my forte.

My first TV OB was of an international table tennis tournament, Australia vs. Sweden, from the Moonah Bowl. Fortunately, I had played the game with my brother at home on the farm and had at least some understanding of the game. Bearing in mind the lessons learned from 'Nugget' May and Paul Murphy, I said very little and got by. In my mind's eye, I can still see the smash of Swedish power-player Kjell 'The Hammer' Johansson. The next weekend we covered Regatta Day, a yachting spectacular on the River Derwent. I had never been on a yacht and had absolutely no idea of the skills and rules involved. The telecast went for most of the afternoon and I said barely more than 'Hello and welcome …' and '… so it's goodbye from Hobart.' Again, nobody seemed to mind.

You learned by your mistakes, and there were plenty of them. At the Tasmanian Athletics Championships, I was given the job of trackside interviews and was thrilled to be the first to congratulate Mexico Olympic gold medallist, Ralph Doubell, on his win in the 800 metres. I rushed up as he crossed the line then, a little overawed, blurted out the first thing that came into my head: 'How do you feel?' Gasping for breath, he croaked: 'How do you think I feel — I'm buggered.' And, with that, he walked away.

These are just a few personal memories from a rewarding career in what I regard as the best job in the world. Fancy being paid to do what you love!

Privilege of the job — chatting with old warhorses — Bill Brown and Alec Bedser, Caloundra, 2007

This is the second edition of this book. The first was published in 2008, and several new names have been added — for example, Kelli Underwood, the only female fulltime sports caller, and Quentin Hull, the only commentator I know who calls all four codes of football.

Sports commentators are a special breed. It's a lifetime obsession, which means that you are never off the job. You have to eat, sleep and breathe sport in order to keep abreast of it. There are wonderful rewards — travel, meeting great people, the excitement of being in the best seats at major events and, above all, the satisfaction of communicating the action to the world — and hopefully, getting it right. There's also a downside, being away from your family every weekend and on almost every public holiday.

In this book I have set out to take the reader behind the scenes with Australia's most famous sports commentators. We love our sport and love to debate the merits, not only of players, but also of the callers. This book is not limited to just one sport; it takes in the whole gamut of sports commentators, on radio and television, both male and female. However, there are two exceptions: horse-racing and motor sport. These are two sports in which, for some unknown reason, I have no deep interest, so I have left them out.

My thanks to all the commentators for their time and for sharing their thoughts with me. We have one thing in common — we all love sport and love talking about it.

Peter Meares

ONE

The Pioneers

'Jones…inside to Jackson…ohhh bless us all, he's dropped it! With the line open! How could you drop a pass like that?'
Frank Hyde

'Now it's Ray bright on to bowl, short and square, with a beard. Not a full beard like Ned Kelly, more like a scribble on an underground poster'
John Arlott

In such a massive country as Australia, with such diverse and far-flung communities, sport created a common bond in the early days of settlement. What's more, Australians excelled at it and the fledgling nation gained international status through the deeds of its sportsmen and women. The first touring team of any kind from Australia was the 1868 Aboriginal cricket team led by Charles Lawrence. They were as popular in England for their spear and boomerang throwing as for their cricket, but they still managed to win fourteen and draw nineteen matches out of 47.

In 1878 Dave Gregory led the second touring side to England and in 1882 came the famous mock obituary in *The Times* after Australia's epic seven-run victory, stating that the body of English cricket would be cremated and the ashes taken to Australia. It was the birth of a sports legend.

In 1896 Edwin Flack became the first Australian to win an Olympic gold medal when he won, not only the 800 metres, but also the 1500 at the inaugural Athens Games. In 1912 Fanny Durack became the first Australian woman to win a gold medal, when she won the 100 metres freestyle at the Stockholm Olympics. Australia is one of only three nations to have competed at every modern Olympic Games.

By the turn of the century, Australia was fast becoming known around the world as a country of athletic champions. In 1899 the Rev. Matthew Mullineux led the first British Rugby team on a tour to Australia and they were soundly beaten 13–3 in the first-ever Test match in Sydney.

On the first Kangaroos Rugby League tour in 1908, James Giltinan's team drew the First Test 22–all with Great Britain and their 46-match tour drew huge crowds, eager to see these brilliant antipodean footballers, especially their star, Dally Messenger, who could kick a goal from the 75-yard line.

A rich history was unfolding and newspapers of the day devoted plenty of space to this national obsession. So it was natural that, when radio broadcasting began, sport would form an integral part of programming.

When the ABC was founded in 1932 one of the first events management decided to cover on radio was the Ashes Test cricket series between Australia and England. As it turned out, this was an acrimonious and controversial series because of the 'bodyline' tactics employed by Douglas Jardine and his team. Len Watt and Monty Noble called the action and their broadcasts proved immensely popular. When they started, they had no idea of what was required, so they just followed their instincts. Years later, reflecting on those early broadcasts, Len said: 'We were told we were on the air, so I started out by talking about the wind and other weather conditions and how I thought it might affect the play. In my headphones someone said "Good — that's what we want", so we kept going. We just described what we saw and, fortunately, it was pretty exciting.'

Thus ball-by-ball broadcasting was born and, 79 years later, little has changed.

The Ashes series in England in 1938 saw the introduction of the 'synthetic' broadcasts. As overseas short-wave transmissions were not reliable enough for 'live' broadcasts back to Australia, the ABC decided to do a fake commentary from telegrams.

With the aid of sound effects, the commentators would use their imagination and cricket knowledge to paint a verbal picture, based on the information received from each telegram. Charles Moses, who later became the general manager of the ABC, was the creative genius behind the concept and headed the commentary team.

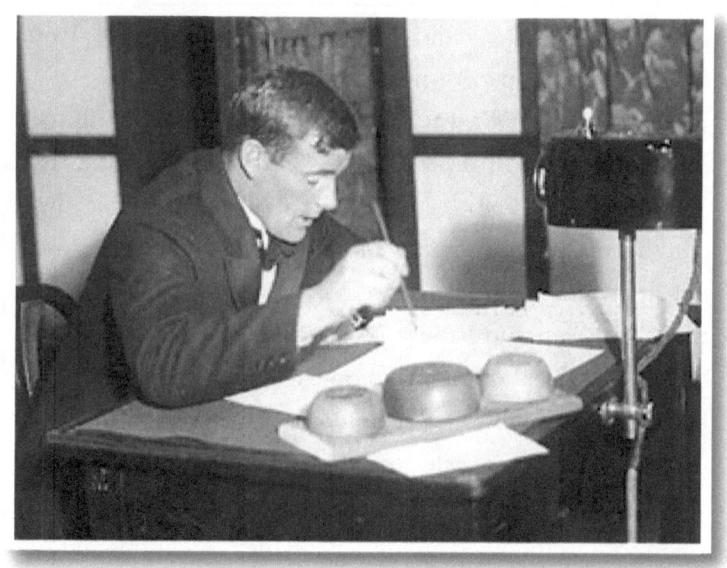

Charles Moses, the creative genius behind 'synthetic' broadcasts

For the 1938 Ashes series, Alan McGilvray joined the commentary team, alongside former Australian captain, Vic Richardson, Monty Noble and Hal Hooker. A cable would be received, relaying all the information regarding weather, crowd and field placings. Another would carry details of the bowler's delivery and the batsman's shot. So you had something like this:

'Farnes bowls to Bradman. It's overpitched and Bradman drives. Compton, at cover, dives but can't cut it off, he's beaten by the pace of the ball, and it's racing away for four. APPLAUSE. Four more to Bradman, taking his score to 101, a century in just 130 minutes, a glorious innings and Australia is now in a very strong position, 1 for 237, thanks to this great knock by Bradman.'

Alan McGilvray, the doyen of cricket commentators

Even though these broadcasts went to air in the middle of the night, they were a great success. In fact, a lot of people thought it came directly from the ground and not a studio in Market Street, Sydney. Moreover, 1938 produced a record year for the sale of radio licences, double the year before — radio was well and truly off and running.

When England toured Australia, a BBC broadcaster was introduced to the commentary. In 1946–47 that man was former England captain, Arthur Gilligan, who teamed beautifully with his Australian counterpart, Vic Richardson. The catchcry from Vic was 'What do you think, Arthur?' NSW captain, Alan McGilvray, had retired from playing cricket to take up commentary in 1935 and, after the war, was a regular member of the team. The three travelled around Australia covering the Tests and became close friends. This rapport came through on air and warmed the listeners to them.

In the 1950s, Johnny Moyes and Lindsay Hassett became regulars. Moyes, a journalist and author, had played for South Australia and Victoria and had a distinctive, nasal voice. Perhaps his attitude to cricket and life could be illustrated by one club innings for Gordon — he scored 218 runs in 83 minutes! Hassett, a whimsical little man who smoked a pipe, had a shrewd analytical cricket brain and a generous nature, which came through on air.

Another famous voice of that era was that of Michael

Two of the author's heroes in the 1950s, Johnnie Moyes and Ray Lindwall

Charlton. Not a cricketer of note, Charlton nevertheless had an urbane, almost English voice and a marvellous vocabulary. He was a professional broadcaster of the highest order and his calls of the 1960 series against the West Indies were memorable.

When Australia toured England, for 40 years after the war, McGilvray went with them. Any baby-boomer with a love of cricket will recall listening to descriptions of Ashes Tests on transistors tucked under their pillows. With the BBC, he joined the likes of Rex Alston, John Arlott and Brian Johnston and, initially, did not fit the mould. The English commentators used a more lyrical style, perhaps best exemplified by Arlott, who was a poet before he became a commentator. He would describe the weather, the seagulls,

Inset: Brian Johnston, the man with a smile in his voice

John Arlott's lyrical, poetic commentary was delivered in his trademark Hampshire burr

the ground and even the attire of women in the members' stand before he got around to calling the ball that was being bowled. His Hampshire burr was known in England as 'the voice of summer'. McGilvray, on the other hand, was more prosaic, describing the ball and the resultant stroke and gave the score at least three times every over. There was some friction at first, even over *how* the score was given — Arlott would say 'That makes it 60 for 2' while 'Mac' would say it the other way round, in the Australian tradition '2 for 60'. However, the public liked the contrast in styles and the BBC had the good sense to allow it to continue. As a listener, I loved it, and actually looked forward to rain stopping play, so 'The Village Glee Club' could have another fascinating discussion about all things cricket.

I interviewed Arlott at his farewell Test match, the 1980 English Centenary Test, at Lord's for ABC TV. I was rather intimidated by the great man and, seeing him struggling to carry a huge black briefcase up the stairs of the pavilion on the first morning, I imagined he had half a dozen copies of *Wisden*, the cricket bible, in it. Imagine my surprise when he opened the case and produced a bottle of red wine, a bottle of port and a large piece of cheese! In our interview he surprised me again when I asked why he called Test cricket in England for 34 years, but made only one tour to Australia, in 1955: 'Because Australians don't like my style.'

'On the contrary,' I protested. 'We love it — or at least I do.' To prove it I quoted two excerpts of his commentary in that game — classic Arlott:

'There's Knott, doing his stretches, turning this way and

that — like a bird looking for an earthworm.' And another gem: 'Now it's Ray Bright on to bowl, short and square, with a beard. Not a full beard like Ned Kelly, more like a scribble on an underground poster.'

Then there was the classic description of that magnificent fast bowler Dennis Lillee, moving in to bowl at Old Trafford, which adjoins the railway line: 'So Lillee moves in to Boycott, as the train moves out of Warwick Road station, elbows and shoulders working like pistons, bucking and heaving, gathering steam ... and Boycott is bowled, no score.'

Another favourite was Brian Johnston, who was a complete contrast to Arlott. Jovial and gregarious, he had a light-hearted style and a wonderful sense of humour. I called my first international cricket match with Brian for ABC TV in Hobart. The match was between a Tasmanian XI, boosted by the addition of Test stars Doug Walters and Paul Sheahan, against the touring MCC in December 1970. Never having called cricket before and being aware that we were 'live' throughout the state, I was extremely nervous. Brian sensed this and opened the commentary: 'Good morning and welcome to the TCA ground in Hobart. The MCC have won the toss and are batting. I'm Brian Johnston and I'm joined by Peter Meares, who's going to run through the Tasmanian side for us.'

Fortunately, I knew who the fieldsmen were by sight and felt emboldened by this recognition, so I ventured: 'Good morning, Brian, and welcome to Tasmania. How did you enjoy Christmas down under?'

'Jolly good, thanks, but very hot for a Pom. Do you know I actually bathed!'

There was a pregnant pause as my mind raced — perhaps the myth about the English aversion to washing was true after all! Seeing my face, Johnners elaborated: 'Perhaps you Australians would say *swam*. Jolly nice it was too.'

I laughed and immediately relaxed. In fact at lunch I suddenly realised we had been on air for two hours and I had forgotten about my nerves. Years later I read Brian's autobiography, aptly named *It's Been a Lot of Fun*. I soon learned the lesson that, if you can relax and be yourself, calling sport is the best job in the world.

Australian Rules was another sport that lent itself to radio commentary and, in turn, the broadcasts boosted the popularity of the sport. Wally 'Jumbo' Sharland, Rod McGregor and Mel Morris called the VFL in Melbourne on ABC stations 3AR and 3LO from 1925 until the outbreak of World War II. The commercial stations realised the drawing power of the broadcasts and followed suit — 3UZ with E.H. Dahlberg and 3KZ with Norman Banks. The latter became one of Australia's greatest callers, even though the VFL tried to stop him calling matches. Worried about the adverse effect of the broadcasts on the gate, the VFL banned Banks from their grounds, so he simply set up a tower outside and called from there. For a few years at Princes Park he actually called from a plank that was stuck into the window of the women's toilet! His career lasted 40 years until in 1965 his eyesight finally gave way.

The popularity of the game can be seen from the fact that four stations covered big games from as early as 1932. 3GL joined the fray with Reg Gray and Geelong secretary Ivan More. In 1950 3DB also started broadcasting football, with the legendary Ron Casey in partnership with former St Kilda footballer and Australian cricketer Sam Loxton. By 1956 there were seven stations calling football, as 3XY (with Doug Elliott and former Collingwood captain, Lou Richards) joined in.

Television began in Australia in 1956 and it didn't take long for stations to realise they were on a ratings certainty with coverage of Australian Rules. Three networks were involved in the first season's coverage, 1957 — the ABC, Nine and Seven. Ken Dakin, the Melbourne sports supervisor, headed the ABC team, while Tony Charlton

AFL broadcasting pioneer and funnyman, Lou Richards.

(the brother of Michael) was at Seven and Ian Johnson at Nine.

With the spread of the VFL nationally, the coverage of the game also increased. When South Melbourne spread their wings to Sydney and became the Swans in 1982, Channel Seven began telecasting games from the SCG. With the introduction of the Brisbane Bears and West Coast Eagles (1987), Adelaide Crows (1991), Fremantle Dockers (1995) and Port Adelaide (1997) the AFL became truly national and the sport confirmed its status as Australia's premier winter sport.

Rugby League is second only to Rules in the popularity stakes during winter and has been broadcast regularly in Sydney and Brisbane since World War II. Perhaps the most famous commentator has been Frank Hyde, the gravelly-voiced former player whose signature line was: 'It's long enough; it's high enough; it's straight between the posts!'

Frank was a good enough player to represent NSW and he captained a premiership-winning Balmain side in 1939. His debut as a broadcaster came about almost by divine providence. He was a member of a Eucharistic choir which sang for the Pope when he visited Sydney and was asked to take the tapes of the Mass to radio station 2SM. He chatted with the station manager, Tom Jacobs, who liked the sound of Frank's voice and said: 'You played Rugby League, Frank. How would you like to try your hand at calling it?' So Frank took a tape recorder along to a schoolboy game and just described what he saw. 'Jones passes to Smith and back inside to Jackson. Oooh, bless us all,

The three faces of Frank Hyde, Rugby League player and broadcasting legend

he's dropped it, with the line open! How could he drop a pass like that?'

It was rough and ready but it had passion and Frank's intimate knowledge of the game. Anyway, he got the job and began a 40-year broadcasting career. His style was all his own, he would call the game as if he was playing it, with an emotional involvement that drew thousands of listeners. As a boy in Sydney in the 1960s I loved to listen to his calls, in his distinctive foghorn voice. He pioneered the 'Around the Grounds' reports and sponsored 'Man of the Match' awards and he also appeared on Sunday mornings on 'World of Sport', a Rugby League show on Channel Nine with Ron Casey as host.

Frank would sit with his microphone on a card table at suburban grounds on Saturday afternoons, flanked by other callers, like 'Tiger' Black from 2KY and Bernie Kerr from the ABC. At one stage there were six radio stations all calling the same Sydney club game.

It was the same in Brisbane where I began calling League in 1971. Sitting next to me on the sidelines, also behind card tables, were Billy J. Smith of 4IP, Fonda Metassa of 4BH, Doug McIntyre of 4AK, Ross Lawson of 4BK and John McCoy of 4BC. The doyen of commentators in Queensland was George Lovejoy. With a distinctive style and a huge following, George ruled the airwaves every Saturday afternoon during the '50s and '60s. He coined the famous phrase: 'Rugby League — the greatest game of all.'

George is said to be the only League caller, other than Frank Hyde, who drew an audience of more than 200 000 within one fifteen-minute period. George was famous for calling a game in Ipswich from a house across the street, after being banned from the ground. When he retired from commentary he employed Ross Lawson, who used to do Lovejoy impersonations at his Goodna pub, to take his place at 4BH — he had a big ego. George was colourful and controversial and his fans loved it.

Rugby Union is another sport that was covered regularly, at least in Sydney, from the early days of sports broadcasting. In fact, the ABC's Saturday afternoon telecast of the Sydney Match of the Day is the longest-running sports program on any Australian network: over 50 years. It began in April 1957, when Norman May and Cyril Towers called the first grade match between Gordon and Manly from Chatswood Oval, and it's been going ever since. Norman called the Rugby for the ABC until 1980 when Gordon Bray took over with Trevor Allan.

Perhaps the reason for the selection of Rugby in those early days was that the general manager of the ABC, Sir

Charles Moses, had been a player and sports broadcaster himself. When he retired in 1964 he was replaced by Talbot Duckmanton, another Rugby commentator, and the tradition continued. Steve Robilliard and Brett Papworth call the Saturday Rugby for the ABC these days and it's a very professional production. No wonder — they've had plenty of practice!

TWO

Ian Baker-Finch

IN THE BIG TIME

What makes a commentator worth listening to? His knowledge of the sport? His knowledge of the players? His ability to capture and enhance the excitement of the event? His credibility? His funny stories? His fearless and controversial comments? Or perhaps just his voice?

To Ian Baker-Finch it's a combination of all these things. He simply tries to make golf more interesting to the viewers.

Ian Baker-Finch — the trailblazer — first Australian to call the world's top golf circuit, the USPAGA Tour.

34 | *Back To The Studio*

'I like to try to tell a story and to improve on the picture you're seeing in your lounge room. I've won a major, so that helps – people tend to believe what I say. Then, if I do my homework, I'm on the ball with my knowledge of the course, the players and the rules of the game. And, if I can relate to the weekend hacker and help him out with his game, I reckon I must be doing a reasonable job.'

What Ian doesn't say is that, in addition to all these other attributes, he's easy to listen to. He has one of those pleasant voices that sounds like fine music to the ear. He's a nice bloke and it comes across. What's more, he has the respect of his colleagues and the audience must like him, because he's still being hired after 15 years in the job. Ian works as an analyst on the high-rating CBS national television coverage of the world's richest golf circuit, the USPGA Tour. Since 1998, when he started with sister stations, ABC and ESPN in the United States, he's never been out of a job.

The youngest of six children, Ian grew up on a farm near Caboolture on Queensland's Sunshine Coast. One of his schoolmates was Nicole Kidman's husband, country singer Keith Urban. After leaving school at 15 to become an apprentice to a club professional at Gympie, Ian has come a long way. Now every weekend, millions of golf fans around the world watch and listen to his commentary. After all, he should know what he's talking about – he won 17 tournaments around the world, including the British Open in 1991 at Royal Birkdale. He still holds the record low score of 130 (64–66) for the final two rounds in the Open.

A strapping 6 foot, 4 inches (193 centimetres), dark-haired and handsome, he turned pro in 1979 and won his first tournament, the New Zealand Open, in 1983. Over the next decade he went on to win at least one tournament each year. Polite and affable, he was as popular with the public as he was with his fellow pros. In 1987, he married his long-time girlfriend, Jennie and settled in Orlando, Florida, where they raised two beautiful daughters, Hayley and Laura. It seemed Ian could do no wrong.

However, in 1993, he started tinkering with his swing in an effort to get more distance. Suddenly he began playing shots he had never played before. Ranked in the world's top 10 players in 1991, he started to slide. He had simply lost his swing. Missing cuts, losing confidence and making no money, he switched coaches. He worked harder, tried hypnosis and sought advice from experts, but nothing worked. The worst thing was that there was no pattern to his problem. Off the tee, one drive would be a snap hook and the next an ugly slice. In 1995, he played 24 American tournaments, missed every cut and broke par only twice.

'When my game went bad, I was looking around for an alternative and in 1996 I was offered a couple of commentary spots at Australian tournaments. As a player, I didn't know the rules. I just called it from a player's perspective, but they must have liked it. I worked for all four networks that summer and then in November 1997 came a fax that changed my life. It was Jack Graham of ABC Sports asking if I was interested in a full-time on-course commentary job in the United States.

I was lucky to start with a producer like Jack, who was brilliant. His attention to detail and simple rules, added to the experience I had working in Australia, enabled me to understand my role as a golf analyst. Working on American television is a bit different to Australia, where you have only three or four voices and about five hours coverage. In the States we have six voices and a more upbeat coverage, with more ads and promos. So you need to have your wits about you and keep your comments brief.

When I first started Jack pulled me up a couple of times when I used a colloquial Australian expression. He pointed out that the other guys in the team didn't understand what I had meant, so I had to explain and that slowed down the coverage. So, over the years, I've learned to compromise – I cut back the Aussie slang but try to keep my own style and accent.'

What I love about Ian Baker-Finch's commentary is that he doesn't back down to the Yanks. He's his own man and proud of it. What's more, it seems the American audiences like him too, so he has the confidence to speak his mind. The mix of accents on the CBS commentary team makes for interesting listening – Irishman David Feherty, Englishmen Sir Nick Faldo and Peter Oosterhuis and Americans Jim Nantz, Gary McCord, Bill Macatee, Peter Kostis and the only female presenter, Kelly Tilghman.

For golf tragics like me, the live coverage of USPGA tournaments is compulsory viewing. It comes through in Australia in the early morning on Fox Sports, so there are occasions when my family wonders why I'm not eating breakfast with them. It's replayed in the evening, so there's the chance of catching up on how the Aussies are going if you missed them that morning. With over 20 Australians playing the US tour there is plenty of interest, especially when the majors, like the US Masters and the USPGA come around. Only nine Australians have ever won a major, so who does Ian think will be next?

'I reckon Geoff Ogilvy, the last Aussie to win one, has another major in him. Then there are the brilliant youngsters like Jason Day and Michael Sim and you can't leave out Stuart Appleby and Robert Allenby, but they're on the wrong side of 40 now. Matt Jones is another one who's playing well over here. There are so many good players and there are only four majors, but I won't be surprised if another Australian wins one soon.'

For a player who had such a traumatic fall from grace, Ian still has an incredible passion for the game. He hits balls on the range or plays almost every day. On tournament days he's up early and, after a workout in the gym, joins the other commentators in checking out the course, pin positions and green speeds.

'We don't get to play the course, but we talk to the guys on the range – we know what's going on. Remember I played the Tour for years, so I know what they're facing.'

Having been through such highs and lows himself, Ian has a rare empathy with players and their emotional rollercoaster. Some players get nervous over a short putt, some over a tee shot.

'If you don't feel nervous on the first tee, you shouldn't be playing. You play and practice enough to conquer those nerves – and that's what's so satisfying when you play well. I understand all these things only too well and I hope I convey those hopes and fears to the viewer, so they appreciate a fine shot even more.'

Ian rates Peter Alliss as the greatest influence on him as a commentator. The urbane Englishman, now in his eighties, has a velvety voice that is a delight to hear and Ian has a similar appeal. He also rates two Australian commentators highly – Peter Thomson and Jack Newton. Strangely enough, he doesn't single out any American commentator but says that he's learned a lot from the hosts he's worked with, such as Jim Nantz of CBS.

His highlight in 15 years of golf commentary in the United States has been working with CBS at the Masters at Augusta.

'Just to be there in the box, poised high above the 11th green and the 12th tee – best seat in the house – it's magic.'

And the lowlight?

'That's not so easy – there have been lots of them,' he says with a chuckle. 'When I first worked with Channel Seven at the Australian in '96 they showed these big carp swimming in the lake beside the 18th green. Quick as a flash I said, "Have a look at the size of those things – they've been nibbling on the members' balls for years".'

Sandy Roberts, Channel Seven's unflappable host, threw to a break immediately.

Then there was the time fellow Aussie, Stuart Appleby was interviewed by CBS's Peter Kostis, who asked what he thought of his mate from Australia as a commentator. Tongue firmly in cheek, 'Apples' quipped: 'He's not bad I suppose, but he's too nice. Sometimes you've got to get tough and criticise the players.'

Shortly afterwards, up came a picture of an Appleby tee shot, hooked into trees, so Ian seized his chance: 'Have a look at that shitty drive by Stuart Appleby, will you.'

Fortunately it was a Thursday and the coverage was limited to The Golf Channel – there were no complaints. It's not easy being a commentator – you need to tread a fine line between colour and controversy. For example, Ian's CBS colleague, Gary McCord was sacked from the Masters' commentary team after his comments on the slick greens at Augusta – 'Smoothed with bikini wax' and with 'humps like body bags'.

Kelly Tilghman was suspended for two weeks by CBS after a comment on Tiger Woods's dominance, saying his rivals might want to 'lynch him in a back alley'.

Ian speaks in measured tones and, like the man himself, is usually thoughtful and courteous. But that doesn't mean he avoids criticism.

'If a guy plays a bad shot I try to analyse why he did it, rather than just lambast him. That might help the weekend hacker at home too, so you're making a positive out of a negative.'

He's outspoken in his views on the game of golf, declaring that there are some laws which need changing.

'Firstly, I think they should not disqualify a player for an inadvertent offence after he has signed his scorecard. For example, if a TV replay shows a guy unknowingly grounded his club in a hazard it should just be a two-shot penalty.

And another rule I would change would be the Out of Bounds (OB) rule. It should be like the Lateral Hazard rule – if you find that your drive has gone OB, you just drop a new ball and take a one-shot penalty, rather than having to go back to the tee and play another drive. If we can shorten the average time of a round to three hours instead of four and a half, then the game of golf will be more popular.'

Ian regards the Ryder Cup, the team event in which America meets Europe, as the pinnacle of the game, closely followed by the President's Cup, in which America meets the Internationals.

'Team events are always more compelling than individual ones, I think. And the Europeans might not earn as much money as the Americans, but over the past 20 years or so they've been dominant. I find it fascinating to watch. It's an NBC event, so I don't work on the Ryder Cup, but I love to watch it.'

Ian has been vice-captain three times in the President's Cup and would love to be captain, but doesn't hold any serious hopes.

'They like to pick the absolute superstars – Jack Nicklaus led the Americans four times, Gary Player led Europe three times and now Greg Norman has taken over. Nick Price will be the next captain and I reckon Ernie Els will be there one day too. I'm happy just to tag along as vice-captain.'

Ian gets a lot of enjoyment out of his job, travelling the length and breadth of the United States with his wife, Jennie.

'She loves the travel and would prefer to be with me than stay at home. The girls are grown up now, Hayley's 22 and

Laura 19, so that means Jennie can come with me. She plays golf pretty well, so we share that enjoyment and try to catch up with friends wherever we go. We also share a love of wine, so we love going to dinner, sharing a good bottle of red with friends.'

They spend nine months a year in America, but relish the chance to come home every year for Christmas. Ian is looking forward to 2011, when he will join Jack Newton and Wayne Grady on the Channel Nine commentary team for the President's Cup in Australia. Moreover, he turned 50 last November and is eligible for the lucrative Champions' Tour in the United States. Is he dreading a return to the 'yips' of the Nineties?

'I played the Australian Senior Open at Royal Perth last summer and, after a poor first round, finished fifteenth, so I'm confident my dark days are well and truly behind me.'

Let's hope so, Finchy, the game owes you a break.

THREE

Richie Benaud

MASTER OF UNDERSTATEMENT

'Say nothing unless you can add to the picture'

If you were to conduct a poll to find Australia's most popular cricket commentator, it would be no contest. Richie Benaud would win hands down. He's been around the longest and, in my opinion, he's still the best. As a player he was a magnificent all-rounder, as a captain he was a brilliant strategist and, as a commentator, he is the master of understatement. What's more, he's one of the true gentlemen of the game.

'I was trained by the BBC and was influenced by three of

'The voice of Australian cricket', the ever-unflappable Richie Benaud

the greats, Henry Longhurst (golf), Dan Maskell (tennis) and Peter O'Sullivan (horse-racing).' Their edict was "Say nothing unless you can add to the picture". Radio commentators paint, for the listener, a verbal picture of everything happening on the field. On television, the viewers know what's happening and the commentator only needs to add to the picture.'

For example, the effusive Bill Lawry, reacting to an exciting passage of play might say: 'Ohh, fantastic catch — it's all happening here at the MCG!' In the same situation, Benaud would simply say: 'Marvellous.' That's the reason why Benaud has entertained and endured for so long.

Richie has called cricket in England for 40 years and is contracted to Channel Nine in Australia for another season. He doesn't want to retire because he still enjoys it so, at the age of 81 (on 30 October 2011), he is saddling up for another season in the sun. There are two things that strike you when you tune in to the cricket, with Benaud behind the microphone: one is the economy of words; the other is the shrewdness of his cricket brain. His father, Lou Benaud, was a schoolteacher who instilled in Richie a love of English and the written word. He had no aspirations of becoming a commentator at first, but always wanted to write.

He worked in an accountant's office for three years after leaving Parramatta High but, in January 1950, got a job in the counting house of *The Sun* newspaper in Sydney. The magazine *Sporting Life* was situated on the floor above and Keith Miller worked there, along with other famous sportswriters, Ginty Lush, Dick Whitington and Johnny Moyes. Richie was a successful player with NSW and every year he would ask whether there was any chance of a transfer to the editorial department. In the meantime, he had to content himself with working on police rounds and writing a weekly sports column called 'Come in Spinner'.

Finally, in March 1956, Lindsay Clinch, the editor of *The Sun* said that if Richie had a good tour of England, Pakistan and India, he would consider the request. As it turned out Australia lost, but Richie emerged as the successor to star all-rounder Keith Miller, finishing second on the batting averages and second in the number of wickets taken. At the end of the English leg of the tour, Richie worked for three weeks on a training course at BBC television. He started at 11.00 am and finished at midnight most days, but he loved it. Television was just about to start in Australia, so Richie simply absorbed everything he could by watching and listening.

That shrewdness is no fluke — there have been few all-round players who have matched Richie, quite apart from his achievements as captain. In 63 Tests, he scored 2,201 runs and took 248 wickets. His all-round performances were outstanding — in Johannesburg in 1957, for example, he scored 100 and took 5 for 84. In Kingston, Jamaica that year he scored a century in just 78 minutes against the West Indies.

After the retirement of Bradman, the Australian team struggled. There was a huge void left by the greatest batsman the game has known — he averaged almost 40 runs an innings higher than the next best player. England won back the Ashes in 1953 under Len Hutton, retained them in

Australia in 1954–55 and again in England in 1956. Benaud made his debut against the West Indies in 1951 and was a member of those teams that suffered at the hands of England. So, when he took over the captaincy, he was keen for revenge. Under Benaud's leadership from 1956 until 1963 Australia never lost a series. The 1960–61 series against the West Indies was perhaps the turning-point in the way cricket was played worldwide. As a fourteen-year-old boy, I watched every ball of the Sydney Test and the tour match against NSW during that series.

Throughout the 1950s, teams often played with a defensive mentality, trying not to lose. In 1960 both Frank Worrell and Benaud threw caution to the wind and attacked, with spectacular results. Dashing batsmen like Sobers and Kanhai, backed by the world's fastest bowler, Wesley Hall, provided the nucleus of a superb West Indies side. Benaud had the free-scoring Norman O'Neill and great all-rounder Alan Davidson at his disposal. The First Test in Brisbane was an incredible tie, which set the tone for the rest of the series. Australia finished up the narrowest of winners 2–1, with a nerve-racking draw in Adelaide and the world's biggest cricket crowd at that time, over 90 000, attending one day's play in the final Test in Melbourne.

Richie began his commentary career in 1960 on BBC radio, while still a player. He worked on the series between England and South Africa, sitting in the box with astute callers John Arlott and Rex Alston. In 1963 he started in television, covering the West Indies tour of England and learned from old hands Peter West and Brian Johnston. To my mind, the

English style was too understated in those days. Sometimes a whole over would pass without any commentary, apart from the score. It was like watching paint dry.

Benaud found a happy medium, a compromise between the extremes of Australia and England. His comments were always pertinent or, if nothing was happening onscreen, he made interesting digressions. I love cricket, but can take only so much of a fast bowler walking back to his mark, polishing the ball on his creams, in silence. One of the difficulties of television commentary is to keep it interesting, while still talking to picture. If, for example, there's a hubbub in the crowd because a pretty girl walks past in a bikini, but the cameras remain steadfastly locked on the bowler returning to the top of his run, what do you say? Generally, the rule is to ignore the crowd, unless the incident is something so important it can't be ignored. Directors have several cameras at their disposal, so they can cut away to an off-field shot for a moment and the commentator needs to be alert, keeping an eye on the monitor, if he does. On the other hand, all callers have a talk-back button on their microphone, which allows them to talk to their director off-air. Thus, one can suggest an interesting cutaway; for example, a shot of the prime minister sitting in the stand. It's a team effort.

Perhaps the best thing that happened to cricket commentary was the introduction of one-day internationals, especially World Series Cricket in 1977. The game was shorter, faster and much more lively, and the commentary reflected this. Under floodlights for the first time, cricket became more frenetic. The introduction of new technology, such as score supers, stump microphones and on-screen telestrators, provided viewers with much more information and changed the whole style of cricket coverage. The cross-pollination of accents with callers like South African-born Tony Greig, West Indian Tony Cozier and Yorkshireman Freddie Trueman made for more interesting viewing — and the odd-ball humour of Max Walker was a pleasant change.

The executive producer of Channel Nine cricket for many years was David Hill, now head of Fox Sports in the United States. Although not a cricketer, he was a brilliant producer who understood the need to make the sometimes confusing and esoteric aspects of cricket more readily understood by the mass audience drawn to the game by the colour and excitement of one-day cricket. In 1977 he wrote a memo on ten commandments for his team of commentators, which still apply today. Perhaps the basic rule is this: 'Remember this is a game of many and varied hues. As a commentator you will keep foremost in your mind that cricket contains venom and courage, drama and humour, and you will not be backward in bringing out in your commentary those aspects of the noble and ancient pastime.'

Kerry Packer wanted his front-man to look distinctive, so Benaud was dressed in a cream jacket in the early days of World Series Cricket telecasts. WSC has gone but the jacket remains, the hallmark of Australia's most famous commentator. Somehow it looks right on the urbane, silver-haired doyen of the microphone.

It hasn't always been beer and skittles, as they say, though. As in every television program, cricket broadcasts have their dramas and, although one of Richie's greatest attributes is his coolness in a crisis, some things are beyond his control. Like the time at the 'Gabba when Channel Nine had designed a brilliant new set for the studio and, as Richie was doing the live tea-break segment, he sensed something behind him. The set had somehow lost a couple of screws and it toppled over onto Richie's head — somehow he kept a straight face and threw to a break.

Richie also loves golf and each Australian winter has, for many years, travelled to the USA and Britain with his wife, Daphne, covering the golf tours. He is a keen player himself and I recall spending a weekend with him at Noosa once when we co-hosted the dinner after the Jack Newton Pro-Am. As a young cricket commentator then, I was in awe of the great man but he put me at ease and, over a drink, answered my queries about commentary with sincerity and warmth. I also recall spending that weekend in close company with the late Fred Trueman, one of the funniest after-dinner speakers I have heard, but a real 'whingeing Pom' in private. He complained about everything, from having to share an apartment with me, to the lack of free golf balls for VIP players.

The sign that you have really made it in cricket commentary in Australia is to have your voice mimicked by the clever satirist Billy Birmingham. For the past 25 years, Billy has cashed in on the enormous popularity of the Nine commentary team by taking the mickey out of them. It's very funny and Billy's CDs are always a popular Christmas present for the cricket tragic in the family, but how do the commentators feel? Richie doesn't mind being sent up, he's been around too long to worry, but he does object to bad language and attempted humour based on the names of foreign players. He also objects when his name or voice is used to persuade people to buy something they believe he is recommending. Such is the price of fame.

The game has changed enormously in Richie's time and he has always embraced any innovation that draws new fans to the game. Even the latest fad, 20/20 cricket, gets his seal of approval. 'Anything which attracts 20,000 people to a cricket match and they enjoy themselves is good for the game. Limited-overs cricket has benefited Test cricket over the past 36 years, so why wouldn't 20/20?'

That's the thing about Richie, he keeps adapting and we love him for it. He is his own man, but you never get the sense of him disapproving of the new-fangled technological gadgets Nine introduces and he's always keen for a verbal joust with his younger co-commentators. Ian Chappell tells how Richie helped him along the road to sports commentary, but only when he asked for advice. His policy is that every caller should develop his own style, and he feels that one of the strengths of Channel Nine's coverage over the past 30 years is that their commentators have all been different.

How does he keep going so passionately year after year? 'More than anything else, just looking into that camera lens and never forgetting that millions of people have invited us into their loungerooms keep me on the ball.'

If you were to ask Richie for a highlight, in all the hundreds of Test matches and one-day internationals he's covered he would opt for the 1981 Ashes series in England. That was the series in which Ian Botham single-handedly turned England's fortunes around with his all-round brilliance, smashing a century when England was following on to set up an unlikely victory. England were 500:1 to win, odds that even the Australian players, Lillee and Marsh, had a bet on — and they collected.

It was the most exciting series Richie had seen, until 2005. He reckons that this series, in which Michael Vaughan's team edged out the world champion Australians, with Andrew Flintoff a modern-day Botham, even surpassed 1981.

In 2008 Richie Benaud was inducted into the Australian Cricket Hall of Fame, along with 24 other greats of the game. A Wisden Cricketer of the Year in 1962, Richie feels this is an even greater honour: 'To be included among the 25 greatest players that Australia has ever produced is indeed a rare honour, as Australia has the proudest Test record of any nation.'

FOUR

Warren Boland

FROM TIGERS TO TAI CHI

'I try to give an insider's view of football. Rather than bag a player for dropping a pass, work out why. He may have been blindsided by a winger or the pass may have been too high'

One of the rare breed of sports stars who have become full-time commentators, Warren Boland is something of a paradox. He played first grade Rugby League with blue-collar teams Balmain and Wests, but has become an accomplished ABC radio personality with his own weekend morning show, 'Weekends with Warren', where he discusses everything from Tai Chi to turnip-growing.

He is still heavily involved with Rugby League, as one of the ABC TV's commentary team for their weekly coverage of the Queensland Cup, alongside David Wright as an expert on ABC Radio's NRL coverage of the Broncos, Titans and State of Origin. Slim and fit, with a bristling moustache,

Warren Boland, from sports star to commentator to radio personalilty

he's affectionately known as 'Merv', after cricket's legendary larrikin Merv Hughes.

I have followed Warren's career with interest — because he took my job. When I left the ABC for Channel Seven in 1985 he took over and has done a fine job ever since in various roles with 'Aunty'.

A lot of footballers try their hand at commentary when they hang up the boots, but not many can call hockey or judo. Warren has, and a lot more besides, in his years with the ABC, Fox Sports and overseas networks. He has covered three Olympics and in 2006 called squash for ten days at the

Melbourne Commonwealth Games. He found that initially daunting: 'I had played a bit of squash but knew nothing about the finer points of the game. I worked with former world champion, Sarah Fitzgerald, who was making her commentary debut, so we were able to help each other out. By the end of 75 matches, I was stealing her lines and she was pinching mine.'

Warren maintains that you can call almost anything as the ball-by-ball describer, solo if need be. 'As long as you know the rules and terminology and stick to the basics of identification, the score and describing the action, you can get by alone. But a good expert obviously helps. When the whistle goes, the analyst comes in and explains the strategy. When you're on your own it can get tricky at times.'

Warren has found himself flying solo at the Olympics and Asian Games, where it's been a real challenge coming to grips with the complexities of sports that he has never played. 'I struggled with judo and hockey at first because I'd never had any experience of them — never even watched them really. On the other hand, when I did tennis or volleyball, I reckon I did a pretty good job because I'd actually played them a bit and had a feel for them.'

Modest and straightforward, Warren is a far cry from some former footballers who move into the media. Big egos and outrageous comments are common in the cutthroat world of commercial Rugby League commentary, but not for this former captain of Wests, who has a rare empathy with players. 'I try to give an insider's view of football. Rather than bag a player for dropping a pass, I try to work out why. He may have been blindsided by a winger a few minutes earlier or the pass may have been too high. Footballers now are so skilful, it's rare for them to drop a pass cold.'

Warren should know. He played in the St George under-23s premiership-winning team in 1974, had three years on the wing with Balmain winning the Amco Cup in 1976, and captained Wests in their 'fibro era' under Roy Masters. He played in the Tigers' reserve grade premiership side in 1978 and led the Magpies' first grade to the preliminary final in 1980. A reliable and speedy winger, he scored 24 tries for Wests in 97 games over five seasons.

After leaving school, Warren had no clear ambition in either his career or football. Having achieved a top HSC pass, he went to Macquarie University where he studied biology and played Rugby League in the University Cup competition before trying out with St George in 1974. The following year he deferred university and football to travel around Australia with a few mates in a Kombi van, returning in 1976 to complete a BA DipEd and join the Balmain club where he cracked first grade. After two years of teaching high school science, he decided he needed to do something else with his life and resigned.

He had brains and ability, but he didn't know what to do. He had a vague idea of becoming a television cameraman, so in 1979 — the same year he joined Wests — he rang TV commentator and radio producer John Brennan, a Balmain committeeman, for advice. Brennan said that there was a job going at his radio station 2SM in the Community Services Department. Meanwhile Warren had obtained some work as a casual stagehand at Channel Nine and they also offered him a position. It was a real fork in the road. Warren chose the radio job because it meant making documentaries. He stayed at 2SM for five years working his way into the newsroom. After retiring from playing Rugby League at the end of 1983, and while still at 2SM, Warren did some 'Around the Grounds' reporting on weekends with ABC Radio but once free of football commitments he was off on a long-postponed backpacking holiday to Europe.

On his return to Sydney in 1985 he noticed a job advertisement for a sports commentator and reporter with ABC Brisbane. He applied and got it. Warren felt that his previous experience with the ABC would stand him in good stead and was confident about his role as the station's Rugby League caller. A week before his first game, he sat in the stand at Lang Park and did a practice commentary. To his shock and horror he found that he couldn't do it. He didn't know the players, he was behind the play and he kept stumbling over his words. Had he made a huge mistake?

The next weekend it was the real thing behind the radio microphone. The star-studded Wynnum–Manly side were playing Valleys in the match of the day at the Cauldron. At least he knew Wally Lewis! He also had one of Brisbane League's most knowledgeable experts in Cyril Connell alongside him. 'I'll be right — just relax,' he kept reminding himself.

When the game got under way, Warren soon forgot his nerves and began to enjoy the experience of his first 'live' football commentary. The call was going well. Wynnum were on top and their slick backline was cutting the Diehards to pieces. 'From the scrum Dowling slips it to Lewis, onto big Gene Miles. He draws two defenders and pops a one-handed pass overhead to … the winger. He's racing away! And the winger … scores!'

Cyril Connell quickly chimed in: 'Great try to Terry Butler — too much pace for the cover defence — and what a pass from Miles. Wynnum now lead 12–nil.'

Warren's mind, searching desperately, had just gone blank. The winger was, of course, Terry Butler but, in the excitement, the name just didn't come and he had no time to look at his program. All the way home he cursed himself — he could have just said 'And Wynnum have scored.' Commentary Lesson One: Don't commit to saying a name till you've got it!

By chance, I bumped into him at the Toowong shopping centre the next week and complimented him on his commentary: 'I thought you did a terrific job in your first call, considering you've just come up from Sydney. By the way, did you ever find out the name of that Wynnum winger?'

Life got better though, and Warren soon settled into the routine of a sports commentator in Brisbane, which included the camaraderie of other sports journalists. What's more he met local girl Sandra and fell in love; they now have four children. It wasn't long before Warren was promoted to the ABC television coverage in Queensland and then late in the 1987 season the phone rang asking him to join the ABC TV's national coverage of the Australian Rugby League. He became an integral part of the Saturday afternoon institution until the ABC lost the rights in 1996.

Summers were spent at the 'Gabba. 'I really enjoyed doing the cricket. As a ball-by-ball commentator you have more time than you do in Rugby League. It really allows you freedom of expression, analysis and a sense of humour.'

Having a background as a player, Warren can call Rugby League either as a describer or an expert. He finds the former role more physically demanding, particularly on radio, as you have to keep up with the pace and energy of the game, living every moment with accuracy and enthusiasm. The latter role is more taxing mentally, as you have only seconds in which to make a precise analytical remark. 'When I sit on the sideline with the Queensland Cup TV coverage it's even harder, because I try to add something the other two commentators haven't already said, and too often they take the words out of my mouth. But I love the challenge.'

When the Super League war divided the game in 1996, Warren was offered a job in Sydney calling Rugby League with Fox Sports. As the dispute moved from the football field to the law courts and back, Warren had to content himself with calling boxing and other sports. Finally after two turbulent years of Super League, he moved back to the ABC in Brisbane. His job in Sport had been filled, but he switched to general radio entertainment, and, to his credit, was given his own statewide weekend show which has proven to be a ratings success.

It's a real team effort calling football and Warren has made some good friends in the commentary box over the years.

He loved working with one of the legends of the game, big Artie Beetson, in the late 1980s. 'It wasn't a myth that Artie loved a pie. He liked to have one before we called a game but was shy about being seen buying it, so I was the pie-fetcher. One day Artie was ravenous and forgot to take off his headset, which had a little microphone next to his mouth. He took a big bite out of the pie, plunging the mic into a bed of hot gravy and gristle! You should have seen our sound engineer's face!'

For someone who didn't really know where he was heading in his twenties, Warren has happily combined a parallel career in two loves, broadcasting and Rugby League. Although his winter weekends are long and full, he loves calling the games. 'Perhaps the one thing I've learned is to relax and not take the whole thing too seriously. I was so intent on not making mistakes before that I probably missed the opportunity for humour. Now I'm a lot more relaxed and I try to remember that while for the players winning and losing is a desperate contest, for the audience sport is just another form of entertainment.'

Hear, hear, Warren.

FIVE

Gordon Bray

THE VOICE OF RUGBY

'My passion is sport in general. In 25 years at the ABC I must have called more than twenty. It was a furphy that I just wanted to call Rugby'

Love him or hate him, Gordon is 'the voice of Rugby'. Starting in 1972 with a commentary of a game between Tasmania and France on ABC Radio, Gordon has now tallied over 300 Rugby Union Test calls, both on radio and television. As Channel Nine have taken over the rights to Test Rugby from 2010 on Australian television, Gordon now freelances. Taking over

Gordon Bray, the ultimate professional

from the legendary Norman 'Nugget' May as ABC TV's senior commentator in 1980, Gordon has polarised rugby fans with his unique style of commentary.

Meticulous in research and preparation, Gordon unearths all kinds of information on players and referees, some fascinating, some trivial. Many of his biographical one-liners have gone down in Rugby Union lore.

Sometimes his lucid lines can annoy the viewer, such as during the 1984 Grand Slam tour when he wanted to let us in on a fascinating insight into the background of Wallaby lock Steve Cutler. Unfortunately, Gordon chose a line-out near the Welsh line as the time to tell viewers that the Sydney University student 'wrote his thesis on the seasonal breeding habits of the ewe' — just as Cutler was winning the ball and sparking a Wallaby attack!

As one who started at ABC Sport in the same year as Gordon in 1968, I have been able to observe and admire his progress closely over the years. A former NSW Combined High Schools half-back who is also a qualified referee, Gordon has a rare empathy with players and a deep knowledge of the laws. As a player he was good enough to play in the Firsts for Waratah Shield champions Homebush High (alongside John Symond of Aussie Home Loans) and for the Wallaby Golden Oldies Over 35s team in Bermuda. However his playing career came to an abrupt end shortly after the Bermuda experience when he volunteered to fill in at half-back at the Hong Kong Sevens and suffered a broken shoulder.

Behind a microphone though, he has few peers. With precise enunciation in the best ABC tradition, Gordon still manages to convey the excitement of a schoolboy watching his first international in moments of high drama. His passion for the game is matched only by his encyclopaedic knowledge and Gordon's economy of words, accuracy and pitch of excitement are object lessons for budding commentators. Who will ever forget his strident 'Campese ... Campese!!' as the flying winger raced away for another try on the 1984 Grand Slam tour. Or his strangled cry of 'Lynagh. He's over!!' as the Wallabies snatched an improbable one-point victory with a last-minute try against Ireland en route to winning the 1991 World Cup? That call was tinged with emotion on a personal level as well, as ABC TV were about to lose the rights to TV coverage of Test Rugby to Network Ten. Yet there were no complaints or bitterness in the commentary; Gordon was as professional as always.

Then there was that spine-tingling World Cup final in 2003, when we all knew that the Wallabies' nemesis, England's Johnny Wilkinson, would try for a shot at a field goal to break the deadlock in extra time. When it came, Gordon anticipated perfectly, saying as he set himself: 'Here's the drop goal for Wilkinson ...' and when it soared high over the crossbar: 'That surely is England's stairway to Rugby heaven.' Gordon never gilds the lily — he lets the pictures tell the story, but adds the right words at the right time.

His technique has been polished by working with some of the great callers; Welshman Cliff Morgan, Bill McLaren of Scotland and Keith Quinn from New Zealand. The Welsh wordsmith was the master of understatement; his mantra for television commentary was simple: 'Silence is golden.'

When Gordon Hamilton scored a runaway try to give Ireland an unlikely lead over Australia in the World Cup quarter-final in 1991, the old grandstand at Lansdowne Road shook to its foundations, and not from the railway line that runs underneath. With only five minutes left Ireland seemed set for an upset victory and the fans went berserk, invading the pitch and cheering their lungs out. Gordon indicated to his fellow commentators, Chris Handy and Gary Pearse, to remain silent. 'We let the crowd tell the story. There was no point in trying to talk over the top of that outpouring of emotion — later I was told that we didn't say a word for 31 seconds.'

From Bill McLaren, the silky-voiced Scotsman who broadcast well into his 70s, Gordon learned the use of team spreadsheets, with informative notes in five different-coloured inks. 'I still do it today, but in the form of a computer printout. I still lock myself away for four or five days absorbing all the information and, strangely enough, rarely look at it during a call. It's just reassuring to have it there.' And from Keith Quinn, he learned how to convey a sense of occasion.

A vital part of any commentary is expert analysis and Gordon worked with some legendary players-turned-commentators. He began with former Wallaby captain Trevor Allan in 1980 and then sat next to Mark Ella, Simon Poidevin, Gary Pearse and Nick Farr-Jones at various times. At Seven he was joined in the box those days by Tim Horan and Dan Crowley and, as always, seemed to bring out the best in them. Some forget that Gordon was trained by the

ABC and therefore is an all-rounder. He called over twenty sports in his 25 years at the ABC and, nowadays at Channel Seven, still fills in during summer on tennis, sailing or golf telecasts.

As in all professions, broadcasters learn by their mistakes and, in his early days, Gordon confesses to more than his share. 'My first television outside broadcast was of lawn bowls in Tasmania. They used to throw us into everything down there and I was extremely nervous, as I knew virtually nothing about bowls. It was the North versus the South and, to distinguish the teams, different-coloured discs had been placed on their bowls. In my introduction, live throughout the state, I came out with something like this: "... and you'll notice that the team from the North have yellow spots on their balls." If I'd been in Sydney, I'd probably have been suspended, but that great ABC broadcaster Margaret Throsby once told me, "If you make an error, don't let it throw you — just keep going." So I did.'

Gordon's boss in Hobart, the avuncular Don Closs, gave his young protégé plenty of opportunities; he called everything from Australian Rules to hot air ballooning. One particular memory still makes Gordon squirm. It was the Australian Marathon Championship, simulcast on ABC Radio and ABC TV, with Gordon calling both. He had been unable to attend the press conference prior to the race but knew that it would be a race between two: world record-holder Derek Clayton against the form athlete that season, John Farrington. Sure enough, the two stars broke away from the field in the early stages and over two hours later came into the Hobart Showgrounds for the finish, locked together. When Farrington kicked ahead of his illustrious rival, Gordon, sensing an upset, began to get excited. 'Here's Farrington, the underdog, and he's forging further ahead of the world number one! It's Farrington leading from Clayton!'

Next to Gordon's open-air commentary position in the grandstand was an elderly gentleman who obviously knew his athletes better than Gordon. 'You bloody idiot — that's Clayton.'

Suddenly the penny dropped — Gordon had them the wrong way round — and had done all race. So he got even more excited: 'And now it's Clayton who's hit the front. He's judged his kick perfectly and the world champion is going to take the Australian title.'

For the TV replay Gordon had to call the race all over again but radio listeners were none the wiser — save for one old man who walked away shaking his head and muttering: 'Bloody commentators — where do they get these blokes?'

Another gaffe came at the World Woodchopping Championship in Burnie. Organisers had given Gordon the start list for the final numbered from station one to five, from left to right but, in fact, they were in the reverse order. With mounting excitement as the woodchips flew and the crowd roared, Gordon described the action for the Tasmanian TV audience. Fortunately for Gordon not only was it a Tasmanian winner, but he was in station three — the only name he called correctly!

Gordon has travelled the world calling Rugby and been privileged to sit in the best seats at the most famous grounds like Twickenham, Newlands, Cardiff Arms Park and Ballymore. Sometimes on tour the accommodation hasn't been quite five star, such as in New Zealand in 1986 when Wallaby coach Alan Jones uprooted his whole touring party in protest against a sub-standard hotel in Thames Valley and shifted them to the next town. The press party remained, however, and Gordon confided to his News Limited colleague, Terry Smith: 'This lot could go up in smoke if someone drops a match.'

Sure enough, the fire alarm rang out during the night and Gordon raced out into the hallway, only to confront Smith, clad in his pyjamas and clutching his wallet in one hand and false teeth in the other.

Rugby is, after all, just a game and Gordon never loses sight of that. He has a wry sense of humour, which was at its best when he teamed in the box with that rambunctious character Chris 'Buddha' Handy — their mutual respect and passion for the game added a new dimension to the Channel Seven coverage.

Now 63, Gordon still likes to keep fit, playing regular tennis and golf. His son Andrew is a fine tennis player and daughter Anna plays first grade hockey, so sport runs in the family. These days, Gordon and his wife, Cathy, live in semi-retirement at McMasters Beach on the NSW Central Coast with their two Jack Russells.

Gordon has also written five books on Rugby and is a columnist with the Sydney *Daily Telegraph*. If Rugby is the game they play in heaven, then surely his press pass will get him in.

SIX

Ian Chappell

ALWAYS HIS OWN MAN

> *'"Wide World of Sports" boss David Hill told me there were three words you don't say on television, and I got three of them out in one sentence'*

For someone who has been one of Australia's greatest cricket captains, Ian Chappell has a lot of critics. On the field and in the commentary box, his abrasive manner has often upset people. Mind you, not everyone dislikes him. It's just that he polarises people with his forthright, almost belligerent, views. For example, he has never been one to praise

Ian Chappell, dapperly dressed as ever

our most famous sportsman, Sir Donald Bradman. As a captain, Chappell crossed swords with the Don over player payments and the rift was never healed. It's almost like swearing in church to criticise such a national icon, but Chappell doesn't care what others think.

That is what made Ian Chappell such a great player and captain. He refused to be intimidated, he was pugnacious and daring and above all, he was a winner. Television commentary is a different thing but Ian calls it like he played it, with a straight bat. Now in his thirty-third year of broadcasting, he's become as much a part of an Australian summer as Pink Zinc and Paddle Pops.

His hero as a boy was Keith Miller, regarded by many experts as the best captain never to lead Australia. Like Miller, Chappell had a larrikin streak, but was a crowd-pleasing batsman. Ian recalls: 'As kids we would play imaginary Tests in the backyard and I was always Keith Miller. When we got out we would actually write our score in an old scorebook and, if Miller got out cheaply, I'd cross his name out and put someone else's name down.'

As a player, Ian was top-notch. An aggressive, right-handed batsman who was both gritty and attractive, he was a brilliant fieldsman and a handy leg-spinner. He had a wide array of shots, with a fluent drive, well-timed cut and glance and, with his quick footwork, was a master of spin bowling. However, the shot that most characterised Ian Chappell was the hook, a fearless, aggressive stroke that showed he was a fighter, a man for a crisis.

Playing in an era before the advent of helmets, he pulled and hooked fearsome fast bowlers like John Snow, Michael Holding, Imran Khan and Richard Hadlee. Batting at number three, he scored fourteen Test centuries and made over 5,000 runs at an average of 42, statistics which don't reveal how he could turn the fortunes of a match. With his collar turned up and his constant fidgeting at the crease, he was a tough competitor who was always entertaining to watch.

It was as a captain, though, that he transformed Australian cricket. Taking over a losing side from Bill Lawry in the final Test against England in 1970–71, he developed a team that bordered on greatness. With an attack built around one of the world's best fast bowlers, Dennis Lillee, and a powerful batting lineup that included his brother Greg, Ian Chappell took the Australian team to the top.

One of his most remarkable efforts in captaincy came in the final Test against Pakistan in Sydney in 1972–73. Australia had collapsed for 184 in their second innings and Pakistan needed only 159 to win. An improbable ninth-wicket partnership between Bob Massie and debutant spinner John Watkins added 83, after they had come together at 8 for 101. It should have been a cakewalk for Pakistan but the dismissal of Sadiq, brilliantly caught by Ross Edwards, ensured that the tourists would have a sleepless night. Next morning it was overcast and humid, perfect conditions for swinging the ball. With Lillee and Massie keeping pressure on at one end, Max Walker bowled his big in-swingers superbly to take 6 for 15 and pull off an unlikely victory. Pakistan was dismissed for only 106. Chappell maintained aggressive field placings throughout, never letting off the pressure — one of the best exhibitions of captaincy I have seen.

On the ensuing tour of the West Indies, the Australian attack was weakened by injuries to Lillee and Massie, so Walker and Jeff Hammond filled in. In Trinidad the West Indies needed only 60 to win with six wickets in hand. At lunch Chappell lay down and rested in the dressing-room — no rhetoric or impassioned speeches — and then said to his team as he pulled on the baggy green cap: 'This would be a good one to win. Let's go.'

Walker dismissed Kallicharran first ball and Australia went on to a famous victory. Chappell would not hear of defeat. He made average players believe in themselves and develop into great players. Leading from the front, he took his team to successive series wins against Pakistan, New Zealand, the West Indies and then England in 1974–75. He retained the Ashes in England in 1975, making 192 at the Oval in his final Test as captain.

Back home for the series against the West Indies later that year, his brother Greg took over for the First Test in Brisbane. The record books show that Greg made a hundred in each innings and led his team to a famous victory, but the reality is that Ian was the hero, shielding his brother from the strike when he struggled against the wily spinners, Lance Gibbs and Inshan Ali. Ian's record as captain was remarkable — fifteen wins in 30 Tests, with only five losses. However, it must be said that Australian cricket in his time acquired a reputation for arrogance and aggression that bordered on bad sportsmanship.

Ian came from a sporting family. His grandfather, Victor Richardson, was an outstanding all-round athlete who captained Australia at cricket. His father, Martin, was a competitive grade cricketer in Adelaide who had three sons, all of whom would wear the baggy green cap of Australia. The three Chappell boys learned their cricket in the family backyard, like most Australian boys of their time, but they had the advantage of some astute coaches: Lyn Fuller, Chester Bennett and Jack Dunning. Fuller laid the groundwork and Bennett, a former South Australian captain, put the polish on the boys at Prince Alfred College, where Dunning, a former New Zealand player, was headmaster. Lyn Fuller gave Ian the best advice he has ever had: 'No matter how good I am as a coach, there's only one person who can help you make runs in the middle — and that's yourself.'

Ian was always his own man — to the point of bloody-mindedness. He refused to conform and his clashes with the establishment led to his suspension and, ultimately, contributed to the formation of World Series Cricket in 1977. Chappell had been agitating for better player payments and found a sympathetic ear in the wealthy media entrepreneur Kerry Packer. Over 60 of the world's best players signed up for Packer's made-for-televison series, including the Australian and England captains, Greg Chappell and Tony Greig. Clive Lloyd led a West Indies team, while Greig captained a Rest of the World side.

When cricket was reunited after two years, Ian went back to playing for South Australia, but was twice suspended for abusing umpires. 'I went back for the wrong reasons.

The second time, when I was out for three weeks, David Hill of Channel Nine asked me to do some commentary. I liked it and I'm still doing it 30 years later.' In fact, he had already done some commentary as far back as 1976, while he was still a player. He called several Sheffield Shield matches for the Ten Network and worked on the 1977 Centenary Test in Melbourne as an expert commentator.

Richie Benaud organised a job for Ian with BBC television during the 1977 Ashes series in England. He found that he relished the role, especially as the expert commentator: 'As a former player and captain I enjoyed trying to work out the strategies of both teams. What would I do if I were in their shoes? It was a challenge trying to think of myself, not as captain of Australia, but as an objective analyst for a change.' He also found that commentary was a lot like batting: 'You can't afford to lose concentration. If you take your eyes off the play at the wrong time, you wind up with egg all over your face.'

He soon realised that it was not a junket. It was a job and, to be good at it, you needed to have a professional attitude. 'There are plenty of guys who ask me for advice about how to be a commentator. I tell them that being a Test player will get them one season, two at the most, but after that it comes back to how good they are at it.'

Well, Ian must be very good at it, because he's been a full-time caller and presenter with the Nine Network for over 30 years. Others have come and gone, but every summer the same voices are in our loungerooms — Richie Benaud, Bill Lawry, Tony Greig and Ian Chappell. There's an old saying that imitation is the sincerest form of flattery. Well, in the case of cricket commentators, if you've been mimicked by Billy Birmingham, then you've made the big time. Richie Benaud reckons Billy does his voice better than Richie himself. The satirist has taken pot-shots at the famous Nine quartet many times and Ian regards it as a kind of back-handed compliment. 'He usually makes me sound a bit thick but it's better than being ignored, I suppose.'

Personally, I prefer the way the ABC blends their commentators, sitting a staff describer like Jim Maxwell next to a former Test player such as Geoff Lawson or Kerry O'Keeffe. The way I see it, a caller who has never worn the green and gold is more likely to be genuinely impressed than someone who played a hundred Test matches. He will react in the same way the listener would, if he was describing a great shot, whereas a former international might be a bit blasé.

Moreover, two former Test players in the box together can lead to a battle of egos, rather than incisive analysis. A ball-by-ball commentator can elicit interesting answers by asking seemingly naïve questions of a former Test player, questions an international would never ask. Having said that, I never cease to be impressed at Benaud's cool understatement, Lawry's boyish enthusiasm, Greig's rapport with teams from the subcontinent and Chappell's strategic analysis. It's a formidable package and it's stood the test of time.

An example of the passion these men have for the game came at the 1996 World Cup won by Sri Lanka. Their openers, Jayasuriya and Kaluwitharana, revolutionised one-day batting tactics by smashing opposition fast bowlers in the first fifteen overs, in a way never done before. Jayasuriya, the powerful left-hander, began the onslaught in a match in Singapore where he took 12 off the first over. Sitting in the box with Chappell, Indian commentator Sunil Gavaskar remarked: 'Well, that was extraordinary, but he can't keep it up.'

When Jayasuriya took 19 off the second over, Chappell inquired: 'Are you sure?'

In fact, Jayasuriya scored a century himself inside the first fifteen overs. During the tournament he set new records for the fastest century (38 balls) and, in the final, the fastest 50 (17 balls.) In the bar of the Singapore Cricket Club after the final, the commentary team, all former international captains, were shaking their heads in wonder at what they had seen. The Sri Lankan team walked through the bar to catch a bus to the airport, with Jayasuriya last of all. The room burst into applause, with Chappell and the other commentators joining in. 'The hairs were standing up on the back of my neck. I thought I'd seen everything, but that was just extraordinary. We were all in awe at what we'd seen,' Ian recalls.

The great thing about having such an elite band of commentators is that, when something outstanding happens in a match, they have the ability and experience to put it in perspective. They've seen so much cricket, you can take their word as gospel. Richie Benaud, for example, has played in, called or watched more than 80 per cent of all Test matches ever played. He started in the 1940s and is still at it, with remarkable recall and an undying passion for the game.

Ian made the transition from player to commentator quite easily, but there was the odd pothole on the road to success. In 1982 he was caught out swearing on live television. '"Wide World of Sports" boss David Hill told me there were four words you don't say on television and I got three of them out in one sentence. I was suspended for three weeks.'

Shortly afterwards Ian and I went jogging together during the Brisbane Commonwealth Games and he asked how I managed to refrain from swearing on air. 'I don't swear — on air or off air — it's as simple as that. If you do it habitually, then it will slip out when you drop your guard.' To his credit, he was never caught out again.

Ian Chappell's style as a commentator is at odds with his hyperactive, rebellious nature as a player. His comments are forthright, but balanced and objective. Perhaps he's mellowed with age — his published concern for the plight of immigrants in Australian detention centres reveals a hitherto-unseen sensitive side. He's aware of the value of humour and occasionally will indulge in good-natured banter with Tony Greig over his background. His newspaper columns are equally thought-provoking and always readable. He was inspired by that great leg-spinner and journalist Bill 'Tiger' O'Reilly, who wrote a witty and incisive column in the *Sydney Morning Herald* for many years. Tiger had a great sense of humour. Once he was asked if he had ever Mankaded (run-out at the bowler's end) a batsman. 'Son, I never found a batsman that keen to get to the other end!'

'He was my favourite old-time player and I always used to pop round and see him when we covered matches at the

SCG,' said Chappell. 'When he announced his retirement I did an interview with him during the tea-break in the corner of the pressbox where he'd sat for 40 years. 'Tiger, you know that we'll all miss you,' said Chappell, choking up.

'Son, I can see from the look in your eye that you mean that.'

Chappell's interest extends beyond cricket and he's called plenty of other sport for the Nine Network. He's covered the US Masters and British Open, the World Series of Baseball and Wimbledon. He even hosted the Superbowl a couple of times. He loves the excitement and immediacy of live television. Recalling an interview he did with Lee Trevino before a British Open at Royal St George's, he had asked why Trevino, unlike many Americans, made the trip across the Atlantic?

'I just love this tournament,' said the colourful Mexican. 'If I couldn't fly, I'd come by ship and, if there wasn't a ship, I'd swim!' The crowd, which had begun to gather, laughed appreciatively. And, when Chappell asked about his prospects, Trevino boasted: 'Son, come Sunday afternoon, you'll be talking to me again — but I'll be drinking out of that old claret jug!'

The crowd roared and burst into spontaneous applause and Ian got the same thrill he used to experience when he smacked a bowler for six in a Test match.

A fit-looking 68, Ian doesn't show any signs of slowing down — and he's till got that competitive streak. Last summer a mate of mine who is a TV director rang me to ask if he could bring some friends around for a game of tennis. 'Sure' I said. 'Who are they?'

'Ian Chappell and Simon O'Donnell.'

When the famous pair arrived there were no niceties and one thing was plain — they were there to win. Hardly a word was exchanged during the two sets, both won by the Channel Nine boys. O'Donnell is a talented all-round sportsman, a natural tennis player. Chappell has only recently taken up the game seriously, but plays as if his life depends on it. Once the match was over, however, a new side emerged. We sat on the deck in the warm Brisbane evening as Ian, drinking his favourite South Australian beer, regaled us with hilarious stories about his career.

The fire is still in the belly but it's settled into a warm glow. When I asked how long he would keep going as a commentator he said he would rather quote his old mate Keith Miller on retirement: 'I'd rather they asked me why don't you, than why didn't you!'

SEVEN

Greg Clark

PAY TV DOES PAY

'I'm a 33% commentator. I just stick to calling the action and leave the opinions to the guys who've worn the green and gold'

Pay television has opened doors for a whole new breed of sports commentators in Australia. Whereas the commentary club on free-to-air TV was limited to the chosen few, there have been lots more opportunities for newcomers over the past decade. One of the most popular is Greg Clark, whose specialty is Rugby Union. Strangely enough, Greg hails from Longreach in western Queensland, real Rugby League country, but by a circuitous route through radio and then television in Brisbane and New Zealand, 'Clarkie' ended up at Fox Sports as their chief Rugby caller. In fact, he never wanted to do anything else: 'From about the age of six I wanted to be a sports commentator. It was my only goal in life. I didn't care whether it was radio or television, or even which sport I called, I just wanted to be a commentator.'

The urbane and professional, Greg Clark

Greg's heroes growing up in Longreach were mainly racing commentators, as his family owned horses and the social hub of the town seemed to be the TAB. So he listened religiously to Ken Howard, Vince Currey and Bert Bryant, trying to emulate their styles. Like many commentators, he got his first break merely by chance. One day, at the Longreach races, word went around that the race-caller was sick and they were looking for a stand-in commentator. Although only 13 at the time, Greg volunteered and got the job.

'I must have gone all right because they asked me back from time to time to fill in and, when I left school at 17, I started with radio 4LG for the princely salary of $15 a week,' Greg recalls.

He called races at places like Ilfracombe and Junda, read the weather report, wrote his own commercials and was the general dogsbody around the station. From there it was a gradual procession — from Longreach to Toowoomba's 4WK, then Brisbane's 4KQ and then, the big step, to New Zealand and 89FM in Auckland.

'I started on a Monday, not realising that the guy who'd hired me had been sacked the previous Friday. And, when they heard my Queensland accent, they nearly sent me back on the next flight.'

So Greg got elocution lessons, to polish his rough edges, and soon the nasal 'strine' was transformed, Pygmalion-like, into the clipped 'fush'n chups' vowels of a Kiwi. 'I remember my elocution teacher advising me to get rid of the second syllable in "pool", so it became "pull" rather than "pu-well" and then to put an "r" into "dance" — which became "darnce" — and I was away!'

After a spell at Radio Pacific, Greg joined the TV network TV3 and began sports reporting and presenting. One day his boss asked: 'How would you like to cover some yachting in America for six months?' At first taken aback, as he'd never set foot on a yacht, the country boy accepted readily. So in 1991 he covered the America's Cup in San Diego for TVNZ as a presenter, where his role required no special knowledge of yachting. On the contrary, he was supposed to ask all the naïve questions that other landlubbers would ask, if they had the opportunity.

Greg stayed in New Zealand for over a decade, covering Rugby, League, tennis, golf and a host of other sports. One of the highlights was the Rugby League World Cup in 1995, where he sat next to the veteran Australian caller Ray

Warren. 'As a boy I had written to Ray and asked for advice on commentary. He had been really helpful, stressing the need for accuracy, research and use of the Queen's English — but above all, to be yourself. I thanked him in '95, about twenty years later and we had a chuckle about that.'

Other influences included Rugby League callers Graeme Hughes and Graham Lowe, with whom Greg worked closely in New Zealand.

Although he was born in western Queensland, Greg fell in love with Rugby Union and was delighted to be chosen to call the inaugural World Cup in 1987 for Radio New Zealand. He worked as a presenter on the next World Cup, in England in 1991, being careful not to show any bias towards the eventual champions, Australia.

When the Super 12 was launched in 1996, Fox Sports won the Pay TV rights. With Rugby League in turmoil over the advent of Super League, there was a demand for more Union, so every Super 12 match was shown 'live'. It was a massive breakthrough for the code, which had previously received exposure only through Tests and club football in Sydney.

A new commentary team was introduced, with Greg Martin, the former Wallaby full-back, included. I was the anchorman, with Sam Scott-Young and Brian Smith the other experts. With a rookie team thrown together at the last minute, there were naturally some teething troubles at first. However, after a while we settled down and were really enjoying the job. One thing was for sure — Greg Martin, the laconic Queenslander, was a natural. Crowds were huge and viewers were signing up in droves to watch this exciting new international competition between 12 teams from South Africa, New Zealand and Australia. However, after 12 weeks, Channel Seven took over the whole production — a move that was never explained to us commentators.

After a season using Seven's production team sanity prevailed and Fox decided to do its own thing. By this time Greg Clark had seen the opportunity to return to his homeland, joining Fox Sports as a Rugby League commentator. As there was precious little League to cover, Greg tried out as a Rugby caller, and got the job. Greg Martin was recalled and joined forces with Phil Kearns. Rod Kafer was later added to the team as an analyst.

Greg's technique is based on remembering that television is an intimate medium — you are usually talking to just one person. So he's fairly colloquial and down to earth in his delivery. He researches meticulously, poring over the team lists when they come out every Wednesday, checking with his statistician and writing cryptic notes next to each name and number, 1 to 22, on a large spreadsheet for the call. According to Greg, 'The stats are there in case you need them but I try not to bombard people with too much. One example was Lote Tuqiri, who had gone 15 games without scoring a try, so I was hanging out for him to break the drought. When he did, the game was in New Zealand and I didn't get to call it anyway!'

How do you cover a mistake? Greg can't recall any clangers, like calling the wrong try-scorer in a Test or Grand Final, but when the inevitable glitch happens his attitude is

'Put your hand up.' He simply apologises and corrects it and carries on. Or if he can't see who actually scored a try he will make a general comment, while he's searching for the try-scorer, like: 'It's a pushover! A great pushover try by the Queensland Reds!'

'Sometimes you can get big props confused, because they tend to look pretty much the same and the fashion for close-cropped hair doesn't help. I wish backs wouldn't wear headgear because they tend to look like forwards, but they can sometimes help. Nathan Sharp, for example, is easy to pick because of his bright blue headgear.'

How do you call teams you haven't seen before?

'This doesn't happen much, as international teams don't change much and you can watch them train. But the Hong Kong Sevens is always a test, as you can get two teams you've never seen before, like Spain and Portugal, for example. There are generally one or two stars in each team, so you concentrate on them at first and hope the others sort themselves out. And you always have your co-commentator sitting beside you — it's a team effort.'

After 15 years in the job, 'Clarky' has developed into a smooth and confident commentator, but he's still content to underplay his hand and defer to his experts: 'I call myself a 33 per cent commentator. I just stick to calling the action and I leave the opinions to the guys who've worn the green and gold.'

The result is a compelling mix. Kearns, with his dry insights into the mysteries of forward play; Kafer, with clever illustrated game analysis, and Martin, the master of the witty one-liner. In fact, if there is a better Rugby analyst than Greg Martin around, I haven't heard him. He has credibility, intelligence, a flair for language and, above all, a brilliant sense of humour — all in all he's an entertainer.

Greg Clark has become a polished all-rounder, covering Olympic Games, the Australian Open tennis and Rugby World Cups as the highlights of his varied 30-year career in broadcasting.

'The Rugby World Cup final in 2003 would probably be the most memorable, although Australia didn't win it. Just the thrill of being there, in the best seats in the house, with a sell-out crowd. It was fantastic.'

The toughest gig for Greg was the Sydney 2000 Olympics, which he covered for Asian Television. He called tennis, water polo, hockey, soccer and table tennis, all on his own. 'I felt sorry for the viewers listening to my pontifications on the finer points of the serve in the table tennis, but calling the Opening and Closing Ceremonies was a thrill.'

Greg is a humble bloke who enjoys a beer and a round of golf. He's married and has a couple of teenage kids. His only passion is his job — 'The best job in the world'.

EIGHT

Gerry Collins

AUNTY'S EVERYWHERE MAN

'In some situations the emotion carries the broadcast. You just have to tell it like it is'

It's not often that a commentator's first effort is his best but, in the case of the ABC's swimming caller Gerry Collins, his first was certainly his most memorable. It was the first finals session at the Seoul Olympics in 1988 and Gerry was making his debut as chief caller for ABC Radio. As if that wasn't enough to give him the jitters, sitting next to him as colour commentator was the country's most famous swimming caller, Norman 'Nugget' May. The event was the men's 200 metres freestyle and it was a hot field.

'It was unbelievably exciting,' Gerry recalled. 'We had the holders of the 100, 200 and 400 metres world records Matt Biondi, Michael Gross and Arthur Wodjat — all up against young Aussie Duncan Armstrong, from my home town of Brisbane, who was only ranked forty-sixth in the world.

Aunty's 'everywhere man', Gerry Collins

'We expected Duncan to be competitive but not to win in a new world record, so I got a bit carried away over the last lap. As he surged past Biondi after the final turn, I started screaming "Australia could win gold." I said it twice. With fifteen metres to go I thought my voice would give in, but somehow I managed to get over the top of all that noise and excitement and wrap it up with "Duncan Armstrong's got the gold medal."

'After the session "Nugget" had to go to dinner with AOC President John Coates, so I walked back to the Media Village on my own and I swear — my feet didn't touch the ground!'

Back at the Village Gerry got a rousing reception from his ABC colleagues, who appreciated just what he had done. Commentators prepare just as athletes do and, when it all comes together, there's nothing better than the recognition of your peers. But today's rooster can become tomorrow's feather duster.

In his call of the 400 metres final, he forecast that Armstrong could do the double and, in his excitement, with Duncan looming again, called the finish of the race 100 metres too early. You're only as good as your last call, as they say in sports commentary.

Since those early days Gerry has become ABC Sport's 'voice of swimming.' A five-times-a-week swimmer himself, he has covered every major championship for the past two decades and called nine Australian Olympic gold medals. After 26 years in the job, Gerry decided to hang up the microphone in 2010 and return to his old stamping-ground at Dubbo, getting married in the process. He goes out in his prime, after an illustrious career. He rates the Armstrong swim as his most memorable, but not by much. There was Kieren Perkins' incredible comeback win from lane eight in Atlanta. 'He had been ill and out of form — it was the swim of a true champion,' says Gerry. Rounding out his top three was the Australian Men's 4 x 100 metres freestyle relay win in Sydney, where Ian Thorpe glided past American sprinter Gary Hall Jr. on the last lap. Heady stuff!

After the Athens Olympics Gerry was honoured by Swimming Australia with a media award for 'Outstanding Contribution to Australian Swimming.'

It's not easy being a swimming commentator, as the meets are so few and far between. Gerry keeps files and updates them all year round, even if Australians are not involved. 'It's just as important to know what the Europeans are doing as the Americans, so I keep tabs on all the major meets.'

Unlike most sports commentators, Gerry made a late start to his career. He grew up in Newcastle where he attended teacher's college and was posted to a tiny, one-teacher school at Byrock, near Bourke in far western NSW. He was transferred to Dubbo, where he completed a BA degree. Like most of his mates, he played Rugby and wrote a column for the local paper called 'Around the Rugby Rucks.'

He met and married Rosemary and they had three sons and two daughters. The manager of Radio station 2DU, Roy Ferguson, was looking for a Rugby League commentator for Group 11 matches, so Gerry made his debut in broadcasting. He worked his way up at the paper and eventually became editor. At the age of 35, he was seemingly content. However, he had always nursed an ambition to become a sports commentator and, after applying unsuccessfully once, he was accepted by the ABC for a job in Canberra in 1984. 'I remember someone asking me at the farewell party what my ultimate goal would be with the ABC, Gerry said. "Without thinking, I replied A Wallaby tour of Britain". Little did I know that I would cover three World Cups. In 1999 when the Australian team did a lap of honour with the Webb Ellis Trophy, I suddenly remembered those words and I actually shed a tear. I've been so lucky really.'

Gerry was profoundly influenced by ABC commentators like Norman May, Alan McGilvray and Alan Marks. He listened and watched as much as he could and, when he came to calling football, tried to be as clear and accurate as he could. 'I have always believed that we should simply try to call what is in front of us. It doesn't matter what sport it is, as long as you can communicate the action and try to capture the emotion.'

A good example of that approach occurred at the Sydney 2000 Olympics where Gerry was thrown in the deep end to do a report on the semi-finals of the tae kwon do, a sport he had never even seen. Australia's Lauren Burns was in with a show, so he spoke at length to the sectional manager of the team, learning all the rules and jargon. When he filed his two-minute report the producer said: 'That's great — now you can call the final tonight.'

Sure enough, Lauren Burns won the gold and Gerry says that the experience, while nerve-racking, was not too daunting. 'I kept my call to a minimum and relied on the expertise of my co-commentator. It helped that Lauren has a terrific personality and she won over the crowd. In those situations the emotion carries the broadcast — you just have to try to tell it like it is.'

Gerry learned a valuable lesson early in his commentary career, after suffering from hoarseness and a sore throat. 'Calling Rugby League in Canberra the crowd noise was such that I felt I had to shout all the time. The worst incident came when I was calling with Paul Quinn, who was a heavy smoker, and I simply lost my voice. Paul blew a cloud of smoke in front of me, just as I sucked in a lungful of air, and I went into a coughing fit. I had to signal him to carry on with the call while I recovered. I just had to lay it on the line — no more smoking in the box. I went to a doctor who referred me to a speech therapist and, for the first time, I actually learned how to use my voice properly. You can get over a big crowd more effectively by clear projection than yelling. And another trick is to drink lots of water.'

Gerry was a true all-rounder. While most callers specialise, Gerry seemed able to turn his hand to anything. Although swimming is his Olympic speciality, Gerry regularly called Rugby League and Rugby Union during the winter and cricket in the summer. It was a busy schedule in the football season, calling the Queensland Cup Rugby League competition on Saturday afternoons and Broncos, Cowboys or Titans games on Sundays. Then there were Test and Super 14 Rugby matches, as well as the club finals. A lot of research was involved, a never-ending task that involves keeping up to date with team changes and learning faces. 'It gets easier as you get older really. I'm lucky that I've got a good memory and I find that certain aspects of a player's appearance will help in a call — the way he runs or kicks, for example. Then, if there's a new name, I make a point of having a good look at him while the team is warming up.'

Away from his commentary duties, Gerry enjoyed media-training young athletes, a role he filled for the past 15 years with the Queensland Academy of Sport. He's very good at relating to budding champions and teaching them how to handle the demands of a high-profile sporting career. I recall a session about 10 years ago when he and I were working with a group of young Queensland cricketers who were to tour South Africa, which included future Test players Andrew Symonds and Andy Bichel. We put the squad through the hoops, testing them on controversial questions about drugs and alcohol, and at Gerry's suggestion, racism. It was no coincidence that Symonds handled himself so well in press interviews in the racism controversy that erupted in India and Australia a decade later.

With a preference for radio over television, Gerry reckons a sense of humour is essential. 'We are in the business of entertainment, as well as being sources of information. I'm no comedian, but I reckon if you see the funny side of something, you can't ignore it.' One incident he remembers, with some embarrassment, came when he was hosting the 'Grandstand Racing Round-up', with David Morrow in Sydney, Greg Miles in Melbourne and Larry Pratt in Brisbane. 'David was preparing to call a race, repeating the names as the horses walked past him down to the starting barrier. I was reading out the list of starters when, suddenly in my headphones I heard David yell: "Oh Geez, Dark Victory's pissed all over the attendant!" I got the giggles and David, hearing me, started laughing too. It was all I could do to get through to the end of the field. Eventually I just had to throw some music on while I recovered. I don't know what it sounded like, but I reckon people must have wondered what the hell had got into me.'

Gerry liked to get away from sport occasionally and one of his recent challenges was trying to learn the French language. He did four years of study at the University of Queensland and must have progressed well. On the 2007 Rugby World Cup tour he was asked to introduce ARU CEO John O'Neill, in both French and English, at a cocktail party at the Australian Embassy in Paris.

Formidable, Monsieur Collins!

NINE

Dennis Cometti

THE VOICE OF AFL

'Liberatore went into that pack optimistically but came out misty optically'

Has anyone in sports commentary ever had a better voice than Dennis Cometti? Some old-timers might say Michael Charlton, some Alan McGilvray and I have always thought Graeme Hughes has a terrific voice but, if you did a poll, I reckon Dennis Cometti would come out on top. Deep, authoritative and calm, even in a crisis, Dennis has the kind of voice that demands attention, that can't be wrong, that delivers a punchline better than anyone else.

In sports commentary, a good voice is half the battle, but it's certainly not everything. I've known plenty of broadcasters with rich, deep voices who are lousy callers. On the other hand, you would never say Norman May had a great voice — it was *what* he said and *how* he said it that mattered. Off air 'Nugget' has always talked at a million miles

The man with always a twinkle in his eye and a voice like no other, Dennis Cometti

an hour but, once the microphone was switched on, he was the model of controlled enthusiasm and elocution.

Ask Dennis about his voice and he'll tell you it's natural, that he's never worked at it. Perhaps the fact that he has been in broadcasting for 40 years has something to do with it. Also that he was a fine footballer and coach in Perth, and that he called fourteen years of cricket before he became a full-time football commentator. Then throw in the fact that he is an intelligent man with a quick wit and a strong work ethic — a man who loves language, lyrics and laughter. Not surprisingly, Dennis is the most popular AFL commentator in the country, whether he's on the ABC, Channel Seven or Channel Nine.

Dennis started out in radio as a disc jockey at Perth station 6KY in 1968. He loved music but he loved football even more and that year he kicked over 70 goals playing for 'Polly' Farmer's West Perth team in the WANFL. It was a golden era for WA football, with Farmer, Barry Cable and Billy Walker among the stars. Dennis might have followed in their footsteps, but fate stepped in. In 1971 Melbourne commentator Ian Major rang 6KY to see if he could find a co-commentator for the upcoming interstate game and Dennis happened to answer the phone.

'Do you fellas call footy?'

'No,' said Dennis, 'but I play for West Perth.'

'Would you like to help me out with the state game?'

'I reckon I'd like to have a crack at that.'

And, just like that, his future was sealed. The following year he joined the ABC and became a full-time commentator. He called football in the winter and cricket in summer, working alongside great callers like Wally Foreman and George Grljusich (who, sadly, both passed away recently). In 1973 he called his first Test match, becoming at 23 the youngest to do so in the history of the ABC. He was deeply impressed by Alan McGilvray and, had he stayed with 'Aunty', may have taken his place as chief cricket commentator. But, after 13 years working alongside the great man, Dennis decided to take the plunge into commercial television with Channel Seven. His football commentary had matured, especially after coaching West Perth for three years, and Channel Seven approached him to join their team. The West Coast Eagles joined the VFL in 1986 and Dennis was keen to be involved, even if it meant giving up cricket.

In 1987 a dispute over television rights for the fledgling AFL saw Dennis call matches for independent broadcaster Broadcom, but the following year Channel Seven regained the rights. He became the chief caller for the AFL and read sports news each night, staying with Channel Seven until 2001, when he switched to Channel Nine. Now he's back at Channel Seven, the only commentator to have called every year of the AFL competition, and better than ever. He's proud of his longevity but, as he has passed 60, knows his days are numbered: 'Not many callers get better after they turn 60 but, as long as I enjoy it and my eyesight holds, I'll keep going.'

What makes a good AFL commentator? In my opinion it's a combination of a whole range of things, not the least of which is credibility. In this area Dennis has an edge over most of his play-by-play rivals because of his background as player and coach. Add to that his great voice and experience and you have the complete package. But there's a bonus: his quirky sense of humour. Dennis has become famous for his clever one-liners. He's even written two books of his best — *Centimetre Perfect* and *That's Ambitious*. Some of his lines are so clever that you can't believe that they are spontaneous — and they're not. Ask the man himself and he will confess that most are preconceived but, occasionally, they just pop into his head: 'There's Alan Didak, with a low centre of gravity. Built like a fire hydrant — which is okay unless you're playing the Bulldogs.' Just too clever to be off the cuff — and Dennis admits it. 'The game is fairly predictable, so there are situations and patterns that you know will crop up — I just try to find something to fit.'

He thinks up the one-liners during the many hours he spends flying across the continent. Then there's this one, after the cameras found hardman Tony Liberatore sitting on the bench, with his head swathed in bandages: 'Liberatore went into that pack optimistically — and came out misty optically.'

Brilliant, instinctive commentary, no less.

In 2003 Dennis was inducted into the MCG Hall of Fame. It must be a tough school — he'd called 13 years of Test cricket there, as well as 18 AFL Grand Finals. He was voted the Australian Football Media Association Broadcaster of the Year for the past eight years and, in newspaper polls, up to 60 per cent of readers in Melbourne and Adelaide named him their favourite commentator. His nearest rival was in single figures.

In 2007 Channel Seven regained the rights to AFL telecasts and the 'Dream Team' of Cometti and Bruce McAvaney enjoyed unprecedented popularity. They are both wonderful commentators, but in different ways. Dennis' delivery is laconic and deliberate; Bruce is up-tempo and excitable. While Bruce feeds off statistics, Dennis shuns them. Dennis sits and calls off the monitor; Bruce stands and prefers to use binoculars. While Bruce has you gripping your chair with the drama of the game, Dennis will defuse the tension with one of his clever one-liners. What's more, they enjoy working with each other, so they make a formidable team.

Dennis is more than just a football commentator. He covered the swimming at the Barcelona, Atlanta and Sydney Olympics and has called more Australian gold medals than any other television commentator. His calls of Kieren Perkins' 1500 metres gold medal swims in Barcelona and Atlanta were sensational. 'The thing about those calls is the pressure — you know the whole nation is watching, so you just hope you don't stuff it up. Fortunately I didn't.'

A good sense of humour is an asset if you're a commentator. When things go wrong, which they are bound to do, it's better to laugh it off than get angry or flustered. Dennis has his bad days like everyone else, but seems to take them in his stride. He tells of a recent presentation night for the WA Racing Hall of Fame when jockey Damien Oliver was to receive a trophy on his induction. Damien, who had celebrated the occasion rather more than he should have, dropped his trophy on stage. Dennis, as Master of Ceremonies, tried to do the right thing and pick it up — then dropped it himself! But, as they both laughed, the audience did too.

I remember when Dennis and I were both young rookies on the ABC cricket commentary team back in the 1970s, we found we had something in common. While most of the boys would head straight from the airport to the pub on the day before a Test match, Dennis and I preferred to go for a jog. We both believed in the old credo '*Mens sana in corpore sano*' or 'a healthy mind in a healthy body'. That philosophy has stood him in good stead and he's still fit and keen to keep going for a while yet.

Living in Perth, married to Vilia, with grown-up children Ricky and Mark as well as young Dan, Dennis is content. The travel wears him down a bit but, when he gets to the ground, the footy invariably arouses the same excitement and adrenalin he felt 40 years ago when he first called a game.

2008 marked the 150th anniversary of the birth of Australian Rules, when Tom Wills dreamed up a game to keep his cricketers fit during the off-season. It was fitting that the only man to have called all twenty years of the AFL should be at the helm of the coverage.

TEN

Peter Donegan

FROM THE HORSE'S MOUTH

'If you can call a Melbourne Cup the Olympic 100m final's a piece of cake'

Anyone who loves Australian sport will remember the 2007 Melbourne Cup. The four-year-old Efficient, brilliantly ridden by Michael Rodd, came from the rear of the field to win the 'race that stops the nation'. It was the best finish I can remember since Kiwi came from last to first in 1983. And anyone who watched the race on television will remember the wonderful interview Michael Rodd did with Peter Donegan. The tiny jockey had tears in his eyes as he spoke about what the win would mean to him.

'Do you realise that your life will never be the same after this?' asked Donegan.

'Yeah — I've never done anything outstanding before, but now I suppose people will say I'm the bloke that won the Melbourne Cup.'

Peter Donegan in his element, hosting a Racing Hall of Fame dinner

The empathy that came through in that interview was no fluke — it came from a lifetime love of racing and a mutual respect between jockey and interviewer. Peter has nothing but admiration for the 50 kg men who ride these 500 kg animals at more than 40 kilometres an hour in such fearless fashion. The jockeys' room is an inner sanctum, normally off limits to anyone except jockeys and stewards, but Peter Donegan's standing in the racing community has earned him a special pass.

Peter's long love affair with racing began when he was four years old and his mother dressed him as a jockey for a birthday party. By the age of seven he was too tall to be a jockey but the youngster loved listening to great race-callers like Bill Collins and Bert Bryant and determined that one day he would be like them.

I think race-callers are born, not made. It takes a special skill to be able to identify horses a kilometre away by the colour of their jockeys' silks. On top of that, big money is riding on it, so you need to be right. None of this deterred Peter.

At the age of seventeen, while still at school, he applied for a job calling greyhound racing at Wangaratta. The veteran caller Ron Hawksworth shifted from Wangaratta to Cranbourne, leaving a position open. It was a three-hour drive from the Donegan home in Albert Park, but the trip was worth it — Peter passed the audition and got the job. Every Saturday night he would make the round trip to Wangaratta and, after a time, was asked to call meets at Geelong on radio 3GL. He did such a good job that Bert Bryant asked him to switch to his racing station, 3UZ, where he not only called greyhounds but horse-racing as well. In his first year with the station, 1983, he achieved his lifetime goal: to call the Melbourne Cup. And what a race to call — that was the year of Kiwi's epic finish. However, a few weeks after the Cup, the management of 3UZ announced that they were opting out of racing, so Peter was out of a job. Having just announced his engagement, he was desperate for work and a stroke of luck fell his way. Channel Seven reporter Max Stevens, who is now a successful football manager, wanted to return to his native Adelaide, so a vacancy came up in the Melbourne Sports Department. Peter applied and in April 1984 was chosen to join Sandy Roberts and Peter Landy in the Channel Seven newsroom, where he covered a wide range of sports, including racing. Executive producer

Gordon Bennett liked what he saw and gave Peter the opportunity to call AFL football, athletics, water-skiing and golf.

Peter is especially good at calling athletics, no doubt because of his horse-racing background. Like Bruce McAvaney, he has the ability to call fast-moving sport clearly and accurately. If you can call a Melbourne Cup, the Olympic 100 metres final is a piece of cake. He said to me: 'I was proud of my calls at Barcelona, where I did the athletics for the Asian Broadcasting Union. Both the men's and women's 100 metres finals were close (Gail Devers in fact won by 1/100th of a second), and I got them both right.' Peter covered those Olympics with fellow Australian commentators Peter Gee and John Hayes-Bell. They called everything, from athletics to tae kwon do, for about sixteen hours a day for the two weeks and were paid the princely sum of $1,000 each! Peter remarked: 'I'd like to have earned more and to have seen a bit of the city but this was the Olympics, the greatest show on earth, and I wouldn't have missed it for anything.'

Peter has a deep and deliberate delivery, ideally suited to race broadcasting, whether it's horses or humans. I sat in front of him at the 2006 Melbourne Commonwealth Games (where I called high jump and pole vault) and enjoyed listening to his calls, especially the men's 100 metres final, where Asafa Powell blitzed the field, and the women's marathon, where Australia's Kerryn McCann won in a sprint finish before a wildly patriotic crowd of 85,000. In each case Peter captured the drama and emotion perfectly. 'That's what we love about sports commentary, isn't it? It's great theatre and we get the opportunity to pass on the whole range of emotions — triumph and tragedy, humour and pathos — to the people of Australia.'

However, we all have days we would rather forget. In Peter's case it came early in his race-calling career at Dowling Forest, a big track in Ballarat. On the way to the meeting, Peter had struck a traffic jam and arrived just ten minutes before the first race. 'I raced to the top of the grandstand just as the eighteen horses, none of which I had ever seen before, passed me on their way down to the barrier. I hadn't had time to grab a racebook, so I asked the judge the names of the horses. He had given me about nine of the eighteen runners when the gates opened and they were off. I was desperate — I just called the ones I knew but, by the 800, I had to flick the PA off and ask the judge for help. I managed to call the winner and about half the field. So, after the race, I announced: "Ladies and gentlemen, there's obviously a problem with the PA, which we hope to rectify before the start of the next race." I thought I'd got away with it. I popped down to get a racebook and saw a mate of mine who's a bookie, watching a replay of the race on closed-circuit TV. Normally they only take a split of the PA, but somehow this one had everything. As I approached I heard my voice yelling: "Hey, George, what's the name of that thing in the orange with black stripes running third?" It was the most embarrassing call of my career and Brian Martin, the race-caller, has a tape of it that he refuses to let me buy, so I can destroy it.'

There's also a lot of fun in broadcasting, much of it contrived by the commentators themselves. An incident Peter recalls occurred when he was at Channel Seven, doing the late evening news. He played a prank on his colleague, Irina Komissaroff, who was prone to the giggles. Just before the throw to the sport break, Peter came into the studio without his pants on and sat next to Irina in his undies. 'She just broke up with the giggles, so they turned her mike off and I did the promo to the sports break by myself. It was all part of the fun but, these days, you'd get the sack if anyone found out.'

That's a sad part of TV presenting these days — it's all deadly serious and there's no time for repartee. I did a TV show called 'Sports Review' on the ABC from 1971 for fifteen years and we always made time for a bit of cheeky byplay. When I first did the show my boss, Arthur Denovan, warned me that the racing commentator, Larry Pratt, was likely to pull my leg, so be prepared.

Sure enough, Larry had a crack at my pathetic attempt to grow a moustache, saying: 'Ah Pete, you've been eating those Vegemite sandwiches again.'

Quick as a flash I came back: 'Come on Larry — you said you wouldn't mention my moustache if I didn't talk about your toupee.' As it happened, Larry's hairline was receding and he was so sensitive about it that he DID have a toupee, and I had accidentally hit the jackpot. So, each Saturday night after that, it was open slather. We had so much fun over the years and, whenever I travelled into remote rural areas, where the only TV station available was the ABC, people would say: 'Larry got the better of you last Saturday, didn't he!' It's a shame that TV programmers and producers seem to have lost sight of the fact that Australians love to have their sport spiced with humour.

Peter is a freelancer these days. He called the Athens and Beijing Olympics for Channel Seven and the Delhi Commonwealth Games on Foxtel covering everything from diving to table tennis. A real all-rounder, he also bobs up on Pay TV calling golf from Asia and the Australian Open tennis. He specialises in horse-racing but nurses one burning ambition: to call an AFL Grand Final. For the past 8 years he has called the Victorian Football League on ABC TV live on Saturday afternoons, but he'd dearly love to do 'the big one'.

He almost got his opportunity in 2007 when Geelong met Port Adelaide and the ABC team's callers, Gerard Whately and Drew Morphett, both had problems with their voices. Gerard lost his at half-time and Drew croaked his way through as far as the final siren, when he too had to give up. Producer Susie Robinson saw Peter Donegan next door where he was calling the AFL Footballer's Sprint at half-time and texted him for assistance. At the end of the game Peter called by and Susie asked if he could host the post-match program for the next two hours. 'I haven't done any research Susie,' Peter pleaded.

'I'm sure you'll get by,' replied Susie.

So well did Peter do that he earned a special mention in a *Herald-Sun* wash-up of the Grand Final media coverage. Affable and easy-going, Peter can turn his hand to any sport. One of the old school, he accepts his lot and just gets on with the job. At Athens, for example, he was asked to call unfamiliar sports, diving and volleyball, but he did his research and did a first-rate job.

If you ask him what he loves doing most, the answer is easy. 'Covering the Melbourne Cup, without a doubt. It's big for racing but it's big for Australia as well. I was interviewing the famous Irish trainer Aidan O'Brien as Mahler went out to the gates at last year's Cup and he said: 'I just can't believe this — there's nothing on earth like this.'

Peter can vividly recall his first Cup, when his Auntie Fran took him to the races for the first time in 1970. 'Midge Didham rode the 25:1 shot Baghdad Note to victory from Vansittart and Clear Prince. I still remember the emerald green silks Midge wore, with grey-striped sleeves. I thought it was the best thing I'd ever seen in my life. So I went back again the next year to see Silver Knight win, and I haven't missed one since.'

ELEVEN

Darrell Eastlake

OVER THE TOP WITH 'DAZZA'

*'It's like an auctioneer in a library,
but it works'*

Huuge!

If ever one word sums up a commentator, then that's the word for the one and only Darrell Eastlake. Outrageous, loud and opinionated, the big man from the NSW Central Coast nevertheless injected so much passion into his calls that he has revolutionised the way sports like weightlifting and sheepdog trials are covered. In Auckland at the 1990 Commonwealth Games, Darrell was famously banished to

Darrell Eastlake loves the sensation of speed, and leather is his favourite winter attire

a stairwell outside the main weightlifting auditorium because his booming voice was distracting other commentators. However, the audience back home lapped it up. He transformed a sport with his enthusiasm and exuberance, so that the public, previously bored by the muted style of coverage, became fascinated by the theatre of big men lifting enormous weights. It was like an auctioneer in a library, but it worked. The big man, now 68, is living in retirement on the NSW Central Coast after almost dying from a blood clot in 2010. A combination of Alzheimers and dementia have reduced that raucous voice to barely more than a whisper. And what a voice — his peers used to say that big Dazza never really needed a microphone.

Not everyone likes his style though. When he called the weightlifting at the 2006 Melbourne Commonwealth Games, he and co-commentator Dean Lukin were criticised on the ABC's 'Media Watch' TV program. When a fuzzy-haired lifter from Nuie Islands matched the lift of Australia's Deborah Lovely, the commentary went like this: 'Here she goes — she needs this to stay in touch with the Australian. YES –SHE'S DONE IT! THAT'LL GET HER ANOTHER PAW-PAW FOR DINNER TONIGHT!'

Starting out doing surf reports on Sydney beaches, Darrell has come a long way in a 40-year broadcasting career. In the 1960s he used to travel to Hawaii each year with mates like Nat Young and Midge Farrelly, taking on the enormous waves and taking some disastrous wipe-outs. They soon learned that the cumbersome Malibu boards were not suited to the seven-metre waves of Waimea Bay or

Pipeline, so Darrell and a mate, Gordon 'Greasy' Merchant, came up with a shorter, more manoeuvrable design, which they dubbed 'Something Incredible'. While Darrell continued to shape boards, 'Greasy' decided to go into business making board shorts with his Filipina wife. A backyard business grew into an empire and Gordon Merchant became a millionaire through his iconic Aussie surfwear label 'Billabong'.

Meanwhile, Darrell began working with Radio 2UW and disc jockeys like Ward 'Pally' Austin and 'Baby John' Burgess, reporting on surf conditions on the southern beaches of Sydney. He would rise at dawn and ride a motor scooter from his home at Bondi to Cronulla, checking out conditions on the way and then he would phone in his report. One day he got a call from Barry Furber, who was launching a new radio station, 4GG on the Gold Coast, asking if Darrell would like to do the same kind of thing in Queensland. Darrell took the plunge and was soon in charge of 'Surfwatch', as well as calling Rugby League on the Gold Coast with former Kangaroo captain Peter Gallagher. He also hosted a one-hour League show every Saturday morning and was heavily involved in surf lifesaving. When the 1974 floods went through his Florida Gardens home, his surf club mates helped out. While they were rebuilding the house, Darrell, wife Julie, three kids and their dog were offered accommodation by generous surf club sponsor Bob Waugh. They paid a dollar a day for the penthouse at the Broadbeach International Hotel, then the tallest building on the coast.

Darrell and his family moved back to the NSW Central Coast, where he became sports director of Radio 2GO Gosford and called Rugby League on weekends. The station manager was Bob Scott, a former player who had called football in an excitable style and he liked what he saw in Darrell. So, for seven years, Darrell 'yelled and screamed' at the footy every weekend, earning a big reputation for his colourful and controversial calls. In 1980 he won a National Radio Award for being judged the Best Sporting Personality in Australia and New Zealand.

The same year, fate took a hand once more in the form of a call from Reg Davis, the boss of TV station NBN3 in Newcastle. He wanted Darrell to audition for a role as Rugby League commentator, taking over from David Fordham, who had left for Brisbane. Darrell was apprehensive at first, as he had never done any television work, and his fears were soon justified. In his audition he had to call two teams he had never seen before from a fifteen-metre tower. Accustomed to sitting on the sideline and calling players he knew by sight, Darrell was lost. He stammered and stumbled his way through the first half and then confessed to Davis: 'I can't do this.'

The sympathetic Davis understood the problem and encouraged Darrell to persevere. He liked what he saw and knew that it was simply a matter of adjusting to the new conditions. Darrell got the job and, with a lot of encouragement and some clever editing, Reg made the replays look fine. Darrell did his homework, watching training and talking to players and coaches and he gradually improved. However, not everyone was happy. After one of his first calls a spectator came up to the box and said: 'Look mate, we love having you call the footy here in Newcastle, but can you do one thing for me — can you just get the teams the right way around?'

Darrell was devastated. He wanted to quit and go back to the Central Coast but Reg Davis was adamant that it was just a matter of time. He was right — by the end of that first season Darrell had settled into the job and the fans were happy.

In 1982 he had another fateful call.

'Hi Darrell. It's David Hill here.'

'Who are you?'

'Have you heard of World Series Cricket? I did that. I'm Chief Producer for Kerry Packer's Channel Nine and I want you to come up to Brisbane to join my commentary team for the Commonwealth Games.'

So Darrell flew to Brisbane, where he was met at the airport by Ian Chappell and Mike Gibson, two of his heroes. At the hotel he was introduced to Ken Sutcliffe — he was overwhelmed. At the first production meeting Hill explained his plans for the Host Broadcaster coverage, which Channel Nine would be sharing with ABC. No mention was made of Eastlake's role, so Darrell asked: 'Excuse me Mr Hill, but what will I be doing?'

'Weightlifting, Darrell.'

'But I've got no idea about weightlifting. I've never even seen it.'

'Well, here's a law book. You've got two days to learn.'

Darrell was a quick learner. At the Chandler auditorium, he introduced himself to David Vine, the famous British weightlifting commentator and asked him to explain the basics of the sport. The quietly spoken Vine, who was weightlifting's answer to snooker's 'Whispering' Ted Lowe, was only too happy to tell him about the finer points. Darrell watched the lifters train and spoke to their coaches. Pretty soon he felt confident that he knew what was going on.

When competition started, Australian flyweight Nick Voukelatis was in contention for a gold medal and Darrell loved the theatre of the competition. 'Here's the little Aussie, Voukelatis, prowling around the bar. He needs this snatch to beat Kombian of India. Look at him — I don't think he likes that bar very much. Now he's ready. OHHH! HE'S DONE IT! HE'S LIFTED IT! YOU LITTLE BEAUTY, NICK!'

After the first morning of competition, Darrell rang Hill. 'Mr Hill, I've got a problem. David Vine, the Pommy guy, tells me that I'm too loud. I can't call this weightlifting because I'm overriding the other callers.'

'Don't you listen to him, Darrell. I'll look after Mr Vine. You just keep going the way you have been.'

So Darrell did it his way. When Robert Kabbas won the 90 kg division gold, Darrell yelled with delight and the crowd seemed to like it too. But, when big South Australian tuna fisherman Dean Lukin outlifted Ironbar Bassey of Nigeria and Bob Edmond of England in the super heavyweight division, Darrell nearly blew the roof off the auditorium.

When he returned to the Channel Nine compound that evening he got a standing ovation. David Hill thumped him on the back and said: 'Let me buy you a beer, Darrell — you've earned it.'

'Thanks, Mr Hill.'

'Don't call me that — the name's David. Now let's talk about Rugby League.'

Hill is a brilliant innovator and now resides in the USA, where he is president of Fox Sports, answerable only to Rupert Murdoch.

By the end of those Games, Darrell had left NBN and had joined Channel Nine in Sydney. He was soon calling Rugby League with Ian Maurice, another Hill innovation. He felt that two commentators were better than one in such a fast and exciting sport. Standing behind Darrell in the box, he would clip him on the head with a program if he felt he was growing too dull. Channel Nine won the rights to the new State of Origin series and Hill told his callers that he wanted to make it something special. 'Channel Seven used five cameras last year — we'll have eighteen this time. We'll have rock music over replays, paint logos on the grass. The fans won't know what's hit them!'

Darrell was an integral part of Hill's revolutionary Rugby League coverage. The more excitable and controversial he was, the better. Brilliant sports director Brian C. Morelli, who pioneered stump cameras in cricket, had some radical ideas for League as well. He wanted more cameras, on rails, in the roof, anywhere to bring the action closer and change the angle of coverage. Ratings for this new concept, the State of Origin series, went through the roof.

Darrell called thirteen seasons of League, Test and Origin games, acquiring a reputation as an entertaining commentator who could make a dull game come alive.

In 1988 Channel Nine took Darrell to the Winter Olympics in Calgary and then sat him alongside former motor bike champion Barry Sheene to call the Grand Prix events. This event was made for a caller like Darrell — thrills and spills at breakneck speed — and Barry was the perfect foil. A laid-back Cockney with confidence and charm, he supplied the credibility and Darrell the colour. Australia was enjoying a boom in the sport, with the success of Wayne Gardiner and Mick Doohan. When Queensland hosted the popular Indy Grand Prix, Darrell was teamed with former world motor racing champion Alan Jones in the box. Since then he has called drag racing and motocross with his trademark passion and flair. These sports are tailor-made for a man like Darrell, who still rides occasionally with Hell's Angels. He loves the sensation of speed and, in winter, leather is his favourite attire.

In summer, you can always find Darrell somewhere near a beach. The former surfboard shaper has had a lifelong love affair with the beach and is a life member of Tamarama Surf Lifesaving Club. He is in his fifty-fourth year as a financial member of the club, where he began rowing surfboats as a fifteen-year-old cadet. He learned the art of the sweep from the legendary Jack 'Bluey' Mayes and Keith 'Spaz' Hurst (grandfather of distance swimmer and ironman Ky Hurst.) Darrell gave me some tips: 'You need to understand how to stand in the chocks above the quarter-bars, so you can steer in big waves. You've got a 20-foot-long sweep oar, so it's bloody hard to get leverage on a 26-foot boat. For example, when you're going down a big wave you yell: 'Trail off and come back.' The crew takes one last pull, lets the oars come back over their heads and runs back up the centre, huddling in the back, to counterweight the bow and bring it up. We all get scared but we love it — it's like catching those big waves in Hawaii.'

It's also extremely dangerous, as Darrell found out at a carnival at Evans Head in massive surf, whipped up by a cyclonic depression off the Queensland coast. Trying to row out, Darrell's boat stalled on a wave and was driven backwards. The sweep oar hit Darrell on the back of the head and he was thrown into the water. When he came to, he was being helped to shore by his crew, but was unable to move his arms or legs. On the beach paramedics were called, as he was feeling pins and needles in his fingers and toes, always a bad sign. The alarm was raised and he was airlifted by helicopter to Lismore Hospital, but there was no improvement in his condition. Kerry Packer himself arranged for Darrell to be transferred urgently to Royal North Shore Hospital, where tests confirmed a severe spinal injury. Fearing the worst, his wife and children rushed to his bedside, to be told that he might be paralysed permanently.

The specialist said: 'You'll go out of here in a wheelchair or at least with crutches.' A young trainee nurse attended Darrell and kept encouraging him to try moving his fingers and toes. Suddenly, a week later, he moved a toe a fraction. The nurse saw it and yelled encouragement. Two toes, then a finger — finally, he was moving his hands and feet. He made a full recovery and proved the doctor wrong — he walked out of the ward unaided.

If that was bad, his heart attack in 1993 was even worse. A young surf lifesaver was killed when two boats collided in a race on the Gold Coast. Darrell was one of the event organisers who decided to go ahead with racing in mountainous seas and he was competing as a sweep in the fateful race. He saw the two boats collide in a T-bone and the nineteen-year-old crewman was crushed. His body was lost in the huge seas and washed up a few days later. It was the first death in a surfboat race in 80 years of lifesaving competition.

After assisting in the fruitless search for the body, Darrell had to rush up the beach to do a motor cycling commentary with Barry Sheene. Carrying his coat and tie over his shoulder, he raced up the beach, only to be confronted by the uncle of the dead lifesaver. 'You bastard. You've murdered my nephew. I'll get you for this,' he yelled.

Out of breath and upset, Darrell arrived at the makeshift studio and asked the make-up girl for a drink of water. Then next thing he knew, he was waking up in Intensive Care in Southport Hospital, with tubes in his nose. Gary Burns, head of Nine Sport, and Heather McCann, unit manager, were there, telling him he had died, but had been revived after a massive heart attack. He said: 'I don't know what the fuss is about — I feel fine.' He remembers hearing the 'beep … beep' of the machine in the corner change its rhythm. When it went 'beeeeep ...' he thought: 'Some poor bastard's had it.' And he died again. Or so they told him later, after he had once again been revived. Kerry Packer again stepped in and arranged to have him flown down to St Vincent's in Sydney, where he was told he had suffered a ruptured aneurism. But quick treatment saved him. He was lucky and he knew it. A high-pressure lifestyle, too much red wine and cigarettes and a love of heavy Italian food had nearly killed him. He changed his lifestyle and his diet, cut back his workload and lost weight.

Last year his wife Julie noticed a strange-looking mole in the middle of Darrell's back. He went to his doctor who recognised it as a potentially deadly, malignant melanoma and removed it surgically, and also cut out part of his lymph nodes. After a lifetime in the sun, Darrell almost paid the ultimate penalty. He helped the Cancer Council use his reprieve as an example to others by delivering a stern message: 'We blokes think we're pretty tough but it only takes a little spot to bring us down. Let me warn you fellas — if there's anything on your skin that looks a bit odd, itches or changes colour — go and have it looked at.'

Now he's fighting another battle, taking his life one day at a time. After a record 23 years with Channel Nine Sport, Darrell's commentary is, sadly, now a thing of the past. One of the last jobs he did on Television was, of all things, a coverage of sheepdog trials in New Zealand, and he still shocked the old conservatives. Can't you imagine it? 'Here's the little border collie from Buller, she's got this flock under control, hasn't she. She's herding them into the yard and ...

WAIT A MINUTE, ONE'S BROKEN AWAY AND JUMPED THE FENCE! HAVE A LOOK AT HIM! GO, SON, GO! OHHH THIS IS HUUUGE!'

TWELVE

David Fordham

A SENSE OF FUN

'Goodness me, another streaker. Yesterday it was a female but today, most obviously, it's male'

Can you imagine it? The Hong Kong Sevens are about to kick off and you're 'live' to a global television audience, about to call a first round match in the famous Rugby tournament. Suddenly, a nude male streaker runs out onto the field, snatches the ball from where it is about to be kicked off, chip kicks over the dumb-founded players, regathers and dives full-length through the mud to score under the posts. This is the second time it's happened in two days — on the previous day it was a female.

The sharp-eyed cameraman has followed the action and it's being shown on the big screen so, for David Fordham, the incumbent commentator, there is only one thing to do — say exactly what happened: 'Goodness me, another streaker. Yesterday it was a female and today, most obviously male.' David's co-commentator, former Wallaby Chris 'Buddha'

Handy, immediately chips in: 'Yes and, as our Australian viewers can no doubt appreciate, he was definitely not born in Israel.'

For once in his life, Fordo is speechless.

Commentary can sometimes be hard work but it can also be a lot of fun. In Fordo's case, it's nearly always fun — especially when he's in tandem with his larrikin mate 'Buddha.' The pair have worked together over many years and shares a roguish sense of humour. They are a regular double act on the Rugby speaking circuit, with Fordo playing the straight man to 'Buddha's' comedian so, in the commentary box, humour is an essential ingredient. As our careers have run like railway tracks, I know David well and have long admired his versatility and professionalism. He is the only commentator I know apart from

Although he's looking pretty serious here, handing Kerrie Meares (a distant cousin of mine) an award, commentary for Fordo is nearly always fun

Quentin Hull, who has called all four football codes — League, Union, Aussie Rules and soccer — in a career with ABC, Channel Seven and Network Ten.

David was born in Bingara, a small town on the Western edge of the New England Tablelands. He had two brothers, John and Bob, and like most Australian boys he played a lot of sport in the backyard. David used to imagine he was Richie Benaud bowling to Ted Dexter, or Reg Gasnier scoring another scintillating try for the St George Dragons, all of which he would commentate as he played. All three boys were good at sport and David played representative schoolboy cricket, league and union for Newcastle. He joined Merewether–Carlton Rugby Club and soon rose to first grade as a long-kicking full-back. In cricket, he showed outstanding ability as a batsman and was persuaded to try his luck in Sydney, where he joined Mosman. He was a hard-hitting top order batsman in First Grade, for over a decade until he became involved in commentary.

The Sydney Cricket Ground holds a special place in David's heart, both as a player and as a caller: 'Dad took me there as a nine-year-old to watch Clive Churchill play and I told him I'd play there one day. So I'm proud that I'm one of the few people to have played and called three sports there: cricket, League and Union.' When it came to broadcasting sport, David got his break, like many of us, through a stroke of luck. He sat on the hill at the Newcastle No. 2 Sports Ground and called the 1971 Grand Final, as his old team, Merewether–Carlton, was playing. The tape was played to the team afterwards, to the delight of the players. One of the team lived next to the ABC manager,

Tom Roberts, so he took the cassette next door and played it. Now, by chance, the famous ABC commentator Norman May was in Newcastle to survey the ground for a forthcoming broadcast. He was invited back to Tom Roberts' house for a drink, where Tom played some of the tape. 'Nugget' was highly impressed and suggested Tom should create a special position for David as the ABC's Newcastle sports commentator. David was delighted: 'It was ironic really because Norman was my mentor. I had never met him but I listened avidly to all the ABC sports broadcasts and, by listening, I learned how it was done. It was the same with Alan McGilvray and John O'Reilly — they were my role models for calling cricket and Rugby League. I reckon the current commentators are good — fellows like McAvaney, Roberts and Cometti — but the true legends were May and McGilvray.'

Taken on as a trainee, Fordo was thrown in the deep end. His first live call came on short notice when regular commentator Rod Allan was ill. David's wife Erica rang him at Muswellbrook, saying that the ABC was after him to call a Rugby match next day between Combined Services and Newcastle. David immediately drove back to Newcastle to watch training at the RAAF base. After the visit by Norman May he had been sent 'Notes on television commentary' in which he was advised to 'overprepare but underuse'. So he took note of players' distinguishing features like red hair, bald heads and beards, all of which helped in identification the following day. He got the job and became a full-time sports reporter and commentator.

The downside was that he had to give up his Saturday

afternoon sport, but it was worth it. 'Looking back on 40 years of commentary,' David reflected, 'I've been so lucky. I've been to Wembley, Newlands, Los Angeles, Nagano — always sitting in the best seats in the house. I've met so many great people and rubbed shoulders with some fabulous commentators, so what does it matter missing out on a few games yourself?'

After only six months in radio, David was offered a job at the local television station, NBN3. 'The station manager, Reg Davis, was a terrific mentor and took a personal interest in me. After every match he would insist I went back to the station to watch the editing, where he would point out any errors. So I learned how to help in post-production by giving edit points in the call and not over-talking.'

'Before every match I would spend a couple of days going over the stats and noting any possible milestones. I would have copious notes on every player, in different-coloured inks, so I knew more about them than any fan. In the call though, I might only use a fraction of it, and only when it was relevant.' A good example of how the 'Nugget' May edict on good preparation came in handy was at the Rugby World Cup in South Africa in 1995.

'We were doing a pool match in Port Elizabeth,' David recalls, 'when the lights went out and we had to fill for twenty minutes. Then, at the semi-finals, torrential rain caused a two-hour delay before kick-off and we had to keep going. All that research about South African history, the teams and the players was a Godsend on those days.'

Calling big tournaments is often easier than minor matches, as the players are more recognisable. One game

Fordo still has nightmares about was in the Commonwealth Bank Cup schoolboys' Rugby League competition, which he called for Network Ten. 'Wayne Pearce and I were calling this game between Katoomba High and Bathurst High, which was tough enough as we hadn't seen any of the players before. But it got worse when, after about ten minutes play, the numbers on the jerseys began falling off. I don't know what had happened — perhaps one of the Mums had put too much detergent into the washing — but soon there were no numbers left. I thought it was a disaster but our producer, John Brennan, told us he once called a game with the teams the wrong way round for the first half!'

For every bad memory, however, there's a good one. For Fordo, one of his favourite trips was to South Africa in 1983, where he interviewed Rugby legend Dr Danie Craven and Cricket Union president Joe Pamensky about the republic's sporting isolation. 'They had been cut off from international sport for twelve years and could see no hope of getting back. Nevertheless, they worked tirelessly to redress the wrongs of apartheid, to give all South Africans the opportunity of playing sport, regardless of colour. I thought they deserved another go but said in my stand-up that it wouldn't happen in my lifetime.'

Twelve years later, David felt a lump in his throat as he watched Nelson Mandela, the charismatic leader of South Africa, come onto the field to congratulate his country's captain, Francois Pienaar, on winning the World Cup. Mandela had fought to erase memories of the apartheid regime, changing the name of the national Cricket team from

Springboks to Proteas but, at the insistence of Pienaar, had allowed the retention of the Boks' Rugby jersey. When he came out wearing a green Springbok jersey, it represented not just a great moment in South African Rugby, but also a great moment in history.

At that tournament, David shared the press box with the doyens of commentary: Scotland's Bill McLaren, New Zealand's Keith Quinn and England's Nigel Starmer-Smith. 'The great thing was that we shared worksheets; there was no jealousy or animosity. It was the same when I worked with Peter Alliss, Bruce Critchley and Renton Laidlaw on golf; they couldn't have been more generous.'

In his early days with NBN3 David would call a Rugby League match each weekend and, compared to nowadays, it was a primitive coverage. 'We had no slo-mo replay in those days so, when a player scored a try, I would call it again from memory and Reg would dub in the replay back in the edit suite later on.'

Although technology has made commentary easier, with player biographies and statistics at the touch of a button, David feels that he was fortunate to have called in an era when there was a closer rapport between players and the media. 'We went on those long Wallaby or Kangaroo tours with them and you used to have a drink with the boys. So later on, when I had to interview them at sportsmen's dinners, they were much more open than they might have been.'

Fordo these days lives with Erica at Hope Island, a golf resort on the Gold Coast, where he hosts events like the Qantas Legends' golf day. This event has been running for nine years now and draws a Who's Who of sports stars: Dawn Fraser, Pat Rafter, Mark Taylor, Ian Healy, Richie Benaud, Tony Greig, Nick Farr-Jones, Robert DiPierdomenico, Nikki Hudson, Vicki Wilson and Natalie Cook, to name just a few. The proceeds go to Rafter's 'Cherish the Children Fund' and the invitees are treated like kings.

In a career full of memorable highlights, David treasures his trips to the Los Angeles and Seoul Olympics, the Winter Games in Nagano, calling the Bicentennial Classic golf tournament in 1988, two Rugby League Challenge Cup finals at Wembley and the Rugby World Cup in South Africa. There are not many sports he hasn't called but he rates his first Australian Rules commentary as the hardest. 'I'd just arrived in Brisbane and Channel Seven threw me in the deep end. I'd called a lot of other footy so I reckoned I'd be okay but, with the first centre bounce, my mind just went blank. Some people might not appreciate that we normally call by numbers and positions, however, in Aussie Rules, that doesn't apply. You have 36 blokes in different numbers and you just have to remember them. Luckily I was working with good blokes, Ken Hose, Andrew Ireland and Alex Jesaulenko, who helped me out.'

If that was tough, so was calling team handball at the Seoul Olympics, a sport he'd never seen before. 'My daughter used to play and I regretted not having gone to watch her. I got hold of a rulebook and just kept my comments to a bare minimum — identification and scores. Again, I relied on my analyst, a guy called Sacha Dimitric, who knew the game backwards.'

Among the best analysts David has worked with, in his opinion, are Rugby League men Peter Sterling and David Wright, cricketers Geoff Lawson and Dean Jones and his Rugby sparring partner 'Buddha' Handy.

The biggest test for David came, not in the commentary box, but in a hospital. Diagnosed with bone marrow cancer, David was dependent on a donor being found but he needed to be of a compatible blood type. A heavy smoker who didn't mind a few drinks, David had time to regret his lifestyle in an isolation ward in hospital. After six months of chemotherapy, David's spirits were sinking but, finally, a donor was found. 'It was the happiest day of my life. I really thought for a while that my number was up — it's the biggest wake-up call you can ever have.' David made a full recovery, retired from full-time work and moved to Hope Island, but keeps busy hosting sports functions and golf days.

He is a likeable rogue and a practical joker. I'm still trying to get square for a trick he played on Gordon Bray and me many years ago, in our single days. We went on holidays together to Great Keppel Island and, from the very first, had a nightmare stay. Transferring from the plane to the island by boat, the roll was called by the staff member: 'Mr and Mrs Smith, Mr and Mrs Jones, Mr and Mrs Bray …'

'Hang on — we're not honeymooners! We're Peter Meares and Gordon Bray.'

'Well you've got the last room available so, unless you want to go back to the mainland, you'll have to take it.'

When we arrived on the island it just got worse. Our room had no air-conditioning and it was stinking hot. There was only one double bed, so we had to sleep head-to-toe. It rained all night and a leaking downpipe kept us awake as it dripped. When morning came, in need of strong coffee and a hot breakfast, we arrived at the dining-room, but were told it was full and to return an hour later for the late sitting. Tired and hungry, we moped around the island, cursing our luck and the lousy weather. When we went back for late breakfast they were cleaning up. 'Sorry, we're closed. No late sitting today. You can always get a snack at the island shop,' said the unsympathetic waitress.

A lukewarm pie and Coke did nothing to improve our spirits and, when we failed in our attempts to rent golf clubs and a catamaran, I'd had enough. I stormed into the manager's office, pouring out our tale of woe: 'I've been to some dumps in my time, but this place takes the cake. It's been a nightmare ever since we set foot on the island. We want to go back to the mainland and, what's more, we want our money back!'

Roger Moyle, the manager, smiled and said: 'That's exactly what Fordo said you'd say.'

Gotcha! Roger had tipped off the entire staff, so they had all colluded in the practical joke, which had caught us, hook, line and sinker. It was the standing joke for the whole week of our stay but, in a perverse way, it made the holiday memorable. The staff went out of their way to make up for our initial misery, complimentary bottles of wine suddenly materialised at our table and we were the only guests granted access to the staff bar.

Nevertheless, I'm going to get you one day, Fordo …

THIRTEEN

Wayne Grady

"YOU BLOODY BEAUTY"

Those three words sum up Wayne Grady. Now 53, the affable Queenslander joined the pantheon of golf's finest players in 1990 when he won the USPGA title at Shoal Creek in Alabama. On being handed the huge Wanamaker Trophy, for the first and only major win in his career, he couldn't restrain himself and exclaimed that memorable, and truly Australian, phrase. 21 years later he's a golf commentator who rarely plays competitively, but he retains that unashamedly Australian accent and commentary style.

"I can't bear hearing my voice on TV. If it comes on, I just turn it off. My voice sounds bloody awful."

Unashamedly Australian and proud of it — after a decade of calling golf in Britain, 'Grades' has finally got his chance on Australian television.

As modest as ever, Wayne says his greatest thrill in a decade of commentary has been working alongside the urbane Englishman, Peter Alliss on the BBC coverage of the British Open. The silver-tongued Alliss has a mellifluous voice and he knows his golf. A Ryder Cup player for 16 years, the 80 year old called his first British Open in 1961. Wayne says Alliss is so clever with words that the director could take a closeup of a cigarette paper and Alliss could give a fascinating word-picture about it. For example, when it began to rain once at St Andrews during an Open telecast, Alliss commented:

"One good thing about rain in Scotland – at least most of it ends up in scotch."

The BBC commentary team also includes Ken Brown, Sam Torrance and Alex Hay, the Scotsman, all with their characteristic British accents. The contrast with Grady's broad Queensland vowels is one of the delights of the Open coverage every year.

It's a peculiar fact that Wayne has called a decade of British Opens before being asked to work for Australian TV networks. Last summer he joined Jack Newton and Ian Baker-Finch in calling the J B Were Australian Masters and in 2011 he will be covering all the major Australian tournaments for Ten's OneHD and the President's Cup on Nine. Those three played a lot of golf together and have a genuine respect for each other, which came across in the coverage. The relative newcomer, Grady sounded like he'd been doing it all his life. But it hasn't always been a given. It was a long a circuitous route via England.

"In 2000 I was playing badly and the Scottish commentator Alex Hay heard me do a spot of commentary on Channel Seven and asked me if I'd like to work on the Open. Of course I said I would be delighted and I got a phone call a few weeks later confirming it. No contract, just a call, and that's the way it's been ever since.

That first Open at St Andrews was the highlight of my career, in more ways than one. First, I got to sit next to the doyen of golf callers, Peter Alliss and loved it. Second, I witnessed the best ball-striking I've ever seen – Tiger Woods in his prime – 72 holes without ever being in a bunker and rarely using his driver. Steve Williams, Tiger's caddy, told me it's the best he's ever seen Tiger play – and I agree with him. What a way to start your commentary career!"

Wayne has worked on the Open every year since and the only surprise is that it's taken the Australian networks so long to approach him.

"One friend of mine said that the reason I didn't get work in Australia was because I was asking for too much money but, as I told him, I'd never even been asked."

Wayne has no rigid philosophy about commentary. His basic rule is to explain to people what they don't know, not what they can see. He isn't overly keen on statistics but makes it his business to know something about each player. He doesn't say a lot but, when he does, it's usually worth listening to. He's forthright in his opinions, without being overly critical.

"It's a lot easier calling it than doing it. But if a player is about to try something foolhardy I'll say so. I try to put the viewer into the player's shoes, analyzing what he's about to attempt to do and perhaps warning the audience that this could be a dangerous shot, or that he's under-clubbed."

Wayne's well aware of the faux pas by veteran American commentator, Johnny Miller, about portly Australian player, Craig Parry, on the 18th hole at Doral's famous Blue Monster course. Although Parry was in a playoff, Miller hated his swing and said so:

"How does this Aussie get away with that swing – it's enough to make Ben Hogan puke."

Parry duly hit a 6 iron into the hole for eagle and won the tournament!

As a player Wayne had a signature pause at the top of his fluid swing. He didn't hit the ball miles like Greg Norman but his accuracy and even temperament meant he had a successful career. He won his first tournament, the Westlakes Classic , at the age of 21 but had to endure a frustrating run of seventeen second places before winning again, in the 1984 German Open. Turning to America, he qualified for the lucrative USPGA Tour at his first try and finished 41st on the 1984 money list. Back home, he beat Norman in a playoff for the 1988 Australian PGA title and the following year had his first win on the USPGA tour, the Westchester Classic, also in a playoff.

Riding a rich vein of form, he led the 1989 British Open into the final round before bogeying the 17th and finishing in a tie with Norman and the American, Mark Calcavecchia. In the 4-hole playoff Norman led early before a miracle shot from the American snatched victory, with Wayne the bridesmaid again.

At the 1990 USPGA tournament in August in Birmingham, Alabama, Wayne tamed the demanding Shoal Creek course to win his first major. Driving like an arrow, he shot the low round of the tournament, a 5 under par 67 in the second round, to take the lead and maintained it throughout, beating Fred Couples by 3 in finishing 6 under 282. It was the turning-point in his career, guaranteeing him exemption from qualifying for the next 20 years on the PGA Tour.

Unlike many of his contemporaries, such as fellow-Queenslander Peter Senior, Wayne is not keen on contesting the rich Seniors circuit, for players over 50.

"I tried it for two years but didn't have the drive to work hard enough to win. It means spending 8 or 9 months a year in the States and I've had a gutful of that, over twenty years. Lyn and I are really enjoying being back home again and I've got my commentary and course design business to keep me busy. "

And why not? They live in an idyllic spot at Ashmore, on the banks of the Nerang River, just a 3-wood away from Royal Pines golf course, where Wayne was touring professional for many years.

He also has a burgeoning golf course design business, along with Paul Smith and Dave Grabham, that is gaining momentum.

"We've got a course in Vietnam we're working on, as well as a re-design at Ipswich and one at Wyong. Dave Grabham is a wealth of knowledge – he did Palm Meadows, Paradise Palms and plenty in Japan – and I just enjoy walking the course and having creative input."

On the use of technology, Wayne's views are simple and forthright.

"Governing bodies in sport are always reactive, not proactive. Manufacturers spend millions of dollars a year on research and development and produce a fantastic new titanium driver; then the R & A ban it. Graphite shafts, square grooves, broomstick putters – you can't stop progress – but you can lay down hard and fast limits for professional players. For example, we should say a driver must be no more than 44 inches long with a maximum had size of 330cc and the ball must have at least 50% of its surface flat.

At Augusta, where they make their own rules about everything, they should introduce a standard golf ball which the longest hitters can only drive 300 metres. That would mean we don't have to keep lengthening holes, which will ultimately save a lot of money. Fair dinkum, the last time I played Augusta I couldn't see the first green (435 yards par 4) from the tee, it's so far. I hit 3 wood into 18 (465 yards par 4) and I couldn't reach the par 4 11th in two shots. They stretched it to 490 yards after one of those guys in a green jacket saw Mickelson bomb his drive over the hill and hit wedge in. That's ridiculous."

Wayne also did his bit in the administration of the game, rising to the rank of Chairman of the Australian PGA at one stage. With over 20 Australian players on the USPGA Tour and the new OneAsia circuit growing, he sees a rosy future for the game in this country.

" Twenty years ago we had six players on the US tour and 20-odd in Europe. Now it's the other way around. We have

13 tournaments on the OneAsia Tour this year and, if we can extend that to 35, we can have a viable third tour. We've always had the talent but access onto the main tour wasn't easy, with a 14-17 hour time difference between here and the States. With the Asian circuit, players can fly over, compete and fly home again because of the smaller time difference.

We have the President's Cup in Melbourne later this year and I really think the Internationals will give it a shake. It's surprising that we haven't won since 1998 down in Melbourne – just the tie in South Africa – but this year it will be interesting. We have the likes of Ernie Els, Tim Clark, Goose, Allenby and Appleby to lead the team and the young lions like Jason Day, Michael Sim and Rio Ishikawa. Then there's Jhonattan Vegas, the first Venezualan to win on the USPGA Tour, who's eligible for the Internationals team. I'm really excited about being down there and calling it.

The Americans don't travel well. They're used to manicured courses in the States and don't like our rough, not to mention the heat and the flies!"

No matter how big the tournament or how tense the situation, Wayne will always sound like he played, calm and relaxed. He will throw in the odd colloquial Aussie comment or make reference to his favourite Queensland sporting teams, the Queensland Bulls and the Brisbane Broncos, without apologizing. We are finally overcoming our cultural cringe. Our commentators are as good as those from America or England, given the opportunity. Why pay vast sums to fly out Bruce Critchley and Renton Laidlaw from Britain when we've got Newt, Finchy and Grades?

However, we all make mistakes and I can't let Grades go with a swollen head. He confesses that his most embarrassing piece of commentary came at the Open a few years back. Asked to analyze the swing of Lee Westwood, Wayne was generous in his praise. Thinking about the perfect railway line alignment of the Englishman, Wayne enthused:

"I really like Lee from behind....I beg your pardon...I mean..."

But the director had already cut away to another hole.

FOURTEEN

Tony Greig

A GIANT OF THE GAME

Tony Greig stands head and shoulders above the rest of the world's cricket commentators, literally. At 200 centimetres or 6 foot, 7 inches he was the tallest all-rounder in Test history and led England in 14 Test matches. Born in South Africa, he played cricket for England and now lives in Australia. As a commentator, even after 34 years in the job, he's as enthusiastic as ever and he retains the same youthful ebullience that he

Much travelled and instantly recognisable, with broad-brimmed hat and cheery smile — Tony Greig.

showed as a player. Now in his sixties, he still gets passionate in commentary but is never biased. When pressed on his choice of team, he says: 'I follow England against anyone at cricket but I follow the Wallabies against anyone at Rugby.'

The son of a Battle of Britain squadron leader from a farm in the Eastern Cape, Tony was a dashing and adventurous cricketer. What he lacked in technique as a batsman he made up in confidence and aggression. He made a memorable hundred against the thunderbolts of Dennis Lillee and Jeff Thomson at the Gabba in 1974, when the rest of the English batting fell in a heap. And he has always been able to see the lighter side of things, such as the story he tells of his English County debut in 1966.

'In my first match for Sussex as a 19 year old, playing against Lancashire, I faced Test paceman, Brian Statham. Playing forward to my first ball, I was struck on the toe by a yorker. A huge appeal from the Lancastrians was turned down by umpire Dusty Rhodes. At the change of ends Rhodes quietly asked me if I knew a Sandy Greig in South Africa.'

"He's my dad." I answered.

"Ah, good decision," said Rhodes with a smile.' He had spent time in South Africa working for an oil company and used to drink with Tony's father in the only pub in Queenstown. Tony went on to make 156 and two years later was playing for England.

Standing erect with his bat in the air, he devised his own radical method, lungeing down the wicket to spinners and slicing bouncers over slips. He was the first English player to score 3000 runs and take 100 wickets in Tests. And he was innovative – when his medium-pacers failed to make an impression against the West Indies on a Caribbean tour in 1974, Tony bowled off-spin. Bowling around the wicket to left-handers, he extracted bounce and spin. In the space of 20 balls he dismissed Sobers, Lloyd, Kanhai and Murray for just six runs and finished the innings with 8/86. He took another five wickets in the second innings and England won by 26 runs.

Sometimes, however, his charismatic confidence overflowed, such as in 1976 when a powerful West Indies team was about to tour England. Previewing the series Tony made the inflammatory boast: 'We'll make them grovel'.

Well, it turned out the other way. When Greig came in to bat the West Indian pacemen would add a few strides to their run-up and bowl ever faster. He had a poor summer and England lost that series 3–0. But the fearless aggression of the blond giant caught the attention of Australia's richest man, media magnate Kerry Packer and, in 1977, after the Centenary Test, he made Greig an offer he could not refuse.

'I had played a season of club cricket in Sydney with Waverley in '76 with a guy called Bruce Francis. After the Centenary Test in '77 he set up a dinner meeting with Kerry at his home in Bellevue Hill and he laid his cards on the table. He wanted me to play and help recruit international players for a professional tournament which would turn the world of cricket on its ear. At 32, I was nearing the end of my career, married with a young family and no job prospects. As captain of England I had made just over $2,000 playing in five Tests before packed houses that summer, and I could barely afford to pay off my house. Something had to be done to improve our lot and Kerry had the concept, as well as the money, to back it up. So World Series Cricket was born.'

Former Australian captains Ian and Greg Chappell were also recruited, as well as West Indian captain Clive Lloyd. In return, Packer wanted exclusive rights to Test cricket, the province of the ABC, to show on his network, Channel Nine. Greig was also offered a future after his playing days were over.

'Kerry offered me a job as general manager of one of his companies, Lion Insurance. When I protested that I knew absolutely nothing about insurance he said 'I don't want you to sell insurance; I want you to lead our company the way you led the England cricket team."

Soon Greig was a familiar face on Australian television, the face of the insurance company, wooing viewers with the mantra: 'For all your insurance needs, get the Lion on the line.'

He and Packer travelled to England to take on the might of the International Cricket Council, who sought to prevent the radical new tournament stealing their players – but they failed. Justice Sir Christopher Slade ruled that the International Cricket Council (ICC) could not prevent players earning a living, even if their rights were damaged.

So, for two seasons in Australia, 1977–78 and 1978–79, there were two competitions, side by side, one on the ABC and the other on Channel Nine. When a compromise agreement was reached, Channel Nine kept the rights to televise Test and One Day International cricket in Australia, with Tony Greig and Ian Chappell in the commentary box. The only member of the team with experience in commentary was Richie Benaud, who had been calling Tests in England for the BBC since 1963.

'Kerry was the one who chose the commentators. He was always very hands-on. He wanted a variety of voices, so that a viewer could tell instantly who was who. There were the Aussies, Chappell and Bill Lawry, Keith Stackpole, Max Walker and Rod Marsh, as well as a commentator from the touring side's country, like West Indian Tony Cozier or Frank Tyson from England. And, of course, there was me, the South African Englishman who lives in Australia. He laid down the rules and woe betide if you broke them. Marsh got the bullet for criticising One Day Cricket in a radio interview.'

Packer may have had his faults but his loyalty was legend and he stood by his people if they served him well. Tony Greig must have satisfied the media baron, as he's been calling cricket now for 34 years on Channel Nine. His forté has always been his ability to capture the excitement of the game, and he's still got it.

'Yesss, he's got him! The finger's up and he'll have to go!'

We take it for granted, watching on television, but it takes lots of experience and concentration to be on top of the action, all the time.

'I just love calling cricket. Next to playing the game, it's the best job in the world and Channel Nine have been very good to me. On top of calling the Australian matches, they have allowed Ian and I to go overseas and work for other networks in the off-season.'

It's remarkable that Tony has achieved so much considering the fact that he's an epileptic. When he was 12 he suffered a brain injury in a car accident and at 14 suffered his first seizure. Fortunately he was under the care of an excellent doctor who taught him to recognise the warning signs and how to prevent a seizure.

Late one night in 1979 I was with him at the Gabba after a day's play and he asked a waitress for coffee. When she refused, saying the restaurant was closed, Tony grew agitated: 'But I've got to have a cup of coffee. Can't you make an exception?'

I took him back to my place and gave him a cup of very strong, sweet, black coffee, which he explained was the antidote to a seizure. Not many of us know it, but 440,000 Australians suffer from the disease. He's now on the board of Epilepsy Australia and is a campaigner for awareness of the problem.

This interview was recorded during the 2011 World Cup and Tony was in Colombo, where he has the status of a demigod. You could not find anyone less like a Sri Lankan than the blond giant in the familiar wide-brimmed hat, but the people of this cricket-mad island treat Tony as one of their countrymen. In fact, he was appointed as an ambassador for Sri Lankan tourism in 2011. In return, he has made it his business to know everything about the players, from their family backgrounds to the correct pronunciation of their names.

Always the innovator, Tony has been involved in many of the technological advances made in Channel Nine's TV coverage, from the One Day circle and stump microphone to the protractor and measurement of sixes. He's a fan of the Umpire Review System, Hot Spot and Snicko – all Channel Nine advancements. And he loves the 20/20 format, which some fear will force One Day Internationals (ODI) out of the sport.

'Just as one day games attracted a new audience to cricket, so does 20/20. Back in the Sixties people flocked to see the experimental Gilette Cup, which was a 40-over game, and then Australia caught on with massive crowds for 50-over World Series Cricket. I don't think we should flood the market with 20/20, but we need to find a balance. The danger is that teams may be decimated, as West Indies and New Zealand have been, by players going for the money in the Indian Premier League (IPL) in favour of playing for their country.'

Love him or hate him, Tony Greig has become as much a part of Australian summers as bikinis and barbecues, and the ultimate accolade is that he's been lampooned by Billy Birmingham. The famous impersonator has released eight chart-topping albums satirising the Channel Nine commentary team since 1984, and not everyone has escaped lightly. The distinctive voices of the different commentators are brilliantly mimicked, so that Richie Benaud once remarked: 'Billy is so clever, he sounds more like me than I do!'

Tony is a favourite target, with his broad South African vowels, and his 'perch inspection' with a car key became the stuff of legend.

However, there have been lowlights. One that Tony will never forget came at North Sydney Oval, where the play was a bit dull, so the director put up a shot of a wedding in a park outside the ground. There was a big burly groom standing next to a very petite, Filipino-looking bride. Tony idly remarked: 'Do you think she's been flown in?'

The media seized on the mail-order gaffe, with the popular TV show *The Panel* making it a highlight, complete with subtitles. The press had a field day and Tony was glad to escape to Sri Lanka for another cricket commentary job. He got a call from Channel Nine CEO, David Leckie saying: 'Don't bother hurrying back – you've been suspended for two weeks.'

Another time Tony's impulsive nature got him in trouble was when he responded to a shot of a very pretty girl in a revealing dress in the crowd with the remark: 'Boy, doesn't she look gorgeous!'

Co-commentator Bill Lawry remained silent until Tony exploded in frustration: 'C'mon – say something, Bill.'

'You dig your own hole – you've got to fill it.'

There was no suspension but plenty of laughs at Tony's expense in the production van and at home.

That's the thing with Tony Greig and it's never changed. Whether playing or commentating, he speaks his mind, with honesty and a genuine love of the game. He's as keen as he was when he started commentating in 1977. Personally, he couldn't be happier. He has led three lives – the first in South Africa growing up on a farm, the second playing cricket in England and the third calling the game in Australia. His first marriage ended in divorce and produced two sons who are now in their mid-thirties. He is now married to Vivian and they have a 9-year-old son and an 11-year-old daughter. Tony is never happier than when he's watching them play cricket or tennis. They still live in the same house he bought in Vaucluse, in Sydney's beautiful eastern suburbs, in 1978.

And the future? Well, Tony doesn't want to retire. He loves calling cricket and will keep going as long as Channel Nine want him.

FIFTEEN

George Grljusich and Benny Pike

'THE ODD COUPLE'

'When Ben Johnson crossed the line in 9.76 seconds George had used 53 words, nine sentences and covered all four favourites'

Broadcasting is a team effort, especially on radio, where the chemistry between those on air can mirror a conversation around the dining table or in a bar. In other words, the most compelling radio is like a mirror to life. There have been many outstanding teams of Australian sports callers, such as Rugby League's 'Fatty' and 'Sterlo', Cricket's Ian Chappell and Tony Greig, soccer's Les Murray and Johnny Warren and the satirical team of Roy Slaven and H.G. Nelson. Another team that endured for nearly 20 years was the boxing

A memory of happy times: a week after this photo of boxing's 'odd couple' was taken George, pictured left, passed away

commentary team of George Grljusich and Benny Pike. Together they covered every Olympic and Commonwealth Games boxing tournament from 1988 until 2006 on ABC Radio. They were brilliant — informative, entertaining and, above all, funny.

Sadly, George passed away as I was writing this book, after a short battle with lung cancer. I spoke to Benny at a golf day on the Sunshine Coast where he is involved with fundraising for the Australian Olympic and Commonwealth Games teams.

Benny was a boxer himself and fought at the 1980 Moscow Olympics and two Commonwealth Games as a light-heavyweight. Always one to look on the lighter side of sport, Benny reckoned he should have sold advertising on the soles of his boxing boots, he got knocked down so many times. He was the perfect foil for George, the professional broadcaster. Benny talks like a boxer — he's no Rhodes Scholar but he knows the fight game. George was a trotting commentator, with a staccato, rapid-fire delivery.

If George made a slip in terminology, Benny would correct him. As George was a strong, opinionated personality, he would usually disagree and a lively debate would ensue. For example, when they first worked together in Seoul, George used the term 'throwing lefts and rights' and Benny corrected him gently, saying they were 'left hooks and right crosses'. George countered by saying that, in a flurry of punches, he didn't have time to go into the details of all the punches. What's more, who was the professional broadcaster? This was Benny's first Olympics. Not to be outdone, Benny came back by saying: 'Well, I'll show you what a left hook is!'

It was all tongue-in-cheek but made entertaining radio, especially on the normally staid ABC. Experienced producer Alan Marks knew his audience and realised that boxing was a far cry from the more genteel sports like cricket, so he let the 'odd couple' have their head. What followed over the years was terrific — down-to-earth and colourful commentary with some hilarious moments.

There were a couple of classic incidents in 1988 in Seoul. First, in a bantamweight bout Korean Byun Jong-Il faced one of the division favourites, Alexander Hristov of Bulgaria. The fight was not pretty, with lots of barging, jostling and general brawling. Referee Keith Walker from New Zealand tried his best to control the bout, cautioning both boxers, but ordered the judges to deduct points from Byun for repeated headbutts. Those points cost the Korean the fight.

On the announcement of the decision, the Korean

trainer leapt into the ring and assaulted the referee. He was soon joined by other disgruntled Korean fans, who pummelled the terrified Walker. Benny, seeing this unfold, called through to the studio: 'Quick, cross out to me — all hell's breaking loose here at the boxing!'

They did, and Benny described the action to a disbelieving audience. Walker fled from the ring but was then also attacked by Korean security guards in the tunnel. Benny raced down to the dressing-rooms, where he found Walker cowering in a toilet. In this unlikely situation, he recorded an exclusive interview with the New Zealander who then left the arena, checked out of his hotel and flew home.

Sometimes, however, Benny's enthusiasm ran ahead of his brain. After a decision went against a boxer from Turkey, he and his trainer staged a 'sit-in' in the ring. On air, Benny volunteered to find out what had happened: 'Just leave it to me, George, I'll go down and talk to those turkeys.'

Another incident in Seoul changed the face of amateur boxing. In the final of the light-middleweight division nineteen-year-old American sensation Roy Jones Junior was an unbackable favourite against Korean Park Si-Hun, who has been the recipient of four 'hometown' decisions en route to the final. Jones was a cocky youngster who boasted beforehand that he wasn't worried about the judging because he would win by knockout.

Although he dominated all three rounds, Jones did not knock the Korean down. However, Compubox, a private company that kept track of scoring punches revealed on the US television network NBC that Jones had registered 86 hits to Park's 32. Incredibly, three of the five judges gave the fight to the Korean. Benny and George were flabbergasted and Dawn Fraser, who is a keen boxing fan and was sitting behind the commentators, was livid. 'Jones was f ...... robbed,' she declared.

How could such a thing have happened? This was the biggest upset in the history of Olympic boxing. As it turned out, a Moroccan judge told *Sports Illustrated* magazine that the Korean was definitely well beaten but, as he felt the other four judges would award the fight to Jones and that the host country had put on such a good show, he would vote for the Korean. Unfortunately, the judges from Uruguay and Uganda did the same thing! In 1989 the International Boxing Federation stepped in and changed the system of scoring, installing a computerised method which allows judges to press a button whenever a scoring punch is made. If a majority of the judges do the same, a point is recorded on the public scoreboard. No more 'hometown' decisions.

Professionally, George was very generous. A former lawyer, the burly, gravel-voiced West Australian had an encyclopaedic knowledge of sport and did an enormous amount of research. After his death, a friend, John McGrath, now a Perth-based member of parliament, revealed how George had helped him out when he covered the 1992 Barcelona Olympics. 'It was my first Games, and I was really nervous, so I asked George for some advice on how to do my research. He told me to come around to his house next morning and he presented me with a full copy of his own painstaking research. He profiled every

Australian competitor, every likely medallist and had background on the laws of every sport and the history of every event at the Games.'

George called 35 sports in a 47-year broadcasting career, which began in 1960 with ABC Radio 720 in Perth. He came from a working-class family of market gardeners and had three brothers and two sisters. To make ends meet, his father was forced to work winters at the Wittenoom asbestos mine or the Albany whaling station.

George played WAFL football for South Fremantle alongside his brother Tom and was good enough to be scouted by Melbourne VFL clubs. However, he had a passion for sports commentary and passed up a career in law to join the ABC. He loved horse-racing, had a tremendous knowledge of the sport and the breeding industry, but it didn't help his punting. Part of his appeal was that his audience was allowed to share in his weekly battle with the bookies, usually a losing one. First and foremost George was a race-caller and his Saturday night calls of the Gloucester Park trots were legendary.

Apart from his penchant for gambling, George's other weakness was his temper. When things went wrong he never held back. One night calling the harness racing he was given a 'sure thing' and had a bet. Sure enough, when George gave the placings his horse was at the back of the field. Livid, he turned off the microphone, tore up his ticket and swore furiously. His female assistant was used to these tantrums, but George noticed her pointing over his shoulder. Turning around, he was confronted by the general manager of

Gloucester Park and his special guest the Governor of WA. For once, George was speechless. He was desperately trying to think of something to say when the Governor said calmly: 'Don't worry, George — I was on it too.'

Having an eye for fast-moving sport, he was a natural at calling athletics. His call of the men's 100 metres track final at the Seoul Olympics is one of the all-time classics. It was a match race between the Olympic champion, Carl Lewis, and the world record-holder, Ben Johnson of Canada. Also in the field were Britain's Linford Christie and American flyer Calvin Smith.

George's call on ABC Radio missed nothing — although he had less than ten seconds in which to describe the action. In fact, when Ben Johnson crossed the line first in a new world record time of 9.76 seconds, George had used 53 words, in nine sentences and covered all four of the favourites. What he said when he discovered later that evening that Johnson had been disqualified for doping was shorter, more colourful and doesn't bear repetition.

However, George's call of the equestrian three-day event double gold at the 1992 Barcelona Games showed another side to his expertise. Called in at the last minute by producer Alan Marks as another commentator was sick, George gave the call of his career. After three days of competition Australia was in second place in the team event and the battle for gold came down to the show jumping final rounds, with Australian Matt Ryan contesting first place in the individual event with Kiwi Andrew Nicholson. George's call was compelling, not only because of the depth of his knowledge of this complex sport, but also because of his agile brain. While others were scrambling to calculate the final scores on computers, George did it in his head and fearlessly forecast what Ryan needed on his final round, building up the suspense as he cleared each obstacle.

'So here's Matt Ryan on Kibah Tic Toc, commencing his final round. After Nicholson of New Zealand knocked down nine rails, Australia has a real chance here of taking the double. I can tell you that Ryan will win if he knocks down no more than one rail.'

'Oh, there's a rail down! ... Ryan needs a clear round from here to win.'

'And there it is ... only one rail down and Australia takes double gold. The team of Andrew Hoy, Gill Rolton and Matt Ryan echo the feat of Bill Roycroft's team in 1960. And the Roycroft name is involved again, through team coach Wayne Roycroft.'

At the Manchester Commonwealth Games in 2002 Kostya Tzu, later a professional world champion, was upset by Ricky Hatton in the gold medal bout, but then Australia's boxers achieved a feat never before accomplished: three golds in a row. Justin Kane, David Beale and Paul Miller all won their finals in succession in the most exciting night Benny and George had ever experienced. 'There was a capacity crowd of nearly 15,000 and they were all going off their heads,' Benny enthuses 'and they weren't even Australians.'

Whether you like boxing or not, the team of Benny and George was one of a kind — forthright, colourful and, above all, entertaining.

George Grljusich was diagnosed with terminal lung cancer on AFL Grand Final Day and he died on Melbourne Cup Day, almost as if the gods of sport had ordained it. His funeral service was broadcast live on Perth radio station 6PR, where he worked for his last eleven years. Among his pallbearers were eminent lawyers, MPs, media celebrities and footballers. A eulogy was delivered by his twin daughters, Jane and Caroline, and his wife Judy, whom he married twice.

Irreverent to the end, George could see the funny side of any situation, even his diagnosis with terminal cancer. After being told that smoking had caused it, he asked the doctor: 'I suppose you don't get much flippancy in your job, do you?'

'No,' said the doctor, intrigued 'why?'

'Because smoking is like adultery — you know you're going to get into trouble but it's wonderful at the time.'

Vale George, one of the greats.

SIXTEEN

Chris Handy
GO YOU GOOD THING!

It's not often that a commentator's favourite one-liners become part of a sport's lexicon but in the case of Chris Handy they have. Phrases like 'Go you good thing!' and 'Overrrr!' are used by players and spectators all over Australia, but they originated with 'Buddha'. The nickname was given to him on an Australian Colts tour of Japan in 1972 when he was seen sitting cross-legged on a bed playing cards, his ample stomach protruding from a kimono. He played six tests for the Wallabies but his deeds in the commentary box have made his name synonymous with Rugby all over the world.

The fifth son of a Brisbane dentist, Chris Handy was a halfback when he started playing Rugby. Even in his final year at school, having grown somewhat in his teens, Chris was a number eight. It wasn't until he began playing club football at Brothers that his coach Jim Kenny switched him

Buddha and I after an interview at ABC studios in 2005.

to the front row. You need to be tough to play there – as Welsh-born actor Richard Burton once described the position: 'Ballet, opera and sheer bloody murder'.

Chris learned in a hard school, alongside state players Mick Freney and Dave Dunworth. After captaining the Colts team to the premiership in 1969 he led Queensland Under 19's and was soon promoted to A-Grade. He played 200 games for Brothers and was involved in winning seven premierships in a golden era for the club.

He made his debut for Queensland in 1972 and was part of the great decade that saw the Maroons (as they were known then) become the best provincial team in the world. Apart from dominating the interstate series against New South Wales, Queensland claimed the scalps of the British Lions, Scotland, Tonga, Japan, Fiji, Wales and, in 1980, even the mighty All Blacks. And 'Buddha' was an integral part of those victories. Moreover, he was a member of the Wallaby teams that lifted the Bledisloe Cup twice, in beating New Zealand. In fact, he belongs to an elite group of players who played in three successive wins over the All Blacks from 1978–80.

With a young family to support, Chris turned to coaching and played a couple of years in the lower grades. In 1982, he was asked to do some commentary for the ABC and a new star was born. He was a natural talker, with a colourful turn of phrase, who knew his Rugby and could get his message across. Off the field he is a larger-than-life Falstavian character who loves a drink, a joke and good company. His sharp wit and fund of earthy Rugby anecdotes soon gained him a reputation as an entertaining speaker, both in the Rugby and corporate worlds.

Although he was busy in his job as a publican, and with coaching at Brothers, he was serious about his Rugby commentary.

'I love television commentary, just as I love my other pursuits. Given that my playing days are over, I can think of no other role in life that I would crave. The combination of commentator, publican and guest speaker are natural extensions of each other.'

He sat for his referee's badge, adding an authoritative knowledge of the laws to his comic talents. Sitting alongside the straightforward Gordon Bray, he was the perfect complement – analytical and funny in turn. His passionate quips became part of Rugby folklore – expressions like 'A face like a squashed grape' and 'The All Blacks – fifteen mongrel dogs in a butcher's shop'.

As a publican he became as renowned for his drinking exploits as for the popularity of his hotels. He owned the popular 'Highway Hilton' at Rocklea, a real truckies pub, and

The Jubilee from 1992. Like a gunfighter in the Old West, he was often challenged by young pretenders. In one such incident, he was having a quiet drink after speaking at a Rugby lunch at Lismore when he was accosted by a rather drunk local in shorts and blue singlet, challenging him to a 'boat race'. With a sigh, he clasped his hands behind his back, lowered his enormous mouth over the rim of his foaming schooner and drank the lot straight down. To the speechless local, he said: 'And I can do that with a rum and coke filled with ice, so piss off!'

And the local did.

'Buddha' called the Rugby World Cups with Gordon Bray for the ABC in 1987 and 1991, the latter tournament won by the Wallabies. With Gordon, he shifted to Network Ten for four years when they won the TV rights to Rugby. Then it was on to Channel Seven. He has combined commentary with the role of tour leader at every World Cup since. And on every tour he takes a blue wrestling suit along. This is for the Falstaff in him, when the serious part of the job is over. He strips off his coat, tie and shirt and is ready for anything – a drink, a wrestle or a celebratory dip in the ocean after a Wallaby win.

He always makes a point of relating to his Rugby audience so, from the sideline at Carisbrook, Parc Des Princes or Twickenham, we have heard cheerio calls to his friends at Rugby clubs such as the Kuttabul Camelboks, the Jindabyne Bushpigs or the Maroubra Sea Lice. It's all in fun, but it maintains his close relationship with the grassroots of the game, still largely amateur.

In much the same way Kerry O'Keeffe broke the mould by introducing offbeat humour to the rather formal ABC cricket broadcasts, 'Buddha' dared to do the same with Rugby. He made his own rules, his own vernacular and talked in 'Rugby-speak'. It has won him legions of fans, enabling him to work as a comments man with four networks, including Fox Sports. It also boosted his profile and made him one of the most sought-after speakers in the country. Every year, for example, he and David Fordham fly to Hong Kong where they host a series of sellout lunches and dinners. How he has managed to combine these activities with commentary on the Sevens is beyond me.

Despite his massive build and rasping voice, he is a kind and thoughtful man. In 1994, when I was at Channel 7, I was asked to call the Brisbane Club rugby Grand Final, at short notice. After five years without calling a game I felt very nervous and tried to do my homework by attending training for both clubs, Easts and Souths. I made notes on every player and went to bed with a Rugby lawbook at night. On Grand Final day, I was two hours early in the box, determined not to blot my copybook, extremely nervous. 'Buddha' was nowhere to be seen.

Ten minutes before the game, still no sign of Chris Handy so the director asked me through the headphones how I felt about calling the game by myself. I said 'Yes, okay' but my nerves became even worse. Suddenly there was a loud clatter at the door of the box. I opened it and there was 'Buddha', a little red-faced and out of breath, carrying a tray of rum and cokes. There must have been a dozen drinks.

'Okay, mate, we don't have long. This is a tradition. These are yours and those are mine. Cheers!'

I protested that I didn't even drink rum and coke but 'Buddha' would not take no for an answer. By the time the game began I was feeling no pain – in fact, my nerves had gone. At half-time 'Buddha' disappeared again. He was back three minutes later, carrying a huge tray of hot and cold seafood, saying: 'Another part of the tradition – get stuck in, mate.'

I've never enjoyed a commentary so much. The big man put me at ease and boosted my confidence. We both relaxed and had a lot of fun, which was probably passed on to the viewers. Therein lies the secret of 'Buddha's' success.

When asked for his favourite Rugby moment, 'Buddha' has no hesitation:

'When I was asked to present the players with their jerseys prior to the final at the 1999 World Cup at Twickenham. For a commentator to be asked to do the traditional address was unusual and I was so nervous I barely slept for four nights beforehand. I was so emotional about what I felt for the green and gold jersey; I just had to get it right. I finished off by saying "Whatever happens – win, lose or draw – today will change your life forever". I spoke of our troops in East Timor and the bravery of the Australian soldiers at Villers-Bretonneux in World War I and I produced a bottle of 1991 Grange Hermitage. The Wallabies had won the World Cup that year and I secretly believed that our small nation could never rise to those heights again. But we had – and these players were like the vineyard from which Grange comes from – the best of the best. The bottle of Grange represented that – to be enjoyed at the right moment.

And, the rest is history, of course. We won for the second time, the first nation ever to do so. And we drank that bottle of Grange after the game in the dressing-room in celebration.'

Now over 60, 'Buddha' lost his place in the commentary box in 2005 to another younger prop, Dan Crowley. Such is the way of the TV world. However, 'Buddha' still appears on Channel Seven every weekend in the lifestyle show, *Queensland Weekender* and, fittingly, he is an ambassador for Queensland Rugby, XXXX beer and Bundaberg Rum.

He makes the odd comeback to commentary such as on the PA at Ballymore for the recent flood relief charity match between Golden Oldies from Australia and New Zealand. One of the high points for me, sitting in the crowd, came when Tim Horan, as sprightly as ever past the age of 40, sprinted away for a try. And an unmistakable raspy voice on the PA yelled: 'Go you good thing!'

SEVENTEEN

Ian Healy

THE HEIR APPARENT

*'I always try to look for a positive comment.
We're trying to entertain viewers not
depress them'*

Not everyone will agree, but I think Ian Healy should be Richie Benaud's successor as anchorman for Channel Nine's national cricket coverage. I know they have a perfectly good presenter in the chair at the moment in Mark Nicholas, but something about having an

Ian Healy had a very impressive Test record, 4 centuries and 396 dismissals in 119 matches, and is now a natural performer in the commentary box

162 | *Back To The Studio*

Englishman hosting our national sport's coverage goes against the grain with me.

What's more, Nicholas never played for England. He captained Hampshire and is witty, urbane and good-looking but, for me, an Australian Test cricketer should be at the helm — and I like Ian Healy.

Named as keeper in the Australian Team of the Century, Ian served his country well for eleven years. Better than well — he scored four Test centuries and played 168 one-day internationals and 119 Tests. As a gloveman he was without peer, taking a world record 395 dismissals in Tests and 234 in ODIs. And we all got to know how important he was to the team's main strike weapon, Shane Warne, via the stump microphone. The mantra throughout an innings would be 'Bowled Warnie' after almost every ball.

All of this, you may say, is irrelevant to my opening assertion. We are talking television presentation and commentary here, not playing cricket. However, I maintain that the tradition established by the peerless Benaud should be maintained, and Healy is the man.

Given that he has the credibility of a great player, what else does he offer? Quite a lot, actually. He is blessed with a forceful personality, as befits a wicketkeeper who began playing open cricket at the age of twelve. He has an analytical mind, having graduated in human movement studies at university and is a level three coach, which combines to make him an excellent communicator in television coaching segments. He is articulate, entertaining and quick witted, essential qualities for a commentator. Moreover, he has an unmistakeably Australian voice, some would say a Queensland accent, but there's nothing wrong with that these days. No offence to Nicholas, but one of my pet hates in Australian television has always been this cultural cringe, whereby we offer our top commentary roles time and again to British and American broadcasters. Jim Courier and Tracey Austin dominate Channel Seven's Australian Open tennis coverage. Can you imagine the same happening the other way around? Benaud cut his teeth on the BBC and worked over there each British summer, but we're talking about a legendary Test captain. Ian Baker-Finch is the only Australian to crack network commentary in the States and he thoroughly deserves it. Wayne Grady gets the occasional gig with the BBC in their British Open coverage, but there's no way an Australian would get regular work with English networks.

I must admit, I'm biased. I had a hand in Ian taking up a media career while still a player in 1996. He was doing some work with us at Channel Seven News as a 'celebrity reporter' and was offered a role when the head of Channel Nine, David Leckie, saw him on television while holidaying at Hamilton Island. 'What's Healy doing with Seven?' Leckie asked his sports department. 'We are the cricket network and he's bloody good — we should sign him up.'

So an offer was made and Ian was tempted, but there would be no commentary work in the near future. Meanwhile, Channel Seven had offered him a trip to the World Cup in India and Pakistan. He broached the subject with me in the newsroom one day and my advice was to get some practical experience as a reporter at the World Cup and then look at the Channel Nine offer. They would still be there when he got back and, if he went well, the contract might be even better.

So Ian took off for India with a handycam and Channel Seven cameraman Gordon 'Sheik' Fuad and they did a marvellous job. Ian recruited swing bowler and natural comic Damien Fleming, and between them they added a lot of personality and colour to the coverage. On their return, 'Heals' was offered a juicy contract and 'Sheik' had become close friends with Australian fast bowler Glenn McGrath. They discovered a mutual interest in shooting and have kept in touch ever since, taking off on pig-shooting expeditions in western Queensland from time to time.

Ian's exit from Test cricket was just as newsworthy as his debut. He had been plucked from obscurity after only six state games for the tour of Pakistan and I was the first TV reporter to interview him at home. It was 31 March when he was informed of his selection by Cricket Australia, but he was convinced that it was a practical joke for April Fool's Day. When our crew arrived he realised it was in fact the real thing.

His relegation was at the other end of the emotional spectrum. Ian's form had slipped, especially with the bat. Averaging 27 in Tests he was a more than handy lower-order player, but over his last twelve Tests he averaged less than 9. Nevertheless, he had played 119 Tests, and was one of only eleven players to have passed the milestone of a century of Tests. He played his last Test against Zimbabwe in Harare in October 1999 and wanted to bow out in front of his home crowd against Pakistan at the 'Gabba in Brisbane. He needed only four dismissals for the 400 and only 39 runs to pass Alan Knott's keeper run-scoring record. The selectors, headed by Queenslander Trevor Hohns, however, were in no mood for nostalgia and Adam Gilchrist took his place.

So Ian's commentary debut was tinged with controversy but Gilchrist made the bitter pill a bit easier to swallow, smashing a brilliant run-a-ball 81 in his first innings. 'The commentary box started to look pretty good from then on', says the genial Healy, looking back.

Ian is a natural on air. He comes across exactly the same as he is off air and has a relaxed and confident manner. So, after a couple of trials with Benaud and Ian Chappell, he soon fitted into the commentary team. Unlike many commentators, he had never been an avid listener or viewer, so he had no preconceived ideas about style or technique — he just called it as he saw it. He is a man of his own mind and he doesn't kowtow to anyone — not even Richie. I recall watching one of his early calls and Richie made a point about how players practised a ritual in the dressing-room, something about lockers. 'Might have been the way in your day, Rich,' said Healy, 'but not any more.' There was no sense of rudeness, it was just a statement of fact, and Richie respected that. Ian said to me: 'One of the greatest things about the Nine commentary team is the way we have all been allowed to develop our own style — nobody is told a certain way to call. I have a lot of respect for both Ian and Mark Taylor.'

Mind you, Ian has had his controversial moments. Like the 'air guitar' incident in 2006 when he was discussing with

Andrew Symonds the pink bat-grips which he and Matthew Hayden use to promote awareness of Breast Cancer. The TV camera focused on the players and zoomed in, to see Healy playing an imaginary instrument while Symonds spoke about the charity. It didn't look good and the public reacted. The Channel Nine switchboard went into meltdown and Ian was asked for a 'please explain' by current affairs shows and talk-back radio hosts. To them all he explained like this:

'I thought Roy was bemoaning the fact that Matty got $20 a boundary while he only got $10, so I was going to pat him on the back, but I realised that he still had a shoulder in a sling, so I did the "air guitar" thing. No offence was meant — I had mentioned Breast Cancer research and the pink grips more than anyone, but I don't want to brag about it. So I just said sorry as best I could and hopefully the whole thing has blown away now.'

There have naturally been plenty of awkward moments, as there were in his playing career. Working for Indian television network Doordashan, he was doing a prerecorded pitch report with former Indian player Sanjay Manjrekar and kept calling him 'Sachin' and muddling the weather forecast: 'It was a bit embarrassing at first but, when I got to the fifth take, it wasn't funny anymore. There are about 40 people involved in a telecast, so for the whole of that match I was the standing joke with everyone on the crew.'

There have also been some proud moments — none more so than calling the World Cup in 1999 which Australia won. It was just after his retirement, so there was an emotional involvement as well. 'When Australia tied with

South Africa in the semi-final, after Klusener teed off and looked like winning it, I was a bit choked up. When Flem ran out Alan Donald in the last over it was so exciting, the crowd went berserk, so I was pleased that I was able to keep a check on my emotions and remember to make sense in my call.'

He has never found a problem with commentating on his former team-mates, even in the first year or so after retirement. 'I always try to look for a positive comment, rather than a negative one. I don't want to bag a player. If he's done something silly he knows it anyway and we're trying to entertain the viewer, not depress him.' Nevertheless, if a hard question is begging to be asked, Ian will ask it. He was a tough and courageous player, one who played a Test with a broken thumb, and he's not afraid of a rebuff. By the same token, he can be generous in his praise, something some former Test players seem to struggle with for some reason.

Ian leads such a busy life that he rejects most offers to work overseas as a commentator. He is president of the Australian Cricketers' Association and runs the Ian Healy Foundation, which raises money for various charities, including the Cherish the Children fund and Prevent Blindness. What's more, he does a seemingly endless round of after-dinner speeches, sportsmen's lunches, coaching clinics and personal appearances. 'I think it's important to give back to the game that gave me so much — and I enjoy it.'

He's hardly ever home and he likes it that way: 'It suits me to travel around the country calling the cricket all summer and then have the rest of the year to work on my businesses. And Helen grew so used to my absences as a player, she likes getting me out from underfoot.' He and Helen have three children: Emma, Laura and Tom. The latter is already taking after Ian; he's a keeper and mad on all sport.

Brisbane poet Rupert McCall penned a tribute a decade ago that sums up Ian Healy superbly:

> A cheeky little bastard
> With a golden pair of gloves.

Perhaps we can change that last line now to 'a golden turn of phrase'.

EIGHTEEN

Quentin Hull

THE ALL-ROUNDER

There are not many commentators who can call more than one sport well. Normally the best are specialists, devoting all their time and effort to their chosen sport. Some have a favourite summer sport and another one for winter. In the case of the ABC's Quentin Hull, he does them all. In summer, it's cricket and tennis and in winter, all four football codes, and you can throw in the odd bit of wheelchair athletics, lawn

Is there a sport he can't call? Quentin Hull is a worthy successor to another fine Queensland all-rounder, Gerry Collins.

bowls or judo. When it comes to broadcasting versatility, he's a genuine all-rounder.

Thirty-four-year-old Quentin grew up in Wagga Wagga, New South Wales, which explains a lot. This large country town in the Riverina district is near the Victorian border, so there is plenty of interest in Australian Rules football (AFL), as well as Rugby League. As a youngster, Quentin attended Tatton Primary and then St Michael's from age seven to 10. All that time he played soccer but at the age of 12, he switched to Trinity Senior High, where he played both League and AFL. 'It wasn't unusual for me to kick a Sherrin around at lunchtime and then make a Rugby League tackle after school.'

It was tennis that took precedence over soccer in the winter months and Quentin was good enough to make the local McDonald's squad.

'I used to lose to guys who were being thrashed by Phillipoussis. I loved tennis but was never good enough to make a career out of it. And, sadly, that was the story with all my sport. But I always wanted to be a sports broadcaster, like my dad.'

Allan Hull was, and still is, a race caller in Wagga Wagga who also does a bit of football, so young Quentin spent a lot of time around commentary boxes and studios. On leaving school he went to university in Canberra and studied sports administration. But it lasted only a year as he was offered a job working in the sports section of the *Daily Advertiser* newspaper in Wagga Wagga. All the while he was playing as much sport as he could – cricket, tennis, footy of all codes, even cross-country running. In 1999 came the decision that changed his life – he applied for and got a job as a sports commentator with the ABC in Sydney. His dream was coming true.

Transferred to Brisbane, Quentin was fortunate to work under another broadcasting all-rounder, Gerry Collins. Like Quentin, Gerry was a country boy from New South Wales and had a background in print media before a late start in broadcasting sport. He passed on a lot of sound advice to young Quentin and gave him plenty of radio broadcasting opportunities. He soon found his feet and, in winter, would often call a League match on Friday night, an AFL game on Saturday and then a Super Rugby game on Sunday. His love of cricket and tennis was rewarded, as he became, at 27, one of the youngest ever to call a cricket Test when he broadcast the Australia/ Bangladesh match in Cairns. He was sent to Melbourne to cover the Australian Open for the first time in 2001and has now done the tournament 11 times. One of his greatest thrills came in 2004 when he was asked to join the BBC commentary team at Wimbledon.

Radio tennis is one of the toughest sports to call. I recall a Davis Cup match in the Seventies when I had to get my mouth around the names of Chile's Pedro Rebelledo and Hans Gildermeister and Australians, Mark Edmondson and John Fitzgerald. Sometimes it just came out as: 'Interchange of volleys – point to Australia!'

But Quentin thrives on the challenge:

'Tennis is hard to call on radio, but I'm lucky because I played a fair bit as a kid. When it comes to describing what's happening quickly and concisely it helps when you've spent a lot of time on the court.'

He's also called four Hopman Cups on ABCTV but he prefers radio:

'I love the fact that it's all up to you on radio. On TV, the real heroes are the director and the cameramen. The commentator is just a small cog in the machine.'

Cricket is another sport that comes easily to Quentin, who was a fair player at school. Even now he plays a bit of indoor cricket and the odd social match outdoors. The long hours at the Gabba covering the Queensland Bulls' Sheffield Shield matches might seem dull, as there are few spectators. However, Quentin's love of the game comes through in his calls and the rewards are there when he covers the big games, like the First Test in the 2010 Ashes or the equally popular 20/20 games. It's not so easy convincing his wife Kirsty that he should be able to listen to the cricket on his days off.

'She likes most sport but finds cricket a bit too long and boring – probably a reflection of what most people think. But the fact that Brendan Julian is hosting the cricket on Fox Sports helps my cause. BJ's a pretty good-looking bloke!'

Kirsty had given birth to their second child, a daughter Isobel, just three weeks before our interview. So this prompted me to ask the obvious – how do you fit it all in?

'It is a busy schedule but having an understanding wife helps. Kirsty encourages me to keep a balance, so I have days when the internet is banned and others when I refuse to watch a footy replay. With three codes of football to call on a weekend, there's a lot of homework but it helps to get away with my wife and the kids and de-frag my brain.'

If you like Brisbane amateur theatre, you might catch Quentin singing in a musical. He also plays the saxophone. Movies and music are his favourite escapes. His taste? Coldplay, Crowded House, Silverchair in their prime and, currently, the British band, Keane.

Quentin estimates that he has called between 30 and 40 sports on radio or television. Ironically, the one sport he hasn't done is horse-racing, his father's specialty. And which is the hardest?

'Well, personally I found that calling judo at the Beijing Olympics was the toughest I've had to do, simply because of the terminology. There are small differences between all the martial arts, so calling wrestling doesn't necessarily mean you can do a good job on judo. Fortunately it was only one session.'

He enjoys the challenge of calling different sports. Being an all-rounder has its advantages, so you know what not to say and how to elicit the correct response from the expert sitting beside you. But it can be easy to get confused, if you're talking about 'the referee and the touchline' one day and 'the umpire and the boundary-line' the next. Also the pace of the call is different. Quentin likens an AFL game to a 3000-metre steeplechase, where you've got to save yourself a bit or you'll run out of steam. There are two describers though, so you know you will get a break.

It's different in League, which Quentin compares to an 800-metre race – flat out for two laps. There's just one caller and one expert, like in Rugby Union, where you have to be in fourth gear for 10 phases but then have to find a fifth gear if a try finally comes.

'It's gratifying to me that I'm accepted as someone who knows what they're talking about – in four different codes. You only have to make one glaring error and you blow your credibility.

The most embarrassing moment I've had was a few years ago when I was interviewing half a dozen players before a State of Origin match and I got two new players mixed up. I started asking questions of this guy which related to the other one. I was so busy I just got confused. Fortunately it was pre-recorded.'

When it comes to highlights Quentin finds it hard to pinpoint a single match or event. On consideration though, he rates the six weeks he spent in China calling the Olympics and Paralympics as the highlight, closely followed by the two invitations he's had from the BBC to join their radio commentary team for Wimbledon.

Like most sports commentators, Quentin feels he's got the best job in the world, but there are sacrifices. You have to be prepared to work long and unusual hours, every weekend and most public holidays. When other sport lovers are out enjoying their game, you are at work. It's an all-consuming obsession and the strain on family life is considerable – there are plenty of divorcees in commentary boxes.

Sport is not a matter of life and death though; there are plenty of lighter moments. One that Quentin recalls with a chuckle occurred one hot Sunday afternoon at Robina.

'We were in the middle of a local derby between the Titans and the Cowboys when the mixer caught fire. Honestly, there were flames coming out of the equipment, so I had to quickly throw back to the studio. Luckily our technician, 'Aussie Bob', had a spare and three minutes later we were back on air. I had to then try to explain what had happened to the audience, which must have sounded a bit far-fetched. But we thought it was hilarious.'

Unfulfilled ambitions?

'Well, I'd love to call an AFL or NRL Grand Final but I know, living in Brisbane, that's unrealistic. I've already done the 2003 Rugby World Cup and several Bledisloe Cup matches, but the one I'd really love to do is an Ashes cricket tour. That's a possibility, so I'll just keep doing my best.'

NINETEEN

Tim Lane

A CLASS ACT

'So here are the two Tanzanians, Ikangaa and Shahanga, taking it in turns to break wind in front'

If I was to pick a commentator to call the World Korfball (see footnote on page 110) Championships, I'd go for Tim Lane. Why korfball... and why Lane? Well, I deliberately named a sport (which I have called incidentally) that is fast-moving, exotic and has a rich history. The reason I went for Tim is because I regard him as the equal of any commentator, radio or television, in Australia. He loves delving into the

Tim Lane's cricket coverage from the sub-continent made mesmerising listening

history of a sport, is a painstaking researcher and has the ability to give an entertaining description of sport, whether it's a blinding flurry of action or nothing is happening at all. What's more, he is a wordsmith with a pleasant voice.

A man who has called the past 27 AFL Grand Finals, Tim loves his footy with a passion and regards it as something of a 'speed test'. 'Your comprehension powers and your ability to translate into words which, hopefully, inform and entertain, is challenged.'

In summer Tim's attention turns to cricket, a sport that he called at the top level for fifteen years on the ABC — and a test of a different kind for the caller. 'There are times when I go to air for my twenty minutes with the score at 4 for 180 and, as I stand to leave twenty minutes later, it's still 4 for 180. There hasn't been a wicket; there hasn't been a run scored in twenty minutes but, if I haven't been making it entertaining and interesting, I'll be disappointed in myself.'

Tim has seen both sides of the fence when it comes to working for the ABC and commercial TV stations. Nowadays he works as an AFL TV commentator with Network Ten, but still calls Friday night games for ABC Radio. A great admirer of Richie Benaud, he prefers to keep his commentary to a minimum on television, letting the pictures tell the story. 'It's the way Dick Mason trained us at the ABC in Melbourne, to keep the commentary sparse. I must admit when I joined Ten in 2003 I felt my natural style was a bit too different, so I have got a bit more wordy, but I think the reason Richie is still so highly regarded is because he found his own way and stuck to it.'

Which is more difficult — radio or TV?

'Most people think TV is easier because you have to say less, but I think it's the other way round. True, you have to work hard on radio to paint a word picture, you can't let up but, on TV, you have a real balancing act. You have to try to complement the picture but, the fact is, the viewer can also see it. So whatever you say, the audience might agree; might disagree. If they agree, you're perhaps stating the obvious; if they disagree, they think you're a mug. So it can be a bit of a no-win on TV. Except in the rare circumstance where the commentator can offer something truly enlightening, not always easy to do, even for someone with a lot of experience. I think that's why you hear so much criticism of TV commentators.'

Like a lot of good commentators, Tim grew up in Tasmania. Born in Launceston in 1951, Tim and his family moved to Devonport in 1963. After graduating from school he attempted a science course at the University of Tasmania, but failed. Not knowing what to do with his life, he found work at the local Edgell factory and had a good time with his mates, playing football and going to the pub. Then fate took a hand. One day he was playing pool with a mate and discussing football, when the local sports commentator overheard him and asked whether he would be interested in helping out with calling the match the following weekend. Tim recalls: 'It was a local Trans-Mersey derby between Devonport and East Devonport, so I knew the players pretty well. I suffered from paralysing nerves for the first few minutes, but must have gone all right because they asked me back. After a couple of games I started to get more confident and decided to inject a bit more colour into the call. When a player made an aimless kick straight up into the air (now called a 'mongrel' punt) I tried to call it by the old cliché — an 'up-country punt' — but somehow ended up with a rather embarrassing spoonerism. Thank heavens the station manager wasn't listening because no reference was ever made to it, but it was a salutary experience.'

After five years in Hobart, Tim got his big break in 1979 — a position in Melbourne as a commentator with ABC Sport. He then called VFL, cricket and athletics, as well as becoming a regular face on ABC TV. I always thought he was a talented caller but, after hearing his track-and-field commentary at the 1982 Brisbane Commonwealth Games, I ranked him with the best ever. In fact he and I shared a commentary box for the men's marathon with Herb Elliott and Dave Power. I was anchorman for the Games and, as such, had introduced the commentators, who called the race from the host studio. It was a memorable race, with Australian champion Rob de Castella making an amazing comeback over the second half to overhaul Tanzanian front-runners Juma Ikangaa and Gidamis Shahanga. At one stage, early morning fog blanketed the runners as they ran around the university campus at St Lucia and prevented the ABC helicopter relaying pictures back to the Broadcast Centre. Disoriented, the commentators were momentarily lost, but quick-thinking Tim called me in: 'You're a local, Pete — what's ahead of the front-runners here?'

'Well, Tim, they are about to encounter the first of several hills. They may look nothing on camera but, at this stage of the race, they're just what Deek needs to reel the Tanzanians back in.'

A week before the race, Tim had come to my apartment at St Lucia for a barbecue, along with Gordon Bray, Peter Longman and Peter Gee. We had all gone for a jog around the beautiful riverside campus and, in describing that race, Tim had the presence of mind to recognise the area and call in a local runner.

He did a marvellous job calling the athletics at those Games and had plenty to work with. On one memorable afternoon, Australia won five gold medals at QEII, capped by Raelene Boyle's epic golden swansong in the 400 metres.

Good as Tim was, not all his comments came out the way they were intended. I kept a list of commentators' gaffes during the long hours in the studio as anchor and I recall this one from Tim in the men's 10 000 metres: 'So here are the two Tanzanians, Ikangaa and Shahanga, taking it in turns to break wind in front.' Shades of the 'up-country punt'!

I asked him about his technique in calling an event like a 10 000 metres, where there may be twenty Africans runners in a field of 25. He replied: 'Peter Booth, one of our colleagues at the ABC in Melbourne, taught me the trick to this. It's never easy, with Kenyans, Ethiopians and Moroccans dominating distance events these days and you can't always see a number. So 'Smooth' Booth advised me to take a handful of texta-colour markers with me and try to find some point of difference, say, in their shoe colours. Then you simply put an orange texta dot on the start-list next to the guy with the orange shoes, a lime one for the lime shoes and so on. Binoculars help and you can check them out as they warm up before the race but, at some stage in a race, you have to commit to names and you just go with your gut until you can confirm the chest number.'

Tim's call of Cathy Freeman's gold medal victory in the 400 metres at the Sydney Olympics was, by his own admission, one of his best. 'There is so much expectation, so much pressure, not only on the athlete in a race like that, but on the commentator as well. It was a once-in-a-lifetime event — I've done heaps of Grand Finals — but this was a one-off. Fortunately, it went according to the script and my words came out as I wanted them to. When you've got a crowd like that, the atmosphere is something special — it's great to be there and to call it — truly unforgettable.'

Tim's career went from strength to strength in Melbourne, a sports-mad city. His thoughtful and incisive football commentary was in contrast to many excitable, garrulous commercial callers and he won a legion of fans. The ABC and Channel Seven had shared replay rights to the VFL but a change of ownership saw Channel Seven pull out. So, in 1987, when the West Coast Eagles and the Brisbane Bears became the thirteenth and fourteenth teams in the AFL, joining the Sydney Swans in the expanded competition, ABC TV got the sole rights for live telecasts. Tim headed the commentary team, which called two games a weekend, or 50 a season. It was a quantum leap for the ABC and for its chief commentator, who became a national star.

In 1988 Tim was chosen to call basketball for ABC Radio

at the Seoul Olympic Games and confirmed his status as one of the best in the business of sports commentary. A former player, he had the rare knack of being able to paint a word picture while still staying ahead of the action. Take it from me (I called the NBL for Channel Seven for five years) it's a tough enough sport to call on TV, let alone radio. Superficially simple, the game has an esoteric complexity in the attacking and defensive strategies, which are not easy to describe. Tim did a fine job in Seoul, where both Australia's men's and women's teams reached the last four.

The ABC in 1989 made a big decision — to split the Sports Department into two halves — radio and television. Tim chose to go with his first love, radio, and became a regular on the Test cricket commentary team. I thought the game suited his contemplative style. When the play was fast he was on the ball: when it was slow he was never short of a topical issue to discuss, an invaluable talent in a cricket caller. He and Jim Maxwell toured India together and their evocation of the vitality and colour of cricket on the sub-continent made for mesmerising radio.

Tim grew up listening to the authoritative voice of Alan McGilvray, whom he rates as the biggest influence on his cricket commentary — 'a towering presence who captured the sound of his sport like no other'. However, being a wordsmith, he also loved listening to that great English commentator, John Arlott: 'He was a policeman and poet first and a cricket commentator later on, so he brought the powers of observation from his early life into his commentary. He also cared deeply about the game and its issues so, for example, he became the president of the Players' Association and championed the anti-apartheid cause.'

When I complimented Tim on his cricket commentary he modestly protested but then explained what he tried to set out to do: 'I had no real playing expertise so I thought, if I was to contribute to the broadcasting of cricket, I would need to find my own way. So I researched the history and the issues of the game and attempted to use language that would communicate best to my audience.' A man of high principles, Tim famously refused a lucrative contract with Channel Nine because he perceived that it would cause a conflict of interest with fellow-caller Eddie Maguire. Tim felt that Maguire's position as president of Collingwood Football Club would put Tim in an awkward position in the commentary box in matches involving Collingwood — and I agree with him.

Without wanting to delve into the politics of the AFL, it's one aspect of a great game that I feel lets it down as an organisation. It's too Melbourne-centric and insular; that's why it will never be an international sport in my opinion. Moreover, there's a culture of arrogance in commentary, perhaps best personified by Rex Hunt and Sam Newman, that is crass and self-serving. What's more, Hunt refers to his ABC colleagues as 'Tobin Brothers', a well-known firm of funeral directors, because of their more restrained style. It's a cheap shot but, in the final analysis, water finds its own level. The democracy of the airwaves enables us to twiddle the dial if we don't like what is being served up, until we find something more to our taste.

It's not all beer and skittles in a sports commentator's life, even one as good as Tim Lane. After his first marriage ended in divorce, as many media marriages do, Tim thought he would remain single for the rest of his days. Then he met Marie and was swept off his feet. A widow with five children of her own, Marie was wary of becoming involved with a man who spent more nights away calling sport than at home. So Tim was at the crossroads. After much thought he made his decision — to give up cricket commentary altogether and spend summers at home in St Kilda with Marie and the kids. His daughter, Samantha, is also involved in football, working as a journalist on *The Age* and on Network Ten's 'Before the Game' AFL show. Tim also writes a column on football in *The Age* every Saturday, which gives him a forum to discuss the broad issues of the game. He is also a regular guest interviewer on Jon Faine's 'The Conversation Hour' on ABC Radio, where he talks with people of all persuasions, not just sportsmen and women.

'I really enjoy the freedom of radio, especially as I grow older and lose more hair!' he admits. Now 60, Tim has recently taken up swimming and found that he's actually quite good at it. It keeps him fit and helps him cope with the stress of a busy media life.

How much longer will he keep going?

'I'm still enthusiastic and my eyesight seems to be okay, so I've got a few years left in me. I still love to perform and while people want me in their lounge-rooms, I'm happy to be there.'

TWENTY

Phil Liggett

THE VOICE OF CYCLING

*'There is no training to be a commentator;
I get a great thrill out of entertaining people'*

If there is a voice that is synonymous with cycling, it's the precise English accent of Phil Liggett. Just as Richie Benaud has become the 'voice of cricket', Liggett has become the 'voice of cycling', not just in Australia, but around the world. His knowledge of the sport is encyclopaedic and his enthusiasm never wanes. He has made the Tour de France compulsory viewing for masses of Australians, even if they aren't cyclists themselves.

Born near Liverpool in rural Cheshire, Phil began riding his bike to school and to go fishing at the age of fifteen. He started racing at seventeen and won his first event in 1961 at Southport. He earned a small pro contract and competed in Belgium in 1966 but was offered a job as a trainee journalist in Fleet Street on his return to England. It was a tough

Phil Liggett, the unchallenged 'voice of cycling', has made the Tour de France compelling viewing

decision for a keen cyclist, but he took the job and never looked back.

A natural talker, Phil picked up a microphone at a race and started commentating. Soon people were calling him to do their races and in 1978 Phil joined ITV. He has now worked on 38 Tours de France and at 68 still retains an effusive enthusiasm for the event. However, Phil Liggett is much more than a cycling commentator. In all, he's worked on 13 Olympics, Summer and Winter, as well as 7 Commonwealth Games. He has also commentated on World Cup ski jumping, speed skating, luge and triathlons. In addition he writes for the *Daily Telegraph*.

Phil travels constantly, each year flying about 180,000 kilometres and staying in a hotel for more than six months! And, yes, he is married, and has been for 39 years — to Trish Tipper, a former Olympic speed skater, who now manages British cycling teams at World Championships. She has worked as a masseuse with Australian riders Robbie McEwen and Henk Vogels, and is currently a university lecturer in dance science.

Why is Phil Liggett so good and so well informed? Well, that knowledge is not innate. It's the result of a lot of hard work over many years. Every morning, for example, Phil updates his records wherever he is. If you ask him, Phil replies like this: 'There is no training to be a commentator and you do something that perhaps nobody else can do almost on reflex. As long as I remain enthusiastic I will continue to commentate, as I get a great thrill out of entertaining people.'

Phil has never asked for a job in television — he has always been approached by others, something almost unheard of in the industry.

He qualifies as an Australian commentator for this book because he's worked here so much, in addition to his international coverage of the Tour de France. From 1988 until 2000 he hosted the Commonwealth Bank Cycle Classic and in 1998 covered the Nagano Winter Olympics for Pay TV network C7.

One of Phil's strengths is his fair-mindedness. He is totally unbiased but, at the same time, realises that Australian riders are of more interest to an Australian audience, so he always keeps us informed on all our cyclists. He does an enormous amount of research, so that he is familiar with the background of all the riders, enabling us to know them as people as well as bike racers. He also has come to know France as well as any Frenchman, informing viewers about points of interest along the famous route.

As a commentator though, his greatest asset is his ability to call a stage finish. This is surely one of the toughest jobs in TV sports commentary, even harder than horse-racing because you have to call off the monitor and the riders are coming towards the camera. There are no identifying numbers or silks as in racing and the caller simply has to know the rider by his team uniform and his reputation. Sprinters like Robbie McEwen, for example, can throw out a challenge over the last 50 metres, coming from the middle of the pack in a twinkling. And Phil Liggett gets it right every time. Well, almost every time. If he's in doubt, his co-commentator Paul Sherwin will confirm the placings — it's a superb team effort. They also use anticipation well to enhance the suspense in a finish. We know beforehand what can eventuate and we are looking for it at the finish. It's a classic technique essential to good television commentary.

Everyone has to start somewhere and Phil's first call was at Crystal Palace, London in April 1978. It was a tough initiation — the biggest race in Britain outside the World Championships — with 88 professionals including Tour de France champion Bernard Thevener. And Phil was a last-minute replacement for regular ITV commentator, David Saunders, who had been tragically killed in a car accident. David was a close friend and, to make matters worse, Phil was the race organiser as well, but he came through with flying colours and he was on his way.

In his long and illustrious career Phil has had many highlights. Two stand out: when American Greg Lemond won the Tour by eight seconds from Fignon in 1990 (and

Phil had predicted he would win by six seconds!); and in 1987 when Stephen Roche appeared from nowhere and saved the day for Ireland against Pedro Delgado on the road to La Plagne in the Alps. Roche went on to win the Tour a couple of days later in a memorable performance.

The funniest moment happened when the tour ended in Blagnac once in torrential rain. The roof of the box collapsed, soaking the commentators and blanking out the monitors. However, as they were live on air, the producer called Phil on his mobile and relayed a description of what was happening. So Phil managed to call the finish without pictures — to the bewilderment of the other commentators.

Phil's love affair with cycling is the reason for his passionate commentary. When he was fifteen he invented his own board game, complete with leader's yellow jersey! He was always fascinated by statistics and used to devour magazines and papers, keeping his own records. Passion is infectious, so he has drawn thousands of people to the sport, simply though his own enthusiasm. His greatest disappointment is that others who don't have the same passion have often misrepresented this great sport.

The greatest cyclist he has seen is the Belgian legend Eddie Merckx. Phil watched him up close from 1973 in Europe and raced against him during his own brief professional career in Belgium. Merckx could win a race any way he wanted to and he won the big races more than once: Liege–Bastogne–Liege, Milan, San Remo, Giro D'Italia and of course, the Tour de France.

Phil once interviewed a Dutch rider at the Amstel Gold

Classic in Holland and, before the start, asked him who he thought would win. The answer: 'If Eddie wants to win, he will, otherwise it will be a very open race.'

Other riders Phil respects are Sean Kelly, Bernard Hinault and Lance Armstrong. In 2003 Phil finished third in a poll organised by *Cycling Plus* magazine to find the group or individual who has contributed most to the sport. The winner was the CTC, of which Phil was president and the runner-up was Lance Armstrong. (CTC is the largest cycling organisation in the world with over 75,000 members.) That year he also published a book *The Tour de France for Dummies* to go with his books on the Tour written in 1988 and '89, *The Complete Book of Performance Cycling*, and *The Fastest Man on Two Wheels — an insight into Chris Boardman*.

Phil Liggett is a global commentator — at present he works for the Outdoor Life/Versus Network in USA, covering all the major races, but he also freelances for ITV in Britain, SABC and M-Net in South Africa, and SBS in Australia.

For his commentaries Phil was awarded an Emmy by the USTV Academy as the Outstanding Sports Personality of 2003 and he was voted Best Commentator at the Lillehammer Winter Olympics by the *New York Times* and *Sydney Morning Herald* in 1994.

Whatever he does, he does well. What's more he's down to earth and completely unaffected. I worked with him for Channel Seven at the 1992 Barcelona Olympics and we shared an interest in health and fitness, a common problem for globetrotting TV commentators. His working year starts in Australia in January and ends in South Africa in December. He says he has the best job in the world but, like everything else, it has its downside: 'I hardly ever sleep in my own bed — I'm lucky my wife Trish is a very understanding woman.'

TWENTY-ONE

Bruce McAvaney

THE MASTER SPORTSCASTER

'I don't think of myself as a great commentator, really. I reckon my best call is still out there'

If you were to ask a bunch of blokes in a pub watching sport on TV who is the best commentator in Australia, who do you think would win? My money would be on Bruce McAvaney. The man with the encyclopaedic memory for facts and figures may not be everyone's cup of tea but I reckon that a man who has been Channel Seven's chief host and commentator for the past twenty years, has called every summer Olympic Games since 1984, hosts the Australian Open tennis and the Melbourne Cup and is a vital part of Seven's AFL coverage deserves to get the nod.

As a mark of his standing, Channel Seven has asked Bruce to host, not just his pet events, but also sports such as Rugby, golf and motor racing. He does a superb job on each and every one, discussing the history, personalities and records of

Bruce McAvaney, here with his children Alexandra and Sam, would probably win a pub poll to vote for Australia's best sports commentator

the sport in such a way that we are convinced he is an aficionado. What sets Bruce apart, really, is this incredible ability to absorb and relate detail, quite apart from his articulate and accurate commentary.

In 1999 *TV Week* awarded the first Logie for Most Outstanding Sports Broadcaster; Bruce won from cricket legend Richie Benaud, race-caller Johnny Tapp and SBS soccer host Les Murray. He was awarded the OAM by the Queen in 2002 for service to sports broadcasting and charity work. Normally a TV commentator, Bruce joined radio station 3AW for the Melbourne Commonwealth Games in 2006 and did a wonderful job. I was calling field events for the host broadcaster and, sitting in the row in front of Bruce, I was able to hear his calls of track events. His description of the men's 5000 metres, in which local hero Craig Mottram tripped and was robbed of any chance of victory, was a classic.

When I recorded an interview with Bruce for this book over the phone, he rang me back later in the day to correct something he had said. When asked about the Beijing Olympics, Bruce had talked about the possibility of Grant Hackett becoming the only male swimmer in Olympic history to win the same event three times. 'Dawn Fraser did it, of course, in the women's 100 metres freestyle and Kristina Egerzecki in the 100 metres backstroke but, no man has won three in a row. Perkins, Salnikov, Burton and Rose all won the 1500 twice but Hackett should become the first to do the hat-trick.'

The phone call that evening was to correct his mistake that morning. Can you pick it? The answer is that Murray Rose only won once, in 1956, and in 1960 he came second behind fellow Australian John Konrads. I actually knew the answer because Rose went to my school, Cranbrook, in Sydney, where he was a hero. I asked him to sign my autograph book, and he signed like this: 'Murray Rose — Cranbrook School, Associated Schools, NSW and Australian schools, National junior and senior, Commonwealth, world and Olympic 440 yards champion.'

Trust Bruce to correct his mistake. Most others would have just let it slide but this is what makes Bruce so good; he is a perfectionist always striving to be better.

'I don't think of myself as a great commentator really,' Bruce confides. 'I try my best every time but, you know,

I reckon my best call is still out there and, at 58, I'm still as keen as ever.'

Some would say that Bruce's call of Cathy Freeman's 400 metres victory at the Sydney 2000 Olympics was as good as it gets, but Bruce doesn't rate it highly. 'It was probably my biggest moment, in that just about everyone in Australia watched that race. There was a lot of pressure, of course. If I'd stuffed up that call, I'd never have lived it down, so I was trying to be very composed. You get nervous, but it was a race that Cathy was expected to win, and she did. So there were no surprises. I was determined not to go over the top too early and I'm happy that I kept my control — but it wasn't my best call, in my opinion.'

Bruce is humble about his achievement and grateful for the opportunities that have been presented to him. 'I've been lucky really to have been asked to perform on the biggest stages, the major events, and I've just tried to do my best. I've worked with some great co-commentators, like Raelene Boyle, for example, and they've made my job easier.'

Raelene and Bruce teamed up in commentary for the first time in 1984 at the Los Angeles Olympics and her dry, authoritative comments are the perfect foil to his animated excitement. When Bruce completed that call of Freeman's epic gold medal victory in Sydney, with the exhausted runner slumped on the track, Bruce gushed: 'What a run… what a moment… what a legend!'

A deadpan Raelene tagged it perfectly, with: 'What a relief!'

That kind of teamwork makes memorable commentary.

Bruce has experienced the same kind of mutual trust with tennis legend John McEnroe. 'I first worked with him in 1998 and I must admit I was nervous. He is a legend and he had an intimidating aura, especially when he turns that icy stare on you. But we got on fine. We had a chat beforehand and I felt quite relaxed working with him. He's an intelligent man with a flair for the medium of television.'

Bruce has interviewed them all — Jack Nicklaus, Michael Jordan, Tiger Woods, Roger Federer — the list is endless. They all treat him with respect because he is such a professional — and he probably knows more about their records than they do!

The one time I can recall Bruce being caught out was when he interviewed Andre Agassi at the Australian Open and asked a question about his relationship with Steffi Graf. At the time their friendship was a no-go zone in interviews, even for McAvaney, and he was told in no uncertain terms to 'mind his own business'. Undaunted, Bruce quickly changed the subject.

It's no fluke that Bruce is so poised in these situations. He has been studying sport — and I mean studying — since he was five years of age. He always wanted to be a commentator, although it was originally in horse-racing, not general sport. His hero was Bill Collins, the silky-voiced Melbourne caller who could turn his hand to Olympic athletics with equal aplomb. 'Bill was the best specialist race-caller that I have ever heard. In fact I would say that he's the best Australian commentator I've heard in any sport. I can still remember his call of the 1965 Melbourne Cup — even though he got it wrong. He called it a dead heat, but Light Fingers got there by a half head in a photo from Ziema. I always wanted to try to follow in his footsteps and my dream was to call a Melbourne Cup.'

Bruce didn't call a Melbourne Cup — he called four, from 1985 to 1988 in his time with Channel Ten. After starting out with Radio 5DN in Adelaide calling trots and greyhounds, he graduated to horse-racing. He used to compere a one-hour weekly show called 'Racetrack' on ADS7 and his big break came in 1980 when he was chosen to host the Adelaide coverage of the Moscow Olympics.

Switching to Channel Ten in 1983, Bruce moved to Melbourne where he read sports news and worked with a young cadet called Eddie Maguire. In 1984 he went to the LA Olympics, where he called track and field and was a secondary host. He made a big impact with his athletics calls and he had plenty to work with: American sprinter Carl Lewis was in his prime, and won four gold medals. Bruce's calls captured the excitement and the majesty of one of the world's greatest athletes perfectly.

In the 100 metres Lewis was beaten out of the blocks by team-mate Sam Graddy and Canadian Ben Johnson and, mid-race, Bruce commented: 'Carl can't win from there.'

Lewis trailed for the first 80 metres but finished with a withering burst of speed to win by over two metres — and Bruce spotted it just in time, adding: 'Oh, yes he can. Lewis will win and win easily. Look at the time — 9.99 — an Olympic record!'

Lewis dominated those Games, adding gold medals in the

200 metres, long jump and 4 x 100 metres relay, in which he ran the anchor leg in an astonishing 8.94 seconds for a new world record of 37.83 seconds.

Bruce learned a valuable lesson about commentary technique at those games. In the women's 3000 metres the clash of America's sweetheart Mary Decker, and eighteen-year-old South African prodigy Zola Budd was eagerly awaited. There had been enormous hype in the American media and Bruce built it up superbly in his pre-race comments. At the 1600-metre mark, with excitement building, Budd led Decker around the turn. Bruce was calling the race using binoculars and had focused on the runners at the rear of the field. Suddenly there was a roar from the crowd as Decker tripped over Budd's leg and crashed onto the infield. Bruce was momentarily bewildered, but soon realised what had happened and said so. In commentary terms though, he had missed the boat: 'I was concentrating on the runners at the back and missed the incident. So I was behind the crowd, which is unforgivable in athletics commentary. You've got to keep an eye on the whole field or at least the monitor.' Bruce still uses binoculars but has never been caught out like that again. If Bruce got noticed for his calls at LA, he was the superstar of the Seoul Olympic Games in 1988.

These were the Games of 'Flojo'. It was electrifying viewing as the controversial American Florence Griffith-Joyner rewrote the record books in 1988 — clocking 10.49 seconds for the 100 metres in the US Olympic trials and 21.34 for the 200 metres. Her time for the 100 metres was faster than the *men's* record in New Zealand, Norway, Iran and Turkey and, when she won the 200 metres final in Seoul, Raelene Boyle commented: 'No *woman* can run that fast.'

Grace Jackson of Jamaica had finished second in 21.72, half a second better than her previous best and only one-hundredth of a second outside the pre-Olympic world record, yet she finished four metres behind 'Flojo'. With her outrageous fluoro running suits, twenty-centimetre-long fingernails and bulging muscles, Flojo was a media sensation. However, her performances were viewed with scepticism because of her sudden improvement at the age of 31 and, in the light of Ben Johnson's disqualification in Seoul, it was thought that she might be on human growth hormones or steroids, though she never tested positive.

Bruce's calls of those races were magnificent. He had already made a name for himself as an athletics commentator, but he cemented his reputation with superb commentary at the World Athletics Championships in Rome and the 1988 Grand Prix finals in Berlin. At the end of 1989 he rejoined the Seven network, where he has been ever since.

Channel Seven used Bruce as a host on such a wide range of sports that they coined the epithet 'the master sportscaster' for him. And he never let them down. Whether it was tennis, golf, motor racing or the lesser-known Winter Olympics events like speedskating, luge or skeleton, Bruce seemed at ease with them all. He was a fund of knowledge, dazzling us with his detail. Bruce said to me: 'I enjoy commentary but I love research. I try to get a grasp of the history of the sport and the personalities, so I can give a sense of perspective to a performance.'

An example was in 2004, when Hicham El Guerouj finally won the 1500 metres at the Olympics. After being tripped and falling in 1996 and being outsprinted by the Kenyan Noah Ngeny in Sydney 2000, he won not only the 1500 metres, but also the 5000 metres in Athens. Favourite both times, as the world record-holder for the 1500 metres, he seemed doomed at the Olympics. When he won in Athens, however, Bruce summed it up perfectly: 'He is a legend — he's gone from the greatest never, to the best of all time.'

When Bruce says 'that's the best performance' you know it's right; he's like a computer on records and statistics. He keeps ledgers on the prominent athletes in each sport he calls. Handwritten, with birth-dates and past performances, these records are updated regularly off the Internet, newspapers or magazines. Bruce marks a good performance with a highlighter and puts a cross next to a bad one, so he can work out an athlete's form coming into a major competition.

Perhaps his only weakness is that he is sometimes too intense and lacks a lighter side. Even the biggest fan needs a laugh now and then.

When he prepares for a major event such as the Olympics or the Australian Open Tennis, Bruce trains like the athletes themselves. He not only prepares himself mentally, with hour after hour of painstaking research, but he also gets as fit and rested as he can. 'When you do the Olympics you don't get a lot of sleep. You work sixteen to eighteen hour days and then you have a couple of hours homework to do for the next day, so you usually get about four hours' sleep a night. For two weeks you live on adrenalin. And I can tell you that, during an Olympics, I won't have a proper evening meal once, usually just a snack like a sandwich. I try to go for a run very early each morning to relieve stress, and look after my health as best I can.'

I can vouch for the run, as I jogged with Bruce each morning in Barcelona in 1992. It was quite a thrill, as expert commentator, former world mile record-holder John Walker, also ran a couple of times, along with hockey commentators David Christison and Richard Aggiss. It was hard work, apart from the heat and lack of sleep, but we jogged up the hill behind our media village in Montigala, an outer suburb of the massive old city. We used to stop for a breather at the top of the hill, where goats grazed near a ruined abbey. All we could see, looking back, were a couple of smokestacks poking through a blanket of pollution, so we nicknamed the spot 'Chernobyl'. On the last morning it was much cooler, it had rained overnight and the air was washed clean. When we reached the top of the hill and looked around we were astonished to see the ocean only a few hundred metres away. We never realised it was there. With pollution like that, no wonder Steve Moneghetti struggled in the marathon!

Despite his fame, Bruce is also a modest and kindly man. When I interviewed him, I asked how he felt about his send-up by Billy Birmingham, 'The Twelfth Man'. In all honesty, Bruce said that he didn't even know who Billy was, or that he had been sent up by the famous satirist. In fact, after the

Sydney Olympics, Billy had released a special DVD, entitled 'Bruce 2000 — A special tribute'. Like many other critics Billy had harped on Bruce's favourite adjectives 'special' and 'clever', but the man himself has never even heard it.

At the Edinburgh Commonwealth Games in 1986 Bruce was with the Ten Network and I was with Channel Seven. The ABC had the TV rights and access to the athletes was difficult, if not impossible. I resorted to combing the bar at the pub outside Meadowbank Stadium, searching for Australian medal-winners — and had a fair degree of success. However, after Rob de Castella had won the marathon I sat in the rain outside the stadium for hours in vain. A big black Rolls Royce pulled up and the window rolled down. It was Bruce, with a sympathetic smile on his face. 'We've just dropped him off at his pub, Pete — he's at the North British Hotel.' My cameraman and I rushed around to the hotel, and asked for a Mr de Castella, only to be told nobody of that name was staying there. Racking my brains, I said: 'How about a Mr Clews?'

Sure enough, Deek had checked in under the name of his wife, Gaylene Clews. Although I woke him out of a deep sleep, I got my interview. Thanks Bruce, belatedly.

Asked whether he is concerned that Channel Seven have lost the Olympics in 2012, Bruce says: 'To be honest, not at all. I've had a good run, and I've been extremely lucky to have been given the opportunities I have over the past twenty-odd years. Also I'm getting older and there's a lot of pressure. Consider what lay ahead of me in 2008 when, in the space of twelve weeks, I covered three of the biggest events in sport: the AFL Grand Final, the Olympics and the Melbourne Cup.

'While we might be losing the Olympics, we've got the AFL rights back and I've loved being involved again. In fact, I didn't realise how much I had missed it until Dennis and I started calling together last season. There's nothing better than doing something you love on a regular basis. I can't wait for Friday nights and Sunday afternoons in winter, calling the footy.'

He would love to call another Melbourne Cup — and Channel Seven has asked about it several times — but he feels that he would need to give up everything else and concentrate on race-calling for three or four months beforehand, and he simply can't find the time.

The one event he has never called, and would give his eye-teeth to do, is the Soccer World Cup. 'Let's face it, the World Cup final is the biggest two hours of sport on the planet. I love the game, the spectacle and its history, but I'm not even a specialist soccer — or football if you prefer — commentator, and it will never happen.'

Bruce's fame as an athletics commentator has spread overseas, and he is perhaps more feted by foreign athletes than Australians. At the World Athletics Championships in Stuttgart in 1993, British superstar decathlete Daley Thompson made a surprise visit to the commentary box to congratulate Bruce and, at the Atlanta Olympics, five-times gold medallist Michael Johnson gave Bruce his running shoe, as a mark of respect.

However, like any high-profile public figure, he gets his

share of criticism. From drunks in pubs to TV comedians, he is castigated and lampooned. Apart from Billy Birmingham, comedians Andrew Startin and Rob Sitch have performed very funny send-ups of Bruce. His attitude to all kinds of feedback, good or bad, is simply to ignore it. He is content living in Adelaide with his TV producer/author wife, Anne Johnson, and their two children, Sam and Alexandra.

We can't let the 'master sportscaster' go without asking the question: what are his favourite sporting moments of all time?

'Makybe Diva winning a third Melbourne Cup in succession in 2005, Ben Johnson beating Carl Lewis in the 100 metres final at the Seoul Olympics and Muhammad Ali's win over Joe Frazier for the World Heavyweight Title in 1971. Mind you, we might not have seen them yet — that's what I love about this job.'

TWENTY-TWO

John McCoy

THE REAL McCOY

*'Wally Lewis is the best player I've seen.
NSW always used to say if you stop Wally
you stop Queensland'*

When it comes to Brisbane football commentators, there have been few better than John McCoy, or 'Macca' as he's known. Best known for his Rugby League radio broadcasts, John is a skilled all-round commentator and still turns his hand occasionally to calling golf, Rugby Sevens and diving on pay TV. He is one of the old school, with clear enunciation and a wide knowledge of all sport. He and I are about the same age and our careers have run parallel, he on commercial radio and I on the ABC, so I have listened and admired his work for many years.

He called Rugby League every weekend during the 1970s and 1980s for Radio 4BC and then, when the Brisbane Broncos joined the NRL in 1988, John called their matches on Channel Nine. He tried his hand in the Sydney market,

John 'Macca' McCoy and Peter Meares at 'practice'. (The boy in the background looks suitably unimpressed.) In his playing days John was happy with a no-training rule

calling League on radio, but didn't develop the same following that he had in Brisbane. John now hosts a daily sports program on radio 4TAB, focusing mainly on horse-racing.

John's Rugby League commentary was accurate and exciting. He has a passion for the game and it came through in his calls. He used his voice well and, while able to command an audience with his excitement, never went 'over the top'. John was never a footballer of note. He grew up in Toowoomba where his father played Rugby League, so that was his favourite sport as a boy. He went to Gregory Terrace, a GPS school, so he played Union at school, and he later played lower grades with Brothers Rugby Club, more for fun than fitness. 'We had a rule that you weren't allowed to train and that suited me just fine!'

Racing was another passion and he loved listening to Radio 4BC on Saturday afternoons, with that great commentator Vince Currey. In the studio in those days was another of John's heroes, the silky-voiced Tom McGregor. Tom was the sports coordinator of the 4BC racing and football panel in the 1950s and 1960s and also anchored Olympic Games broadcasts. Shortly after returning from the 1968 Mexico Olympics, Tom passed away and there was a vacancy at 4BC.

John had applied for a job in Mt Isa on leaving school and, after a year as a disc jockey with 4LM, he was transferred to Brisbane's 4IP. While in Mt Isa he had worked alongside an old schoolmate, Billie J. Smith, who was four years older. Billie called the football for 4LG, and when he came down to 4IP as their League commentator, John applied for the position at 4BC to pursue his love of sports broadcasting. His boss was Vince Currey, who had a profound effect on John's career. John appreciated this break: 'Vince was a wonderful commentator and not just on racing. He called Olympic Games, Davis Cup tennis, boxing, you name it — and on top of that he was a great bloke. I couldn't have had a better mentor.'

John took over the sports coordinator job on Saturdays at 4BC but also called the Rugby League. He was one of the sideline brigade in the 1970s, when I used to call the League for the ABC and, of all the commercial callers in that era, I admired John's commentary most. He always called the game as he saw it and never fabricated excitement. Some callers seemed to think that you had to have the audience on the edge of their seats all the time, so they screamed their lungs out.

John rarely called by the numbers. He was so familiar with the players that he could pick them by their hair, running style or distinctive clothing. He used to concentrate, not only on the ball-carrier, but also on the players most likely to receive the next pass. 'You have to stay ahead of the game, to beat the crowd', John says. Even when he couldn't study players beforehand, John rarely made mistakes in calling them. He and I teamed to call the Rugby Sevens at the 2006 Commonwealth Games in Melbourne and I was able to appreciate his skill. When you call Sevens tournaments you need your wits about you, as you call over 50 games in two days, with only a few minutes between them. John organised our team sheets in such a way that we soon picked up the key players, even with obscure teams like the Cook Islands and Kenya.

All great commentators use 'light and shade', skilful use of the voice to transmit the rise and fall of excitement during a match. John was one of these — when play moved into the attacking quarter his voice would rise, until there was a try, or possession changed hands. So, if you were outside washing the car or watering the garden, you could tell something important was about to happen and rush inside to listen.

Asked for the highlights of his Rugby League broadcasting career, John picks the first State of Origin match in 1980 and the 'Invincibles' unbeaten Kangaroo tour of

England in 1982. 'That moment when Arthur Beetson walked out onto Lang Park was electric. Although there wasn't a huge crowd for what was then really an experimental match, the roar from them was deafening. I can still see Artie in that old Queensland jersey with the big 'Q', the sleeves cut off and white chalk all over the front of it.' John's brilliant call of Chris Close's match-clinching try in that 20–10 victory was recorded for posterity by singer Danny McMaster in 'The Rugby League Song' which was played for many years on match days at Lang Park.

One of the strangest broadcasts of his career came when he was asked to call a game at Nambour, while on holidays at the Sunshine Coast. John recalls: 'A mate of mine, Mike Prenzler, was station manager at 4NA and asked if I could call a country trial match at Nambour Showground. It was between South Zone, coached by John 'Cracker' McDonald, and North Zone, under Ray Laird, to pick the team to play City. I hadn't seen either team and only knew one player, Greg Platz from Toowoomba, but the idea was that the players would arrive late in the afternoon, have a light run and then an early dinner, before kick-off at 7.30. I could have a look at them then and make a few mental notes, as I always did. However, something caused them to be late and the players changed in the bus and went straight out onto the field for the game. On top of that, our commentary position was on the roof of the pavilion behind the deadball line at one end — and then the fog rolled in!

'Barry Muir and I tried to call the game but we simply couldn't see anyone past halfway, so we sent a couple of kids to find out who scored when there was a try. It was the worst call in history. To make matters worse, we were supposed to give a Man of the Match award, but Barry said he had no idea because he hadn't seen enough to make a judgement. Well, we had to do something, so I suggested that the North Zone winger who scored a try might be a fair choice — I knew his brother Ian, who played for Wynnum–Manly. It was Kerry Boustead, the flyer from Innisfail, who went on to play for Country, Queensland and Australia that season.'

John considers himself lucky to have called in such a great era in Queensland Rugby League, especially because he got to see one of the greatest players of all time, Wally Lewis. 'He could do everything. He had great hands, feet, strength, a terrific kicking game and amazing vision. NSW experts always used to say that, if you could stop Wally, you stopped Queensland — but they couldn't.'

John's opinion was backed by two of the most respected names in Queensland Rugby League, Jack Reardon and George Lovejoy. Reardon, who played for Australia in the 1930s and was the *Courier-Mail* League writer for over twenty years, and Lovejoy, the commentator John most admired, both agreed that Lewis was the best ever.

One of the worst moments John can recall involved Lewis, when he was a youngster running around with Valleys. Playing against Norths, he was accidentally hit in the windpipe in a tackle by raw-boned Kiwi international Mark Graham and couldn't breathe. For what seemed an eternity, Lewis lay writhing on the turf, clutching and pointing at his throat. Fortunately, quick thinking by the experienced

Valleys doctor, Tom Dooley, saved the day. 'Tom gave him mouth-to-mouth, but for a while there I thought we might see the first fatality in Brisbane football. It was an awful incident.'

There are plenty of funny moments too. One story John loves to tell concerns the rough and tough Queensland prop John Barber. John played for Redcliffe and later joined 'Macca' as a commentator with Channel Nine. As a player he had developed a dislike for Ipswich: 'Every time we played them we not only lost the match, we lost the fight as well.' One day, calling a State League match in which Ipswich had been beaten, John forgot himself momentarily and said: 'Ipswich — not the end of the earth — but you can see it from there.'

Next day 'Macca' had a call from the station general manager, Hugh Cornish: 'John, we had switchboard meltdown after that comment about Ipswich by Barber yesterday. That's one of our big ratings areas — you'll have to get him to apologise.' So, next weekend, JB dutifully said he was sorry but somehow finished by saying: 'Don't take it to heart. Ipswich aren't the worst team in the world, but they'd be in the Grand Final.'

That was the end of John Barber's commentary career. Eight years later, 'Macca' was getting into his car after watching a game in Ipswich and heard a familiar yell: 'Hey, "Macca", how are you?' It was Barber.

'What are you doing here?' asked McCoy.

'I live here.'

John McCoy has had a rich and rewarding broadcasting career but, like most commentators, there's one event that he'd love to call, or at least, watch: the US Masters. To golf fans this major is like Wimbledon is to tennis, rich in history and different to all the other majors. A few years ago, John was travelling with his wife from Charlotte to Atlanta and passed through Augusta. Now there's not much to recommend the actual town but, being a golf tragic, John had to see the famous Masters course. So he drove up to the front gate, which was closed. With nobody around, John was gazing wistfully down Magnolia Drive when a voice called: 'I'm afraid we are closed, sir.' It was an elderly man, obviously one of the ground staff.

John replied: 'No problem. I was just having a look.'

'Are you Australian?'

'Yes I am. I'm from Brisbane.'

'I owe my life to Brisbane. If you are from Brisbane, be my guest.'

It turned out that the old guy was wounded in the Battle of the Coral Sea and was evacuated to the Yeronga Military Hospital, where he felt the doctors and nurses saved his life, so he gave 'Macca' the full guided tour.

Fringe benefits — one of the joys of being a sports commentator.

TWENTY-THREE

Jim Maxwell

A LIFE ON THE BOUNDARY

'Well, the crowd that's been let in free today is really getting its money's worth'

I go back a long way with Jim Maxwell, back to the days when he was known as James. We were at school together at Cranbrook, in Sydney's eastern suburbs, and I was five years older. My first memories of Jim were in the cricket nets, when this little fellow with glasses would hang around the Firsts' practice session, hoping to be allowed to bowl. Jim bowled off-breaks

Jim Maxwell called his 200th Test in 2008, a remarkable performance. Kerry O'Keeffe says Jim has a voice that's 'roasted over burning fire'

and he was so keen that he was usually there until sunset. 'Were you one of those unfortunates picked up at slip playing for the break?' Jim asked. Looking back now, Jim recalls that his passion exceeded his ability and, truth be told, he bowled 'straight breaks' most of the time. He was an all-rounder and captain of the school 15As and Firsts, where he enjoyed the tactical battles.

However, his forte was writing and at school he used to produce his own publication, *Cricket Chronicle* on a regular basis. When he left school he joined the Old Boys and became club secretary, producing a detailed annual report every year. It would all help in producing the always excellent *ABC Cricket Book*, which he has edited since 1988.

ABC Radio's 'voice of cricket' has (at April 2011) racked up 240 Test matches as a commentator, a phenomenal record dating back 30 years. His passion for the game, shrewd analysis and distinctive voice have become part of the fabric of Australian cricket.

Jim was always bent on becoming a cricket commentator and had been beaten twice (once by yours truly in 1968) for a position as a specialist trainee in the ABC's Sporting Department. Persistence paid off eventually in 1973 and I like to think I had a hand in his success. Cranbrook Old Boys' Cricket Club embarked on their first overseas tour in January 1973 and I managed to get leave from the ABC, where I worked for the Brisbane Sporting Department, to join the tour. Jim had again applied for the position as trainee and wanted to practise his cricket commentary, so I helped him out. We would sit on the boundary calling the game into a tape recorder and replay it to the boys over a beer after play, much to their amusement.

Occasionally I would stop Jim and correct him, saying that you don't say it like that, you say it like this. When he asked why, I said: 'Because that's the way McGilvray does it.'

So that was the way we all learned our trade in those days and nobody disputed the guidelines of the guru. 'Mac' used to say: 'Copy technique, not style. Make your own style.'

Alan McGilvray had started calling cricket for the ABC in 1935 and carried on until he was 75, an incredible 50-year career. He was a living legend and woe betide anyone who disagreed with him, even in a friendly bet in the pub. 'We were a lot more formal in the way we presented the cricket in those days,' says Jim. 'There were these half-hour windows of cricket description and it didn't matter if someone was on a hat-trick at 29 minutes past the hour, you still crossed back to the studio for the news.'

One of his early jobs was to type up what were called 'Program Presentation Sheets', which were written introductions for studio announcers — and they were very formal. Someone like Peter Dawes-Smith would intone: 'And now, for descriptions of play in the match between NSW and New Zealand at the Sydney Cricket Ground, we cross to Alan McGilvray ...'

This was the atmosphere in which Jim found himself in the early 1970s, so his style then was rather stiff and restrained, compared to nowadays. He would sit next a former Australian opening batsman, the late Jimmy Burke, calling the Sheffield Shield, mindful that he was to stick to the facts and leave the opinions, and the jokes, to Jimmy. Maxwell recalls: 'I wasn't any good for the first ten or fifteen years really, because I was too tense. We were all in awe of "Mac" I suppose and fearful of making mistakes. He was a potent personality and a bit pontifical towards the end, as older people can be. It wasn't really until I worked on the World Cup series in England in 1983 that I loosened up. Brian Johnston was a bit of a leg-puller and he made me realise that you shouldn't take life too seriously. He had the same impish sense of humour as Kerry O'Keeffe, and he used to delight in sending up new boys, like Jonathon Agnew and myself. It was all great fun.'

After McGilvray retired in 1985 he would spend his days either at the cricket or in his favourite pubs, the 'Lord Dudley', near his home in Woollahra and 'The Strand', just down from the ABC in William Street. These days there is a plaque on the bar at the 'Dudley' in his memory. Cricket lovers, including Jim, would often seek out the venerable broadcaster for a beer and a chat. However, his relationship with 'Mac' deteriorated when Maxwell was chosen to cover the 1983 tour ahead of him. 'It wasn't until a couple of years after he retired that "Mac" softened in his attitude towards me. Until then he was always like the old bull elephant, jealous of his turf, but he mellowed and became quite helpful eventually.'

'One thing "Mac" stressed was that you set up the play before a ball was delivered, so that you were on top of the action if something dramatic happened. So you might say: "To this ball from Lillee, Boycott is ... [pausing as the ball is bowled] ... on the back foot, cutting and it's gone for four." You can't say all that after the delivery before the crowd applauds — it's a dramatic technique.

'Another McGilvray trick was to lower his voice almost to a whisper to build up suspense, such as for the first ball of a Test match. Then, when something happened, he would bellow it out and the listener would sit up and take notice.'

Jim's first call was in 1973 of a match between NSW and New Zealand and he can still recall the details. 'They had brought out a new bloke called Jeremy Coney to replace the injured Mark Burgess. I was called in to do a stint and I remember how he was having trouble timing the ball, probably because the pitch was so much faster than he was used to. I had just toured New Zealand and at least had some idea of what I was talking about.'

Jim admired the English commentary team of that era, with John Arlott, Trevor Bailey and Freddie Trueman alongside 'Johnners' and he loved the light-hearted banter between them, especially when rain stopped play. The apochryphal lines: 'The bowler's Holding, the batsman's Willey' and 'There's Harvey, crouched at short leg, legs apart, waiting for a tickle' have gone down in the annals as classic 'Johnners', but his modern equivalent, Kerry O'Keeffe, has a growing legion of fans. Jim thinks the present ABC team is a similarly well-balanced unit.

'They had a great rapport but I think these days we have a pretty good team in the box at the ABC. Kerry is the comedian of the group, of course, a great observer of life and analyst of the game — he's the full package.' Then there are

Peter Roebuck, the erudite analyst who once captained Somerset and batted between Barry and Viv Richards, Geoff Lawson, who can read a bowler like a book, and Glenn Mitchell, the West Australian with a computer-like head for cricket trivia. The other interesting aspect of the ABC coverage each summer is the addition of a visiting commentator to the team. So we have been treated to the differing styles and accents of Harsha Bhogle of India, Jonathan Agnew from England and Reds Pereira from the West Indies.

One of the fringe benefits of sports commentary is the travel and Jim loves it. However, the accommodation in some places on the subcontinent is not always what it might be. We have come a long way from the time in 1969 when Doug Walters had to sleep in a hammock on the tour of India — these days players are accustomed to five-star digs. The Taj Mahal Hotel in Bombay is as good as you would see anywhere in the world. However, on the last tour, the game at Nagpur was memorable for more than Adam Gilchrist's magnificent innings, which secured a series win for Australia for the first time in 27 years. The ABC commentary team was unable to find accommodation because of a medical conference in the town, so they had to be content with a government hotel which was the equivalent of minus four star.

To make matters worse, the broadcasting line failed and the first day's play was relayed to Australia via Jim's mobile phone. In India, broadcasters are expected to put their equipment together and, on this occasion, the connection from the local phone company had not been made. Despite regular promises a technician from Indian Telecom was not forthcoming until the next day. Nevertheless, the show must go on, as they say, and listeners were too happy about the result to worry about the quality of the line.

There are other pitfalls for the unwary or the inexperienced on cricket tours — the self-inflicted kind. Even before he became a commentator, Jim had been introduced to the hard-drinking culture at ABC Sport. McGilvray and Norman May led the way and it was a kind of rite of passage for young would-be commentators. While Jim found it fascinating to listen to these broadcasting icons, it had an adverse effect on his work next day. McGilvray had one party trick that Jim fell for a couple of times, to his regret. After a session at the pub 'Mac' would invite a select band back to his place in Woollahra and then, at about 11.00 pm, he would flick off the top of a bottle of Black and White whisky and say: 'Right. Nobody leaves until this is empty.'

On his first tour to the West Indies in 1984, Jim's constitution was tested to its limits. The press box included journalists from the afternoon papers, Sydney's *Mirror* and *Sun* and Melbourne's *Herald-Sun* for the last time. 'The crew included the late Peter McFarlane from Melbourne, Phil Wilkins, Jim Woodward and Ray Titus, the photographer. Woodward played hard and his favourite party trick was to sing 'Good King Wenceslaus' standing on his head, while drinking a beer. One memorable night in Barbados, Ray drove our Mini Moke into the dining-room, shaving off the wing mirrors. The fact that his co-pilot was Bob Radford might have had something to do with it.'

But those days have gone now. On his last tour, for the 2007 World Cup, Jim was accompanied by only three other journalists, such are the wonders of computers and syndication. Radio broadcasters are now also expected to write for papers or online cricket websites, so a free night is a rarity these days.

Jim has made his share of blunders, as we all have. One he likes to tell is the time in 1982–83 when England was in a strong position to win the Boxing Day Test, only to be stalled by stubborn batting from the last Australian pair, Allan Border and Jeff Thomson, who took play into an unexpected fourth day. There must have been 20 000 people at the MCG the next day, as Border and Thommo crept slowly towards an unlikely victory. In the box, Jim was feeling the tension too and perhaps didn't think, as he said: 'Well, the crowd that has been let in free today is really getting its money's worth …'

Another incident might have sounded embarrassing, but was really a set-up. The BBC had a special spot every Saturday during a Test for a non-cricketing celebrity — Nigel Havers, Hugh Grant and Elton John, for example. This day they has a lady called Michelle Verockin, who was from the British Anti-Doping Agency and Jim, as the only Olympic commentator in the box, was asked to interview her. Unknown to the listeners, she and Jim had met the night before and concocted a plan. She spoke about the use of 'live' doping tests and, hearing Jim's apparent interest, said: 'Let's do one with you right now.'

Apparently the regulations stipulated that she had to witness the sample being provided, so Jim made a few undressing noises, said he was ready and proceeded to pour some wine into a glass next to the microphone, gradually increasing the speed of pouring.

'There you are,' said Jim and she ostensibly went off to test the sample.

On returning to the mike, she said: 'Right, we've been unable to find any prohibited substances in your sample, but we think you may have a drinking problem!'

We tend to take our commentators for granted, much the same as the newspaper being delivered on our doorstep, but every now and then something happens to make you realise how good they are and how long they have been a part of our lives.

At the Sydney Test in 2006, Jim was surprised but delighted by a tribute to mark his 200th Test. The only other caller to pass that mark was Alan McGilvray, who broadcast 219 Tests over 50 years. It strikes you how much more Test cricket is now played, but also what a great job ABC Radio, and Jim in particular, have done. He regards Peter Walsh's tribute, which took the form of a collage of comments from his peers, and even Australian captain Ricky Ponting, as one of the highlights of his career, but is very modest about his achievement. 'We are just the conduit. It's very satisfying but I'm not going to get pontifical about it.'

Perhaps the ultimate accolade came from that brilliant mimic Billy Birmingham, who said about the veteran broadcaster: 'Channel Nine's team should be listening to Jim, but they're too busy listening to themselves.'

A less public tribute came from his colleagues. Kerry

O'Keeffe organised a dinner at a local hotel and, to Jim's delight, a special guest was the former Seekers' singer Bruce Woodley. After a magnificent meal and copious bottles of red wine, someone found a guitar and Bruce performed two of the Seekers' hits, 'I am Australian' and 'The carnival is over'.

When one considers Jim's remarkable career, it might have been more appropriate for Bruce to perform 'I know I'll never find another you'.

TWENTY-FOUR

Norman May

A PRICELESS NUGGET

*'Three! Two! One! Gold!
Gold to Australia!
Gold!'*

He was the first; he's done the most and, in the eyes of his peers, he's the best. He taught me how to call sport. Norman May, better known as 'Nugget', began his broadcasting career just after the advent of television in Australia and over 50 years later, he's still at it. He went to Beijing for the 2008 Games, which gave him a round dozen Olympics to go with his twelve Commonwealth Games. At the age of 83, 'Nugget' still retains an encyclopaedic memory and can rattle off statistics with the best of them. So good is his memory in fact that the University of NSW Psychiatry Department is including him in their study of memory and ageing. He attributes this to his philosophy that the mind needs regular workouts as much as the body, so he completes the cryptic crossword in the *Sydney Morning Herald* each morning over breakfast.

Some say Norman 'Nugget' May, seen here with Gerry Collins, left, and ironman legend Grant Kenny at the Barcelona Olympics, 1992, is the best. 'Nugget' started broadcasting over 50 years ago, and will be an ambassador in Beijing, 2008

'Nugget' was born in Melbourne in 1928, but grew up in Coogee where he developed a love of the surf. His earliest memory is of the voyage from Melbourne to Sydney on the *HMAS Manunda* — that was in 1931 when he was only three! There are fond memories of cracking waves at Coogee at the age of four but horrific ones of an accident at the age of six that cost him the sight in his right eye. A playmate, Alan Reynolds, the son of a bookie, shot an arrow into Norman's eye and he was rushed to hospital. A glass eye was inserted, which had to be replaced every two years until the age of twenty, as the eye grows like any other organ.

Despite that handicap Norman grew into a fine all-round sportsman, playing cricket for the Combined GPS Firsts, Rugby Union for Randwick and representing NSW at surf lifesaving. He won three Australian championships in rescue and resuscitation and teams racing. How he could identify footballers so accurately in his commentary career is a mystery, but says a lot for one-eyed commentators!

Norman got his break merely by chance. In 1954 he was interviewed by ABC Radio's NSW sports supervisor, Dick Healey, about surf lifesaving, as part of the Queen's Christmas Message. In 1956, just three months after television had started, Norman was on his way by bus to a surf carnival at Freshwater. Healey spotted him and asked: 'What are you doing on Saturday fortnight? Would you like to be a commentator for our telecast of the Metropolitan Surf Championships?' As luck would have it, Norman's team had failed to qualify, so he was in.

On the day, 9 February 1957, he and Bob Richardson sat on the roof of a boatshed on Dee Why Beach to call the action. However, as the sun was shining brightly over their shoulders they couldn't see the pictures on the monitor so someone found a blanket and, for four hours, they called the carnival, dripping with perspiration, covered by a blanket! The general manager of the ABC, Charles Moses, saw the coverage and asked if Norman would like to call the first-ever telecast of Rugby Union. So, on 6 April 1957, he called the match at Chatswood Oval between Manly and Gordon. Fifty-four years later the ABC is still covering the Sydney Match of the Day every Saturday afternoon. Norman was employed by the ABC full-time for 26 years and called over 40 sports. His versatility was extraordinary — he could turn his hand to anything. Following the Charles Moses edict that ABC Sport should cover some sporting event every weekend, Norman was called upon to broadcast everything from rhythmic gymnastics to glider flying, with equal aplomb. He was so convincing that viewers would swear he had been covering that sport all his life. Although his colleagues didn't know it, Norman did painstaking research. He has a mischievous sense of humour and loved to give the impression that he simply did everything off the top of his head. He also had an unnerving habit of arriving at the last minute, to the consternation of his fellow commentators.

Gordon Bray tells the story of one such day when Norman was to call the Rugby Match of the Day from Coogee Oval but, half an hour before kick-off, had not appeared. With only ten minutes to go, even unflappable producer Bill Phillips was worried and asked Gordon, then a young trainee who was acting as scorer, if he could take over. A delighted Gordon accepted gleefully but, suddenly, Norman appeared, leapt into the commentary position, put on the headset and said: 'May here, standing by.'

And away he went, never missing a beat, even commenting on the magnificent game in reserve grade that the audience hadn't seen. Puzzled, Gordon asked: 'How could you say that, when you weren't even here to see the reserves, Nugget?'

'Yes, I was. "Catchy" and I were across the road in the club — great view from there.'

Ken Catchpole, regarded by Norman as the best Rugby player he has ever seen, is one of many legendary sportsmen with whom he has worked in commentary. He was always careful not to usurp the role of the expert, but cleverly elicited opinions from those who had worn the green and gold sitting next to him.

One of Norman's most remarkable achievements came in tragic circumstances, when eleven Israeli athletes were killed by Palestinian terrorists at the 1972 Munich Olympics. Norman had called the swimming and, oblivious to the horrific event, had enjoyed a night of carousing with the German media. After consuming more than his fair share of schnapps with beer chasers, he was carried to bed to sleep it off at 2.00 am. Next morning he was shaken awake at 6.00 am by a senior producer, telling him of the tragic events of the night before. 'There's a Ceremony of Mourning at the Olympic Stadium and we want you to call it.'

With a capacity crowd of 84,000 at the stadium and over 1000 athletes gathered on the infield, the IOC President Avery Brundage made the simple statement: 'The Games must go on. Otherwise the terrorists have won.'

For Norman, it was a challenging assignment, even without a hangover. The ceremony was conducted in four languages: Hebrew, German, French and English, but the heavy German accent of the interpreter made his commentary incomprehensible. So Norman trusted his instincts — if in doubt, say nothing.

'It was an eerie atmosphere,' Norman recalls. 'Normally a crowd like that made an enormous amount of noise but, that day, you could feel the silence. It was an unforgettable experience, but the toughest job in my career.'

Norman's professionalism drew praise from the ABC bosses but, as any commentator knows, you're only as good as your last broadcast. At the same Munich Games, Norman was also called upon at the last moment to broadcast the canoeing at Dachau, near the site of the Nazi concentration camp. Having already done the rowing, Norman was confident that he could handle the call, even though he had never been to a canoeing event before.

The bus from the media village arrived at 9.28 and the canoeing started at 9.30, so Norman grabbed a start list and began his commentary. After a while it was apparent that Norman's call was nothing like that on the big result board. What was going on? Then the penny dropped. At the rowing, the numbers had been from 1 to 8 from left to right but, at the canoeing, they were from right to left, so the broadcast was a total shambles. Fortunately it was not a live telecast, so Norman, now armed with the correct start list, dubbed the call again — much to the amusement of his international colleagues.

Eight years later in Moscow Norman did a call that has gone down in the annals of Australian sports commentary. In 1980 Australian sport was at an all-time low, after failing to win a single gold medal in Montreal four years earlier. At Moscow, American President Jimmy Carter had boycotted the Games in protest at Russia's invasion of Afghanistan, along with 25 other nations, so it was thought that Australia would win more medals. However, after the first week and only a couple of bronze medals, the drought had still not broken.

Then came the 4 x 100 metres medley relay. The quartet representing Australia was thought to have a chance of a medal, but few thought it could be gold. Mark Kerry, the backstroker from Wollongong, put Australia into fourth place, barely a body length behind the leaders, Russia. Mark Tonelli, normally a backstroker, then swam the butterfly leg two seconds faster than his personal best. Peter Evans, a breaststroker from WA, swam 63.01 seconds for his leg, the fastest breaststroke time of the Games. However, the surprise packet was seventeen-year-old Neil Brooks. The gangly boy from Perth was an asthmatic, who had never swum the 100 metres freestyle in less than 51 seconds, but he clocked 49.86 to out-touch Kopliakov of Russia.

Calling the race on ABC Radio, Norman timed his finish as well as Brooks:

'With 20 metres to go it's Kopliakov ahead of Brooks... Australia has a chance for gold... 15 metres and Brooks is catching... Now they're level... Brooks and Kopliakov... Australia and Russia... Brooks in front, it could be Australia's gold medal!... 5 metres! Four! Three! Two! One! Gold!... Gold to Australia!... Gold!'

What a call! What excitement there was for everyone listening at home in Australia. It was such a momentous occasion, our first Olympic gold medal in eight years, and such a wonderful commentary, that TV news programs dubbed Norman's radio call of those epic last stages onto Channel Seven's pictures for their bulletins. And, 31 years later, Norman still gets asked to sports functions to talk about that race.

Of course, Norman was much more than just a swimming commentator. In fact, he will tell you that his favourite sport is cricket and he still watches every ball of Sydney Test matches from the top deck of the Noble Stand. Much as he loved radio, he was regarded by ABC bosses as a television commentator. This suited him fine, as he travelled around Australia calling the cricket for seventeen years with the man he regards as the greatest cricket commentator of them all, Alan McGilvray. 'In my day there were three great callers: McGilvray, John Arlott from England and Charles Fortune from South Africa. But McGilvray had captained NSW, he was a player and the other two were not. That was the difference — he knew the game.'

When Norman first worked on cricket he was very much the junior. McGilvray had been calling cricket for over twenty years, so Norman did a lot of listening and learning. But one thing he learned was that even great men can make mistakes. The occasion was a match between the touring MCC, led by Peter May, and NSW at the SCG. There were four Australian players, Benaud, O'Neill, Simpson and Davidson in the NSW team, so there was an air of nervous anticipation as the match began, both in the stands and in the commentary box. McGilvray began the broadcast as always and then it was Norman's turn. 'Mac' said: 'And now to continue the commentary, here's Peter May.'

Norman chuckled but said nothing — if anything it eased his nerves. At the end of his twenty-minute stint, McGilvray was waiting outside the box, apologising profusely: 'I'm terribly sorry — that won't happen again.'

Well, after McGilvray's next shift, he threw once again to Norman, saying: 'Now, to continue, here's Norman O'Neill.'

One thing Norman learned from that experience is that we all make mistakes, but not to let it throw you. He also learned a lot about the game from his friendship with McGilvray. They got up to some mischief, but were the ultimate professionals on air. On the first morning of a Test match they had a ritual they called 'Prayer Service'. This entailed gathering in McGilvray's room, usually with fellow commentators Norman O'Neill and Keith Miller, for a couple of cold beers with breakfast. Some of the younger commentators, including me, were invited to join them but I couldn't face alcohol at that time of day. They would have an animated discussion on the tactics to be employed, so that when they went on air a few hours later, O'Neill would have his answers ready to McGilvray's queries on each team's strategy.

Norman May was the pioneer of cricket commentary on television in Australia. His first call was in 1958 of a grade match at Mosman Oval, alongside McGilvray. He had a chat with the producer and advised him that there would be two main areas on which his three cameras should focus — the batsman and the fielder who pursued the ball. A feature of his cricket commentary was the enthusiastic way in which he would describe the race between the fieldsman and the ball: 'This one from Lillee is overpitched and Boycott cracks it through the covers... Walters is after it... he's very fast... they have two... will Walters stop it... yes! That's a great piece of fielding... but three more to Boycott, who moves to 47.'

Calling another favourite sport, Rugby Union, Norman

was a perfect blend of enthusiasm, knowledge and controlled excitement. He spoke in clear and concise language, added to the picture and never stated the obvious — in other words, he was a model for other commentators. His pitch of excitement got you involved but he never went 'over the top' — as he wrote in his notes for trainees: 'A dull commentator at an exciting match is just as inappropriate as an exciting commentator at a dull match.' Norman wrote the rules and they still apply today.

As a presenter, he was just as good. He hosted the ABC Sports Award for twenty years from 1967 and was equally at home interviewing boxer Lionel Rose or yachtsman John Bertrand as he was talking with Richie Benaud or Dawn Fraser. His effusive nature endeared him to the TV audience, and his knowledge of all sports was incredible. Woe betide any young trainee who took on Norman in a trivia competition at the pub. Someone would be dispatched to the office to fetch *Wisden*, *Miller's Racing Guide* or the *Laws of Golf*, to settle the argument, but 'Nugget' was always right.

His capacity for alcohol was legendary and he rarely appeared to eat anything. His memory wasn't always so good. One memorable time he called in at The Dolphin, a pub in Surry Hills owned by former dual Rugby international Dick Thornett. 'Nugget' had won a packet on the races and bought a carton of his favourite tipple, Moët champagne, to celebrate. He put the champers in the boot of his cab and popped inside to invite his mates to come around to his flat for a party. However, when he went outside, the cab had gone, along with the booze! And, for the life of him, 'Nugget' couldn't remember anything about the driver to track him down.

He has friends everywhere, even in the police force. When we were trainees, he used to get us to put coins in the parking meter for the 'Red Rocket', his battered old Datsun. Sometimes, however, we were too late and there would be a parking ticket. 'No worries — I'll just put it with the others.' In his glove-box was a stash of unpaid tickets, but we all knew why.

On a personal level, Norman's life has been far from enviable. He's never married and lived with his ageing mother for many years. He drank too much, ate poorly and his health suffered. He was plagued with gout, which meant that he often wore carpet slippers, even with a suit. His only lasting relationship, with a woman doctor, ended several years ago and he now lives alone in an apartment overlooking Bondi Beach. The single-minded dedication needed by sports commentators takes a heavy toll on personal lives.

It wasn't until he contracted late-onset diabetes in his seventies that he slowed down, but he's still full of energy. For the Beijing Olympics he prepared a series of 55 Olympic profiles, one for each Australian gold medallist, starting with Edwin Flack and ending with the men's hockey team, the Kookaburras. These were shown on the Australian Olympic Council website, one each week, leading into the Beijing Games. Norman was offered a fat fee for the series but, instead, asked for a ticket to the Olympics. He was an ambassador in Beijing, a fitting swansong for a man whose whole life has been bound up in sport, and especially the Olympics.

After that, at the age of 80, he said he was retiring. Can you believe it? He actually retired from the ABC in 1984 and has covered five Olympics since. He still listens to and watches a lot of sport, but prefers his old favourites, cricket and Rugby Union. One sport he doesn't watch is Australian Rules, probably because of his background as a Rugby player. He likes going to Melbourne though, where they love their sport, and if anyone asks him: 'Which team do you follow?'

'Nugget' simply smiles and answers: 'Australia.'

TWENTY-FIVE

Drew Morphett

THE LIKEABLE LARRIKIN

'They had big old bikes that looked like Malvern Stars. You'd reckon they were delivering mail for the PMG'

A great survivor who has never lost his schoolboy enthusiasm for sport, Drew Morphett is still one of the best around — just ask the fans. These days, he calls cricket in summer and AFL football in winter for ABC Radio, after going full circle via Channel Seven for

Drew Morphett, a likeable larrikin, is part of a team described as 'an easy-to-listen-to mix of men happy to focus on the real stars — the men in boots'

thirteen years. I recorded an interview with Drew just after he had called the cricket series with Sri Lanka in late 2007 and was astonished to hear that this was his Test debut on radio.

'I did Tests on ABC TV for eight years, but never on radio. The closest I ever got was when Australia played the World XI in 1971 and Dennis Lillee took 8/29 at the WACA. So it was quite a thrill to call those Tests at the 'Gabba and Bellerive,' Drew recalls.

With over forty years' experience in sports broadcasting, Drew can do a fair job on any sport but cricket is one of his passions, so, not surprisingly, he was a great success alongside the likes of Kerry O'Keeffe and Peter Roebuck. Some of his lines were classics — such as when rain stopped play in Hobart:

Morphett: 'There are some planets in the solar system where it doesn't rain — perhaps we could use them as neutral venues. We could play cricket on Mars.'

Roebuck: 'It hasn't rained on Mars for over 250 million years, you know.'

Morphett: 'Imagine the turn you'd get on the ball there!'

That's vintage Morphett — irreverent but always entertaining. And there are years of experience behind seemingly-flippant remarks, such as when he went in to bat for WA spinner Brad Hogg ahead of Stuart MacGill before the First Test. It turned out that MacGill got the nod, but bowled poorly. At the end of the Sri Lanka series Drew mischievously put a call over the air: 'Come on, Hoggie, start warming your arm up. You'll be there for the Boxing Day Test!'

ABC colleague Damien Fleming fielded an irate call from Australian selector Merv Hughes, advising Morphett to stick to calling the action and leave the selections to those better qualified. Drew's response was that he is not a describer, he's a commentator and he has opinions. 'Mark my words, Merv. You'll come around to my way of thinking by Christmas.' And he did!

It's all tongue-in-cheek and entertaining, but a quantum leap from the way we young trainees were taught to call in the days of Alan McGilvray. Things are a lot different now. The stiff formality of those old ABC broadcasts has evolved into an entertaining blend of drama, humour and whimsy — a pattern that suits Drew perfectly.

The extraordinary thing is that the man himself hasn't changed in 40 years. Perhaps, with age, he's mellowed a bit and doesn't stay out until 3.00 am the night before a Test these days, but the impish sense of humour, enthusiasm and voice are just the same.

I remember when we called the cricket for ABC TV in the 1970s; I would stay with Drew in Melbourne and we would go out every night. Next morning we would arrive at the ground, bleary-eyed after four hours' sleep and no breakfast, where I would have to do the pitch inspection, and sometimes the toss, before play. Meanwhile Drew, happy in the knowledge that he played second fiddle to Norman May on the commentary roster, would curl up under the scorer's bench, saying: 'Wake me up at drinks, won't you?'

Then he would come on for the second hour of play, bright-eyed and bushy-tailed, full of the joy of life. Drew could get away with anything, it seemed. In his first year as a trainee he had to record a summary of each day's play from the Ashes in England, in case Alan McGilvray's wrap-up from the ground was of poor quality, something fairly common in those days of radio broadcasting. One Sunday morning his mother woke him up, saying: 'Aren't you supposed to be at work this morning?'

'No, Mum, leave me alone,' Drew said, curling up again.

'Then why is your boss on the phone?'

After a mercy dash to the office, Drew grabbed the cables from Lord's, wrote and recorded his summary and got it to air, just in time.

Another time, Drew was calling the Australian Lawn Bowls Championships in Perth, where the last match was dragging on and on. Extra ends had to be played and Drew rushed from the club back to the studios, where he was to broadcast the evening sports program, 'Sporting Highlights'. Stuck in traffic, he heard the familiar opening theme being played and the announcer came on: 'At this time we were to have "Sporting Highlights" but, as nobody is here to present it, let's have a some music.'

Red-faced and panting, Drew rushed into the studio, mumbled his apologies and did the program. Somehow he got away with it.

As a youngster growing up in Sydney, Drew always wanted to be a sports commentator. At school at Scots College, he was a more than useful left-arm spinner and won his colours in the First XI, but he was never destined to play for Australia. He applied for a job with ABC Sport as a trainee in 1968, armed with a reference from a family friend, popular 2UE disc jockey Gary O'Callaghan. To his surprise and delight he got the job and, at the age of eighteen, began work alongside his heroes, Alan McGilvray and Norman May.

'In those days I would take a recorder out to a Sheffield Shield match and sit at the back of the M.A. Noble Stand, calling the play. Then I'd take it back to the office and, if I was lucky, get "Mac" to listen to it. I still remember him saying the most important thing was to be ahead of the crowd. You had to set up your description of a delivery so that you weren't describing the action after it had happened. And, even after a 200-run partnership, you had to be alert because a wicket could fall at any time.'

With 'Nugget' May the best advice came in the pub, over a beer. He once pointed out that Drew talked too quickly — he was a 'bit of a gabbler'. This was ironic as 'Nugget' himself talked like a machine-gun, except when he was on air. Then he became the ideal model of elocution, with perfect diction. Drew listened to this advice and became much more articulate.

His polish came, however, when he moved to Perth and came under the tutelage of one of the best sports mentors in the business, Jim Fitzmaurice. The dapper 'Fitzy' showed Drew the ropes and introduced him to the finer points of WA's winter obsession: Australian Rules football. Drew admits: 'When I went to Perth I didn't even know how many men there were in a Rules team, so Jim sent me to Lathlain Park, the home of Perth Football Club, to talk with a legend of the game, Ern Renfry. My brief was to ask any question at all, no matter how elementary. So, after ten minutes or so, I asked what this big fellow was doing, moving from the centre to the far end.'

'He's going for a rest in the forward pocket,' replied Ern.

'Hang on, this game goes for two hours, doesn't it? And he's going for a rest already!'

'You'll see.'

A few minutes later Drew noticed something else.

'What's that other big bloke doing, moving from the boundary to the centre?'

'He's going for a run on the ball.'

'The ball's been bouncing through legs and over shoulders and this six foot seven giant's gonna have a run on the ball — this I've gotta see.'

'Another mug from the eastern states,' Ern sighed.

To his credit, Drew learned fast and, on moving back to Melbourne, became the host of 'The Winners', which became a Sunday night institution for a decade. Drew recalls: 'That show was the brainchild of Dick Mason, the ABC's sports boss in Melbourne and a brilliant producer. He unashamedly stole the format from that great English soccer program "The Big Match", which featured all the highlights of the weekend's round of First Division (now the English Premier League) in an hour. It was a bit tougher condensing Aussie Rules into that time, with so many more goals but, with good editing, it became a terrific show. We began the Mark of the Day and Goal of the Day long before the commercials got onto it and that show rated its socks off.'

The late Dick Mason was different to most ABC Sport commentators. He loved American sport and was a capable baseball coach and basketball commentator. He deplored the funereal pace of cricket in the 1960s and never attempted to hide his contempt. One day, calling a Shield match on a flat pitch at the Junction Oval, Victoria was playing for a draw. Bored and frustrated, Dick said: 'Allan bowls, Lawry defends and the ball is fielded by a Queenslander in a white hat.'

'Next ball... and it's played down into the gully where its picked up by a Queenslander in a white hat.'

'Over-pitched this time, Lawry drives but another Queenslander in a white hat is there to cut it off. I can't tell who these players are — they must have had a fire sale of white hats at Bill Brown's Sports Store.'

When the ABC lost the rights for VFL to Channel Seven, Drew joined the commercial world in 1988 — and ran into the inimitable Christopher Skase. 'It was fair dinkum Hollywood. We'd have these cocktail parties with champagne flowing, flashing lights and gorgeous models and on match day we'd get picked up in stretch limos — but I don't think the drivers ever got paid!' Drew laughed.

Drew has always been one to speak his mind and got into hot water when he clashed with a Channel Seven producer. Drew had said that a goal in the final quarter had been 'the clincher', which promptly drew a rap over the knuckles from the producer. 'We don't say things like that here at Seven. We want the audience to be kept in suspense until the final siren.'

Drew exploded: 'What do you mean? Don't tell me how to call football. Everyone knows that the crowd starts to leave when there's a three goal difference and only three minutes left.'

Well, that may have been the way it worked at the ABC, but Drew was carpeted on Monday morning and told to change his ways.

'It wasn't all bad, though. Gary Fenton, the executive producer, gave me some advice early on: "Don't get involved in arguments about umpires. If you bag an umpire because he's made what you consider a bad decision in a Carlton/Collingwood match then you'll alienate 50 per cent of your audience. A minute or two later you bag him for a decision which favours the other side and, bang, in two minutes you've lost your whole audience." I know he'd never called a game in his life but that was sound advice and I still follow it.'

With his ABC training, Drew is an all-rounder and he rates his cycling commentary at the 1984 LA Olympics as the highlight of his career. 'The Yanks cheated in those Games. In a hundred years of the Olympics they had never won a cycling gold medal and in LA they scooped the pool — from the road races to the sprints, USA won everything. They used blood doping — the same trick as the Finnish runner Lasse Viren — where you completely replace your blood with a fresh supply the day before you race. What's more, the Yanks had the carbon fibre disc wheels, teardrop helmets and skintight suits. Fair dinkum they looked like men from Mars. So when we came to the team pursuit, there were the Yanks, who had the gold and bronze medallists from the individual pursuit, the greatest living certainties ever in a sports event.

Then in the final we had the Aussies — a team of unknowns — Michael Turtur (SA), Michael Grenda (Tasmania), Kevin Nichols (NSW) and eighteen-year-old Dean Woods (Victoria). They had these big old bikes that looked like Malvern Stars — you'd reckon they were delivering mail for the PMG!

'On the start line Australia had a stroke of luck — one of the Yanks pulled a foot out of the pedal when they said "Go", just like Shane Kelly did in Atlanta, and they were down to three.

'The Aussies started really fast — too fast I thought — and at halfway they led by two seconds. Everyone was expecting the Yanks to come back but they didn't and we won Australia's first gold in cycling since the 1956 Olympics. It was also the first gold for Australia at the LA Games and twenty minutes later Jon Sieben won the second in the butterfly. The cycling got the momentum started though and I still get goosebumps talking about it today.'

Drew knew his cycling — he hosted a popular ABC TV program called 'Flashing Pedals', which was shot at Coburg Velodrome each weekend and he knew Dean Woods personally. That just made it all the more special. They say that TV commentary is glamorous and exciting but it can be trying. In Atlanta in 1996 it was blazing hot at the cycling and the commentary position was in the open, so Drew opened an umbrella. However, officials told him to take it down and one of his colleagues subsequently suffered badly burnt forearms.

There was a similar situation in Barcelona in 1992 where Drew called the diving at the spectacular venue on Montjuïc

Hill, overlooking the city. Once again, it was so hot that Drew and Steve Foley called the action off the monitor under a tarpaulin. And you don't get paid danger money. Drew recalls how he and Steve watched an NBC America commentator do eight takes before he got his piece right. He had wardrobe, make-up and a personal assistant, all for a brief summary of the day's event. The hard-working Australian pair was there on their own for the whole day.

When Channel Seven lost the rights to the AFL in 2001, Drew went back to the ABC and to where he started, on radio. He works on the cricket during summer and the football in winter. In between times, he and his wife Caz run a horse agistment business on their farm at Pakenham, an hour east of Melbourne. Drew explains: 'It all started by chance really. It was just a hobby for Caz, who loves horses, being a country girl. A farrier we knew asked if his brother-in-law, Robbie Griffiths, could put some horses on the farm. Then word got around and Peter Moody, the former Queensland trainer, and Colin Alderson, the president of the Trainers' Association, are now with us. I'm on the Pakenham Race Club committee and Caz is a vet nurse, so it all fits. I love the balance between the excitement of calling sport and the tranquillity of the farm.'

For a man who's called sport on television most of his life, Drew has a rare appreciation of radio. The old lessons are still remembered and he will tell you that the most valuable weapon in a caller's armoury is silence. 'You have Trueman bowling to O'Neill. This broad-shouldered Yorkshire miner with the shock of dark hair and his sleeves flapping as he moves in. And O'Neill, brilliant player, but a nervous starter — still yet to score. And, to this one from Trueman ... [pause] he's bowled! [Crowd roars] O'Neill out for a duck — Australia in trouble — 3 for 24.'

'That pause makes all the difference', Drew says, 'because the listener has the chance to form his own image in his mind of what's happening.'

With his laconic, earthy nature Drew has a wide appeal to an Australian audience. He hates people who 'bung on side' or allow their ego to get in the way of the game. He has a genuine interest in a wide range of things outside sport, especially rock music. I vividly remember sessions in the beer garden of the Melbourne Hilton, with a gaggle of commentators engaged in music trivia contests. The idea was to play a series of tunes on the juke box and the contest was to be the first to name the song and the band. Invariably it came down to two finalists: Drew and Peter 'Smooth' Booth, another ABC veteran. Their knowledge of music was incredible. After a few drinks, Drew's favourite party trick was to jump on the bar and belt out Van Morrison's 'Gloria'.

If you press him on which commentator he admires most, Drew will opt for Norman 'Nugget' May, his old mentor. 'He may not have the greatest voice but his knowledge and ability to call almost any sport is mind-boggling. Have you ever tried to call a surf race, for example? How you identify different swimmers 200 metres away in all that white water is beyond me — yet Nugget did it time and again. He must have called 50 sports in his career and you'd swear he was an expert at every one of them.'

The same could well apply to Drew, and unlike many of his counterparts, he is as down to earth and humble as ever. A recent article by Michael Horan in the Melbourne *Sun* on Melbourne football commentators sums it up: 'The understated ABC team, led by Drew Morphett, Gerard Whately and Dan Lonergan, is an easy-to-listen-to mix of men happy to focus on the real stars — the men in boots.'

TWENTY-SIX

David Morrow

A LEAGUE OF HIS OWN

'I hope your listeners don't understand French because they've just had a guided tour of the best brothels in Perpignan'

'The game is all about passion and anyone who says he doesn't follow a team doesn't have any passion.' That's what David Morrow reckons. He is the chief Rugby League caller for ABC Radio and is always being accused of bias towards St George–Illawarra by listeners. 'I don't deny it. I am a staunch supporter of the Dragons but I deny any bias.

'Old commentators never die, they just lose their voices' says multi-skilled David Morrow

In fact, like a lot of referees, I tend to bend over backwards towards the other team, in order to avoid this kind of criticism.'

Having called Rugby League myself on ABC Radio for 15 years, I can identify with David's feelings. You are always under the scrutiny of the listening public and, if you get any feedback at all, it's normally bad. But David recalls a positive response: 'I once got a letter from a bloke who reckoned listening to me had made him think the world was a better place. It came after Kerryn McCann won the women's marathon with a sprint finish before 85,000 people at the MCG in the 2006 Commonwealth Games. It was one of those precious moments every commentator loves to call and I just did my job, trying to convey the excitement and emotion. Obviously he got something out of it and was moved enough to send congratulations — little things like that make it all worthwhile.'

Mind you, ask any sports commentator what drives them, and it's generally not money. That's the thing with the best commentators: their whole lives are bound up in watching, reading and talking about sport, even when they aren't at work. It's a 24/7 occupation, which requires total devotion but has enormous rewards.

'My favourite sporting moment would have to be 'Flojo' breaking the world 200 metres record twice within two hours in Seoul in 1988,' David recalls. 'I was lucky enough to be calling those races and, whether you believe she was on drugs or not, to see how she demolished the field both times was breathtaking.' That's what they say about life, isn't it?

It's not the number of breaths you take, it's the number of breathtaking moments. For people like David, they are worth more than money. He should know, as he was lured away from the ABC to join Channel Ten in 1990, but came back to the ABC fourteen months later.

'Although I was being paid a hell of a lot more money, I simply hated my time at Ten. I was bored out of my brain most of the time, just reading the news.'

The one thing David did enjoy though, was the 1990 Kangaroo tour of Britain. His call of Mal Meninga's match-winning try in the Second Test has gone down in the annals, but for all the wrong reasons. David recalls: 'When Ricky Stuart broke clear, ran 70 metres and fed the big fella, I lost my voice. The box had a tin roof and I'd been yelling all game, trying to make myself heard, falling for the old trap. So, when the big moment came, I was reduced to a croak. For some reason people liked it and nowadays at sports dinners I'm forever being asked to do it again.'

David was born at Walcha and then moved to Uralla, in northern NSW. 'I went to the Armidale School where I was an average student and an ordinary footballer. My one claim to fame, though, was that I was in the same year as a bloke who scored four tries in a Rugby Union Test: Greg Cornelson.'

David always wanted to become a broadcaster, so he applied for a position as a trainee with the ABC in 1972, but lost out to Jim Maxwell. 'One of the interview panel was Rugby League commentator John O'Reilly, whom I regard as the best caller ever. I worshipped him so, when he suggested I go to university until another job came up, I took his advice.' David completed an economics/law degree at Sydney University and finally broke into radio in Kempsey, on the NSW North Coast. His father helped him write to 46 radio stations throughout NSW and he finally got his break. 'Vern Hart gave me a job and I cut my teeth in country radio, doing a bit of everything, including horse-racing and football.'

In 1980, another job came up at the ABC and this time Head of Sport, Derek White, chose David. He began calling harness racing every Friday night at Harold Park and, when Geoff Mahoney retired in 1990, he became the ABC's Sydney racecaller. But League was always his first love. 31 years and 7 Olympics later, he's still mad about Rugby League, even though every winter it means he sees more of his co-commentators than he does his family. 'Warren Ryan and Craig Hamilton are terrific company so I don't mind, but the commitment is much more than it used to be when I first got into this game. In the old days you'd start at 2.30 and go home at 5, but now we get to the ground before the players and are still there long after they're gone. "Wozza" hates flying, so we spend a lot of time driving to and fro, but it's a lot of fun.'

The ABC Rugby League commentators' appeal is such that they are the top-rating team on Sydney radio. They call Friday, Saturday and Sunday games, with the odd Monday night as well. On top of this, there are 'Grandstand' previews, reviews and talk-back — all adding up to hundreds of hours in a season.

They make a terrific team — with David's deep voice and authoritative call, Ryan's perceptive analysis and Hamilton's quirky sideline comments. Above all, their mutual love of the game is what comes through strongest.

David doesn't mind admitting he uses anything he can to help identification. A TV monitor is a bonus and, at big grounds like Lang Park, he always uses binoculars. 'In the modern game, where you have four or five tacklers sometimes, it's almost impossible to see a number. It's not so bad at Leichhardt, where you can see the pimples on the football, so I don't need anything there, but it's a team effort and, if I miss something, Craig will generally pick it up from the sideline.'

David is more than just a League caller — he also specialises in racing, trotting and cricket, but is a fine athletics commentator as well. I know, because I sat in front of him at the 2006 Commonwealth Games and enjoyed his calls of the track events. David comments: 'It's certainly helpful to have a background as a race-caller. Getting your head around a twenty-man field in the 10 000 metres isn't so bad when you've called a seven-race card every Saturday for a couple of years.'

Like most good ABC commentators, David can turn his hand to almost any sport and is one of the few Rugby League callers in Sydney who covers soccer. His call of the Sydney FC friendly against David Beckham's LA Galaxy was like the match itself — classy, fast and entertaining.

David prefers radio to television, although he admits to enjoying working with former ABC TV director Ray Hume, who now produces cricket in India. 'Ray is a great director — quiet and efficient. He lets you get on with what you're good at, which is calling the game, without screaming abuse in your headphones because a cameraman's framed his shot wrongly. That's the thing with radio — you just need a voice.'

In all those hours in the box, there are plenty of lighter moments. One of David's favourites occurred in France, where he was calling a Test at Perpignan in 1986 (the Second Test, in which Garry Jack became the first Australian full-back to score three tries in a Test).

'When I got to the box it was empty. No operator, no microphones, just a couple of wires coming out of the wall. Fortunately this bloke arrived, really nonchalant, although we only had half an hour before the broadcast. Although he didn't speak a word of English and I only had a few phrases of French, he got us wired up and I thought everything would be okay. So, a few minutes before the cross I'm enjoying a cup of coffee while he's chatting away to some mate of his in Paris. Suddenly I hear an Australian voice in my headphones, a fellow from master control in Sydney who understands French: 'First David — I'd better tell you — the lines are open and they have crossed early. Second, I hope your listeners don't understand French, because they've just had a guided tour of the best brothels in Perpignan!'

There are also embarrassing moments, the ones when you wish you could take back what you just said, and David has had his share. He recalls: 'When the great trotting driver Laurie Moulds died I was asked to record several tributes, of varying lengths for different programs. As you know, you occasionally have the odd stumble and have to do them again. Well, of the five that I did, they played the one that I stuffed up on the national news, warts and all!'

The most difficult sport he has called on radio is, surprisingly, not horse-racing — it's tennis. 'That's one reason I admired John O'Reilly so much. He was fast and accurate and always ahead of the crowd. An A-grade player, he had a remarkable ability to read the game and anticipate what would happen. Especially in doubles, it's really hard to stay on top of a rally when there's an interchange of volleys at the net.'

David loves horse-racing and enjoys picking a winner. He admits to being chuffed when we did our interview, the week after the Melbourne Cup. Not only did he pick the winner, but he also picked seven horses in a box trifecta and they finished first, second, third, fourth, fifth, sixth and eighth. What's more, he backed his tips — that's what I call 'Efficient' tipping!

How long will he keep going? With digital radio around the corner, there will be an even greater demand for sports coverage. 'Jim Maxwell and I were discussing this the other day — we reckon they might carry us out in a box.'

Old commentators never die — they just lose their voices.

TWENTY-SEVEN

Les Murray

THE FACE OF FOOTBALL

'It's such a hard game in which to score, so when a goal comes, especially if it's an extraordinary play, like a backwards scissor-kick, you just go berserk'

When it comes to soccer in Australia, there's only one name that matters, when you talk television: Les Murray. But that's not his real name, it's Laszlo Urge. Born in Hungary, Les migrated with his parents to Australia in 1957, bringing with him a love of the round ball game that was the most popular sport in Europe and, indeed, the world. Yet in

Les Murray has had a lifetime's love affair with football

Australia it wasn't — Australian Rules and Rugby League held sway in the 1950s and Les would get into fights in the schoolyard with League-mad kids who called him a 'wog', simply because he loved soccer.

It was a big cultural leap from Budapest to Port Kembla, but Les vowed at the age of eleven to convert his adopted country to 'the beautiful game' and now, 54 years later, he's done it. Soccer may not be the dominant football code in Australia but at least it now stands proudly, shoulder to shoulder with the three other codes in what is surely the toughest market in the world. Australians love their sport but, due to the sheer size of the country and diversity of ethnic and cultural influences, they are divided in their loyalties. At least Australians are now proud of their national team, the Socceroos, and the most-watched TV program of 2006 was their World Cup match against Italy, the eventual champions. Qualifying for the FIFA World Cup for only the second time, the Australian team played skilful and exciting football, winning the respect of even the diehard AFL and League fans.

Hosting the SBS coverage, as always, was 'Mr Soccer', Les Murray, who seems to have been the face and voice of the game forever. We have watched him age gracefully on air and now, at 64, he is grey and wears glasses, but he's a natty dresser and still retains a boyish enthusiasm that is the hallmark of his work. Despite his Hungarian accent, Les has overcome schoolyard sledging, racist attitudes and entrenched media policies to put soccer on the map. In fact these days, thanks to the urging of the late Johnny Warren, it's known more often as 'football', bringing the terminology into line with the rest of the world.

Les and Johnny Warren were thrown together as a commentary team in the 1970s, after Johnny finally succumbed to a knee injury and retired from playing. A former Socceroo captain and star striker, Johnny was the perfect foil for Les and, driven by a common passion, they worked together for more than 30 years.

Les was persuaded to change his name by a producer at Channel Ten when the network held a press conference to promote its coverage of the fledgling National Soccer League in 1977. 'You can't have a name like Laszlo Urge, it's too complicated. We'll just call you Les Murray; that has a nice Aussie ring to it.'

Coming from Budapest, Les had followed St George Budapest in the NSW competition and their star player through the '60s and '70s was Johnny Warren. So it was natural that they would get on well together. 'There was a mutual respect and, what's more, we shared common interests, apart from football. We both loved good food and wine, so we'd sit and talk for hours in restaurants and cafés when we were away, always discussing the one thing: football.

When we covered the World Cup in Italy in 1990 we wouldn't finish work until about 1.00 am but we'd always buy a bottle of Grand Marnier and sit and drink it, looking over Rome and talking football, before we went to bed.'

One thing about Les, he's a stickler for correct pronunciation. Being from Europe he has a better understanding than most Australians of how to pronounce foreign-sounding names. As Head of Sport at SBS TV, he has passed this on to his commentators and presenters, who do a fine job covering global football.

These days Les takes a back seat when it comes to football coverage, leaving the commentary to others. He occasionally presents the excellent 30-minute daily sports program on SBS as well as hosting 'The World Game' on Sunday afternoons. 'I don't mind taking a production role with football coverage these days, but as long as they want me and I still enjoy it, I'll keep presenting sports programs.'

Les took a gamble when, in 1992, he started Toyota World Sports on SBS each weeknight at 7.00 pm. Channel Ten had tried it with 'Sports Tonight', but soon reverted to a late-night timeslot, so it was seen as a risky programming move. However, SBS have never been ratings-driven and their soccer-mad audience lapped up the longer bulletin.

As a player Les was no superstar, but he found his niche in commentary, just when soccer in Australia needed someone like him. His knowledge and passion for the game came through and satisfied Australian fans who, by and large, came from multicultural ethnic backgrounds. When Australia opened its doors after World War II to migrants in order to provide labour for massive engineering projects like the Snowy River Scheme, thousands of Europeans came to the country. Unfamiliar with traditional Australian football like Rugby and AFL, they formed their own soccer clubs and gave them ethnic names. So the Czechs had 'Prague', the Italians 'Apia' and the Jews 'Hakoah'.

I remember covering an NSL match for the ABC in 1969

when our regular commentator, Martin Royal, was sick. I felt totally lost, not just because I didn't know much about soccer, but because Arlington Oval seemed to be in a foreign country. Apia was playing Yugal, but there were no programs left and it seemed that nobody spoke English. Fortunately one of the managers wrote the team lists out for me, so I could give my reports on the match — but I wasn't sent back to the soccer again!

My experience probably reflected that of most of the media who simply felt that covering soccer was too hard. The barriers of language and culture were too much, so they reverted to more familiar territory. That's where Johnny Warren was a saviour. He had the clean-cut, all-Australian look, spoke with an Aussie accent and had been a Socceroo star. He hosted a children's program called 'Captain Socceroo', held coaching clinics and, alongside Les, commentated and presented soccer on television every week. In fact, they did so much together that they became known as 'Mr and Mrs Soccer' (with some debate as to who wore the skirt!).

Australian soccer changed its image when David Hill took over. The former ABC boss perceived the ethnic nature of the game to be a source of violence and racism, so he banned ethnic names and emblems. There was some resistance at first but, in the long run, the sport has won over a new audience because of the move.

In fact the 'sheilas, wogs and poofters' image of the game is misleading. True, the first postwar teams were ethnic-based and many players couldn't speak English well. However, when

I called the soccer at the Barcelona Olympics in 1992, I was surprised how few of the players with European names spoke with foreign accents. We had names like Zelic, Blagojevic, Markovski, Mori and Longo but the only one I couldn't understand was Eddie Thomson, the Scottish-born coach!

Les Murray and Johnny Warren formed a team that covered the world of soccer, not just the Australian game. So, in any given week, they would call European Cup, Copa America, Spanish or Italian league matches, as well as the local NSL game on the weekend. Les did enormous amounts of homework, so that he could call matches 'off tube' (from the monitor) not merely by players' numbers, but by the colour of their hair, their height or the way they ran. 'You would write out reams of notes on their backgrounds, their personal lives and stats, but in a game you would probably only use 5 per cent of it. It was really just a comfort drug that gave you confidence in your call.'

One match Les recalls being especially difficult involved a Macedonian team, Vardar, who wore blood-red shirts with black numbers. Calling off the monitor, Les simply couldn't tell one player's number from another, so he had to watch the tape over and over until he knew the players by their appearance.

We all make mistakes, but Les recalls one particularly embarrassing commentary. In Italy the Socceroos were playing Udinese and not having a good day. They were down 2–0 at half-time, but at least they restored some pride in the second half by scoring the only goal, a header by John Kosmina. Les and his co-commentator, Mike Hill, had both analysed the Australian goal, intently watching the monitor, as the producer ran several replays. Later, in the hotel bar, Les remarked to Socceroo goalkeeper Terry Greedy that a 2–1 scoreline wasn't too bad really against a crack Serie A team like Udinese.

'2–1!' said a startled Greedy. 'No, the score was 2–0. That Kossy goal was disallowed. Didn't you see the ref?'

Horrified, Les rang producer Dominic Galati in Sydney to relay the news. Fortunately for Les and Mike, the match wasn't shown live and Galati was a brilliant editor. 'Somehow he cut out our commentary when we gave the wrong score and it went to air with Australia losing 2–nil, but we never lived that one down.'

Naturally there have been plenty of career highlights as well, such as the World Cup qualifiers against Israel and Iran in the days of Frank Arok and Eddie Thomson. 'They were fantastic matches to call — high pressure, big noisy crowds. Whether they were in Tel Aviv or Melbourne, we really loved calling those matches.'

Les found commentary immensely rewarding. 'It's such a hard game in which to score, so when a goal finally comes there is this tremendous feeling of gratification and exuberance, especially if it's an extraordinary play, like a backwards scissor-kick. You just go berserk.'

There is a difference in calling Socceroos games to NSL or A League games, Les maintains. 'It's okay to want Australia to win but when you start accusing the referee of bias you can go too far. I've sacked commentators for that, you simply have to retain your objectivity.'

Simon Hill did a wonderful job in Germany in 2006 under some duress. It seemed that the referees simply didn't respect the Socceroos and every time there was a foul in the games against Japan and Brazil, it went against Australia. As it turned out, the English referee Graham Poll, who officiated in the Japan game, later admitted his bias and flew home. However, in the crucial match against Italy, Les thinks Australia may have been hard done by. 'The jury is still out on that Lucas Neill tackle on Fabio Grosso, but I find it mystifying that a referee could award a penalty on a 50/50 ball with only seconds left on the clock. Having said that, I think Australia has finally earned the respect of the football world from their display at the 2006 and 2010 World Cups. Martin Tyler, David Basheer and Craig Foster did a fine job in South Africa, but the Socceroos were disappointing. Their tournament was all but over after their first game — a 4-0 thrashing by Germany.'

Les Murray has a lifetime love affair with football and even now will stop the car and watch a junior match when he sees a game under way at a suburban ground. 'I just want to see how the kids play, how they're being coached and if the game is in good hands.'

It will be as long as you're around, Les.

TWENTY-EIGHT

Jack Newton

THE ONE-ARMED BANDIT

'Right in the Mayor's office!'

Golf is one of my favourite sports to watch on television. I love playing the game and have always enjoyed seeing how the pros do it. I think that Australian networks cover the sport better than anyone else in the world and our commentators are generally first-class as well. The urbane Englishman Peter Alliss is in a class of his own and Ian Baker-Finch is doing a terrific job calling the US PGA Tour but, of the Australian-based commentators, Jack Newton has no peer.

Jack was born in Cessnock, NSW and was a fine player himself before a horrific accident in July 1983 (he walked into a plane's propellor) cost him an eye, an arm and his golf career. Undaunted, at the age of 33 he began a new challenge as a commentator and, to his credit, has achieved even more in the commentary box than he did on the fairways. He was a better

Jack Newton mellows with age — and life looks pretty good here, with Georgie Shew, right, and Laura Csortan

than average professional, after a brilliant junior career in which he won the Champion of Champions at sixteen and the NSW Amateur at seventeen. A long-hitting, aggressive player, Jack won the 1979 Australian Open and lost the 1975 British Open to American star Tom Watson in a thrilling play-off by a single stroke. He also finished runner-up to Seve Ballesteros in the 1980 US Masters and had the golf world at his feet when he had his accident.

On leaving hospital he was offered the chance to do a commentary stint for ABC TV at the Australian PGA tournament at Sydney's Concord Club. Although still weak and weighing only about 65 kg, Jack revelled in his role as an expert analyst and thoroughly enjoyed his half-hour session. The producer, Bill Pritchard, came out of the OB van to congratulate him, saying: 'Jack, you're a natural at this. You should give some serious thought to doing more of it.'

Jack did and, after a couple more operations, his strength returned. During his recuperation, he was amazed at the kindness of so many people in the golf world, sending cards, letters and offers of help for him, his wife Jackie and their two small children. He says that the game of golf also helped him through the ordeal of facing the end of a promising career and such devastating injuries: 'Golf is a tough game and you play it under the microscope, so you learn to be mentally tough. I think that discipline helped me through those dark days when I felt like sulking in a corner.'

Offers for more TV work came thick and fast and Jack freelanced all over the world as a commentator who wasn't afraid to speak his mind. An early example of his forthright attitude came in 1984 when he was working at the British Open for the BBC. Jack recalls: 'A Scottish guy working with me took exception to my comments. The group of Fred Couples, Ian Baker-Finch and John Bland was coming up the eighteenth into a headwind and all three played out to the left on the adjacent first fairway. The Scot said they had pulled their drives but I said that it was intentional, so they could hit their second into the wind and get a better angle to the flag, thus avoiding the Valley of Sin, the gully in front of the green. He then said he disagreed. When Freddie holed his chip to lead the Open into the final round and the other two made birdies, I turned to this bloke with a big smile, but no apology was forthcoming. So I said: "That's why I played tournament golf and you're a teaching pro".'

Jack never worked for the BBC again. However, this kind of blunt, but honest, assessment was seen as an asset by

Australian TV producers, and Jack got plenty of work back home. Christopher Skase knew talent when he saw it and offered Jack a lucrative contract to work exclusively for Channel Seven and he's been with them ever since. Sporting his trademark bow tie and sunglasses, he has become a sporting icon in this country. His raspy accent is in contrast to the rounded vowels and clipped tones of British commentators like Henry Longhurst and Peter Alliss, but Jack has a common touch, which has won hordes of fans in Australia. Not just golfers either — Jack has a simplicity in the way he calls which appeals to non-golfers and older people — and everyone likes a bit of humour, something the loveable rogue is always on the look out for.

Having been a top player himself he has an empathy with those on the course and he shows a rare ability to get the viewer involved. An example might be at a short par 3, which looks straightforward to the viewer but has more to it than meets the eye. Jack might say: 'Well, this hole is only 158 metres but is playing more like 170, with the wind from the right and hurting. With the pin cut back left he needs to start this right and let it work its way back to the flag. But left is a no-go zone because you short-side yourself in that deep bunker.' And, on seeing a magnificent shot land about a metre right of the pin, 'Right in the Mayor's office!'

That's what I love about Jack's commentary — it comes from years of playing experience and it's often spiced with humour. Golf can be a frustrating game, as we all know, so it's good to lighten up proceedings with a quirky comment every now and then. All over the country people are now saying, as their ball lands on the green, 'Commercially sound' (or other Newton-isms).

Jack is more than a sports commentator, he is a very successful fundraiser and administrator. The Jack Newton Junior Golf Foundation, which he started in 1986, has steered many youngsters towards a career in the game and Jack's Celebrity Classic, now in it's thirty-first year, has raised over four million dollars for junior development. On top of that, Jack's Corporate Cup has raised about $500,000 for diabetes research. For his services to golf and youth development, Jack was honoured with the Order of Australia. For a decade from 1990 Jack was Chairman of PGA Tour Australasia, perhaps the most influential job in the game in this country.

Jack is especially proud of his two children, Clint and Kristy, who are both successful athletes. Clint is a Rugby League player, who won a premiership in 2006 with the Melbourne Storm, and Kristy is a budding pro on the LPGA tour. 'I think the discipline kids get from sport is important. Anything that can get them away from the computer and out in the fresh air has to be a step in the right direction.' His mother and father were big influences on his career. His dad was a footballer who didn't take up golf until the age of 28, but was down to a scratch handicap at 33 and played to it until his late forties. According to Jack, his mum is responsible for his stubborn nature and determination and she was no slouch as a player either, getting down to a handicap of six.

Jack's dad always loved to caddy for him and, both being strong personalities, they occasionally clashed. One story Jack recalls is about the time they were at the Australian Open, played at the Australian Golf Club. Jack was three off the lead coming to the eighteenth, the famous double water-carry hole. After a big drive Jack had 200 metres to the flag over the water and was keen to go for it with his trusty persimmon three-wood. Dad was having none of it though and tried to grab the club back. 'There we were at the Australian Open, with a huge gallery and a national TV audience, having a tug-o-war.'

Eventually Jack got his way and, as if to prove a point, hit his second shot to within a metre of the hole, canned the putt for an eagle and led into the final round. 'It was the shot of my life, I reckon. And, in the bar afterwards, Dad was telling everyone what a job he had to persuade me to hit the three-wood!'

On occasions Jack doesn't mind giving players a bit of stick because he has been through it all himself — and he's not shy about his own awkward moments on the course. 'Playing the Wills Masters once at Victoria Club I was teeing off on the short par four first and a fly crawled up my nose as I was on my backswing. I hit behind the ball and it ballooned high in the air out to the right. There was a girl who was selling programs next to the Pro shop and it landed in her lap — and I still had a four-iron to the green!' But that wasn't as bad as an incident in South Africa. 'I got tangled up with some Matabele ants that crawled up my trousers and I had to drop my daks in the middle of the eighteenth green. The commentators must have had some fun with that!'

At 61 Jack is mellowing with age and thinks he's a bit

softer these days. He still loves what he does and, as Channel Seven has lost rights to Australian golf, he freelances. It was wonderful listening to him at the JB Were Australian Masters in 2010 alongside two other fine commentators, Ian Baker-Finch and Wayne Grady. Despite his handicap he still takes on all comers on the course and, being a good judge of form, he doesn't mind a bet. His skill is unbelievable — just try hitting a three-wood with just your left arm sometime — and he still loves the competition and the banter. He is more involved these days in golf course design with the firm of Newton, Grant and Spencer and is a board member of the Australian PGA and PGA Tour Enterprises. On his time off he likes to follow his local Rugby League team, the Newcastle Knights, or spend a day at the races. Although he feels that he may soon be replaced by one of the younger brigade, I hope that he keeps going as a commentator for many more years. As I see it Jack, you've just finished the first nine …

TWENTY-NINE

Kerry O'Keeffe
THE CLOWN PRINCE

'If you took his (Shane Warne's) mobile phone away he'd be speechless!'

'Biomechanically you (John Howard) have got the perfect action. Pity you can't bowl!'

Who would have thought that an infectious laugh could lead to a successful career? In the case of Kerry O'Keeffe it has. Of course, there's more to Kerry than

Kerry O'Keeffe's self-deprecatory sense of humour and infectious laugh have found a wide cricket-listening audience

just his snorting, wheezing trademark but it's what makes him so readily identifiable. I hosted a sportmen's dinner in Brisbane recently and as soon as that familiar laugh emerged, the audience simply broke up.

As a cricketer, Kerry was no slouch. A leg-spinning prodigy with St George, he played for NSW as a teenager. I played against him in first grade in the late 1960s and he got me out — along with most of my Sydney University teammates. In fact, he applied for a position with the ABC as a sports trainee broadcaster in 1968. When he discovered that meant working, instead of playing cricket on Saturdays he withdrew — and I got the job. He went on to play 80 matches for NSW and took 53 wickets in 24 Tests for Australia in the Ian Chappell era. He could bat well enough to open the innings, which he did in the Centenary Test in 1977 at the MCG. Kerry recalls: 'Rick McCosker had his jaw broken by Bob Willis and our skipper, Greg Chappell, asked me to open the batting in the second innings — as if my life depended on it! Seeing poor old Rick, my life could well have been in danger.'

He batted for 30 minutes and shared an opening stand of 33 with Ian Davis. He chipped in with three wickets in England's second innings as Australia went on to win by 45 runs — exactly the same margin as the Test 100 years before.

Kerry did not adapt easily to life after cricket and struggled for many years, both financially and personally. He worked as a security guard and a futures trader, all the while searching unsuccessfully for his niche. His wife, Veronica, supported them both at times in her job as a legal secretary. Then, in the late 1990s, came a chance to work in the media. After doing bits and pieces on radio, he got his chance on TV in an obscure program called 'Between the Wickets' on Channel Seven's now-defunct pay network C7. He was incredibly good, so it was no surprise when he became a regular panellist on that marvellously quirky ABC TV show, 'The Fat'. He was a sensation. His knowledge and insight into sport, not just cricket, allied to his off-beat humour, won him hosts of fans. Finally, he won a seat in the ABC Radio cricket commentary box, a place reserved in the past for icons like Johnny Moyes and Victor Richardson and, of late, for the esteemed Peter Roebuck and Geoff Lawson. How would the conservative ABC audience react to the mischievous wit and unorthodox style of O'Keeffe? He was, of course, an instant success.

It's hard to put a finger on Kerry's appeal but, basically, it's his sense of humour, often self-deprecatory. It's the one dimension that was lacking in the superb ABC Radio cricket broadcasts. When play becomes slow and boring, Kerry will invariably come up with something witty and irreverent. Sometimes it will be startling, like the time when Indian commentator Harsha Bhogle was reflecting on the late-night vigil of cricket fans listening to Ashes broadcasts from England. It went something like this:

Harsha: 'In India we also like to sit up during the night and listen to the Ashes Tests, but it's hard to stay awake, so I have a Scotch. I might have a couple of stiffies, in fact.'

Kerry : 'Me too.'

Harsha: 'How many stiffies would you have in a night, Kerry?'

Kerry: (snorting) 'One, if I'm lucky Harsha — I'm fifty bloody years old!'

That certainly woke me up. Whether the ABC establishment approves or not, I don't know, but the vast majority of the audience loves him.

When necessary, Kerry can fill the role of the analyst and his comments are based on sound reasoning. He has for many years had the habit of videotaping bowlers' actions, so he can look at their strengths and weaknesses biomechanically. He is the perfect foil for a straightman such as Jim Maxwell or Glenn Mitchell, providing moments of comic relief amidst the drama. Somehow I don't think Alan McGilvray would have approved, but times have changed. The rather stuffy formality of ABC cricket broadcasts stemmed from the days when newsreaders donned dinner jackets to read the national bulletin. Michael Charlton, one of the most popular callers on the ABC in the 1960s, had a fruity British accent and there was a rigid formality in cricket broadcasts.

Kerry fluctuates between serious analysis and bizarre contemplation, so the listener never quite knows what to expect. Some of his one-liners are so clever, one suspects they have been rehearsed, but who cares? One that I recall came when Sri Lanka were touring Australia some years ago and their fast bowler Dilhara Fernando was no-balled. When the bowler questioned the call, the umpire went into a rather lengthy discussion. Then-ABC commentator Tim Lane mused: 'What do you think the umpire's saying to him, Kerry?'

'If I had to do the same again, I would my friend, Fernando.'

And another, discussing the merits of often-underrated Queensland bowler, Michael Kasprowicz:

'He bowls a lot of Rock Hudson balls; they look straight but they're not.'

But perhaps his funniest joke came during a one-day international against Sri Lanka at the Gabba in 2006. During the course of an over, he told this joke between balls: 'A frog goes into a bank and approaches the teller. He can see from her nameplate that her name is Patricia Wack.

'Miss Wack, I'd like to get a loan of $30,000 to take a holiday.'

Patty looks at the frog in disbelief and asks his name. The grog says his name is Kermit Jagger, his dad is Mick Jagger and that it's okay — he knows the bank manager. Patty explains that he will need to secure the loan with some collateral. The frog says, 'Sure. I have this,' and produces a tiny porcelain elephant, about half an inch tall, bright pink and perfectly formed. Very confused, Patty explains that she'll have to consult the manager and disappears into the back office. She finds the bank manager and says: 'There's a frog called Kermit Jagger out there who claims to know you and wants to borrow $30,000 and he wants to use this as collateral. She holds up the tiny pink elephant.

'I mean, what in the world is this?'

The manager says:

'It's a knick-knack Patty Wack. Give the frog a loan. His old man's a Rolling Stone.' The play was forgotten for the next few minutes as Kerry, co-commentator Glenn Mitchell and the audience burst into uncontrollable laughter. The joke, is obviously rather corny but because of the way Kerry told it, in such an incongruous context, has become a classic. It's now gone around the world on YouTube and Kerry is always asked to re-tell it at Sportsmen's dinners.

Kerry has also written three best-selling books and is one of the most sought-after speakers in the country. On the release of his first book, *According to Skull*, I hosted a question-and-answer session on a book tour in Toowoomba and the publishers were delighted, selling every copy they had. The audience was mixed, all ages and both sexes, the line for autographs stretching out the door and down the road. Kerry was in fine form, playing all my deliveries with ease and breaking up the audience every time he laughed.

His humour is a curious mixture of clever satire and sardonic self-deprecation, and it works.

THIRTY

Sandy Roberts

SMOOTH AS SILK

*'Ladies and gentlemen,
I would like to introduce Miss Australia 1981,
Leanne Cock ... I mean, Dick'*

One of the best-known voices on Australian television, when it comes to sport, is that of Sandy Roberts. The deep, affable tones of Channel Seven's 'Mr Versatile' have been filling people's loungerooms for the past two decades covering everything from golf to gymnastics. His avuncular manner puts one in mind of

A young and debonair Sandy Roberts displays his country boy charm

a genial Santa Claus, spreading hearty enjoyment and goodwill. One can't imagine anyone getting upset about Sandy, who comes across as he is, a down-to-earth nice bloke, but he is on record for possibly the most embarrassing public faux pas in Australian sporting history. Covering the Mt Gambier Cup race meeting in 1981, he attempted to introduce the current Miss Australia, Leanne Dick, to the crowd: 'Ladies and gentlemen, I'd like to introduce Miss Australia 1981 — Leanne Cock ... er, I mean, Dick.' (Strangely enough, her married name is Cockerill!)

After a gaffe like that, one might imagine Sandy being quite happy to return to his family's sheep farm at Lucindale in South Australia, but he shrugged it off to become one of our foremost commentators and presenters. That's his appeal, with his country boy charm and gentlemanly nature, it's almost impossible to dislike Sandy. Add to that his vast experience, and you have the complete package. In this era of shock jocks and inflated egos, he is something of a rarity: an articulate, polite and scrupulously fair professional.

For a sports commentator, Sandy is unusually well-spoken. Without wishing to be derogatory, most callers get no formal training and are chosen through their reputation and knowledge as players. By contrast, Sandy was a keen participant but not an outstanding sportsman. He started out his broadcasting career as a general announcer and newsreader, joining radio 3CS Colac as an announcer and then switched to television as a newsreader with BCV8 in Bendigo. In 1973 he joined ADS7 in Adelaide, again as a newsreader, but soon was calling football, and hosting everything from midday movies to 'It's Academic', great all-round training for a rookie broadcaster.

Sandy's big break came in 1980 when, out of the blue, he was asked to cover the Moscow Olympics. It was hard work with a team of only 49 compared to the 350 they take to the Olympics these days. At 30, the youngest and least experienced commentator, he called everything and anything. 'I called the diving for the first week and was reasonably comfortable doing that. However, it got tougher in the second week — I recall sitting next to race-caller Bill Collins at one of our early morning production meetings. Ron Casey read out the commentary roster for the day. Collins — Greco-Roman wrestling, Roberts — archery ... I had never seen an archery contest and Bill hadn't a clue about wrestling, so we spent the next few hours boning up on the rules and went out and did it.'

He must have done a good job as, halfway through those Games, Sandy was invited by Head of Sport, Ron Casey, to move to Melbourne to work with HSV7. Sandy was thrilled: 'It was great — all my dreams come true — but they sorted out young blokes like me on "World of Sport" (the three-hour Sunday morning sports show). Blokes like Doug Elliott and Lou Richards were always looking for practical jokes. I remember doing one of my first "live read" commercials — as they had no autocue we used to read the script off giant cue cards next to the camera. Well 'Uncle Doug' crouched down next to the camera and set the card alight with his cigarette lighter, so I had to read faster and faster before the script went up in flames! It was a lot of fun and you had to have a thick skin, but terrific training.'

When Sandy started calling the VFL he worked with some of his heroes, people like Mike Williamson, Jack Dyer and Peter McKenna. At first he was intimidated but found that they were just normal human beings who loved football, just as he did. Conditions were sometimes a bit rough and ready — at the Western Oval they had cats roaming around in the commentary box and Lou Richards would invariably spill his coffee all over Sandy's jacket — but he loved it.

Sandy's favourite players were Leigh Matthews, Malcolm Blight and Gary Ablett. He loved watching Simon Madden and Paul Van Der Haar. Listening to Butch Gale and working with Mike Williamson and Ted Whitten, he learnt the tricks of the trade and became one of the best callers around. He's now called over 700 games and ten Grand Finals since his first in 1990. It was like losing a relative when Channel Seven lost the rights to the AFL but Sandy still maintained his links with the game, hosting Grand Final breakfasts and the Brownlow Medal count. 'When we got the football back I realised just how much I'd missed it. But I always kept busy with other sports, like tennis, golf and the Olympics.' A bonus came in 2010 when he was signed along with Rex Hunt, to call AFL games every weekend on 40 regional radio stations throughout Australia. Hunt and Roberts — what a contrast in styles!

Sandy admits that golf is his favourite sport to cover, although he enjoys the tennis as well. Sandy has been Channel Seven's face of golf for the past twenty years, covering over 100 tournaments, including the Australian Open and the

Masters. He's also hosted coverage of two President's Cups, two US Opens and a British Open. He rates the 2001 President's Cup his most thrilling golf telecast: 'We had "Tiger", Jack, Greg — all the best were there — and it was 90 degrees one day and freezing cold and blowing a gale the next. We beat the Yanks in a huge upset — it was unforgettable stuff.'

So what was it like working with the legends of the game in the commentary box?

'I must admit I was a bit overawed when I first sat in the box with Jack Nicklaus and Mark McCormack, the head of IMG, but they were so easy to work with, true gentlemen. I was thrilled to call with Englishman Peter Alliss, whom I consider the best golf commentator of all.'

Greg Norman, Australia's leading player over the past three decades, was another big name who became a personal friend. When Sandy's son, Sam contracted AIDS from a blood transfusion and died a painful, lingering death, Greg was a tower of strength. On the day Sam died in 1993, Norman wore his name on his hat at the Australian Masters. To this day, he keeps in touch and recently visited Sandy at his farm with Greg's new love, Chrissie Evert.

The strain of Sam's death contributed to the break-up of Sandy's first marriage. However, he and his new wife, Carolyn, have a six-year-old son, Angus, and his eldest son, Ben, made him a grandfather in 2006.

Tennis is another sport Sandy really enjoys — he has covered the Davis Cup and the Australian Open for over a decade. This has brought him into partnerships with former stars like John McEnroe and Jim Courier, an experience he finds challenging, but fun. 'McEnroe is a unique individual, very different. However, when the red light goes on he's the ultimate professional. We've spent a lot of hours in the bunker down in the Rod Laver Arena and never had a problem.'

Sandy's preparation for something like the Open starts after the Melbourne Spring Racing Carnival and he's constantly updating his profiles and statistics. 'When the tournament starts, the days are long and you don't get a break for two weeks. It's hard work, but I wouldn't swap jobs with anyone. A mate of ours the other day asked me whether I grew tired of it, after all these years and I said: "How could I get sick of it? I'm about to pop down to the Rod Laver Arena and sit with a legend to call Federer and Gonzales — how good is that!"'

Sandy still has one burning ambition. After ten Olympics he has yet to call an Australian gold medal, believe it or not.

Sandy has called gymnastics with Liz Chetkovich at the past five Olympics and they have made the sport eminently watchable. Liz is a coach with enormous knowledge of the sport and Sandy has become an enthusiast — together they make an entertaining team. The problem Sandy faces is that he is such a consummate host he rarely gets much time for commentary these days. Unlike some, who are showing their age, Sandy is looking much younger than his years, with just a few grey streaks among the blond.

How long will Sandy keep going? At 61, he has just signed another three-year contract with Channel Seven, but he feels that he's got at least another five years in him. He's been with the network now for 38 years, but has no thoughts of retiring. Perhaps a new spin on an old cliché is relevant: 'If you're good enough, you're young enough.'

THIRTY-ONE

Steve Robilliard

MR NETBALL

'Greg Norman said "It's only a game". I try to remember that when I call sport — to err is human'

There are many fine Australian commentators whom we take for granted, professionals who do a terrific job, week in, week out, who hardly ever get any publicity. One of these is the ABC's excellent television commentator Steve Robilliard. Best known for his knowledgeable coverage of netball, Steve is actually an all-rounder who does an equally good job calling

The calm and articulate Steve Robilliard loves his job, and actively encourages more women commentators

tennis and Rugby Union. A calm and articulate man, Steve has a particular passion for netball, Australia's most popular female sport.

Now 54, Steve has been with ABC TV since 1989, based in Sydney. Like many good callers, he came from the country, being born in Port Kembla, a hundred kilometres south of Sydney. He always wanted to go into the media and, as soon as he left university in 1979, got a job with radio station 2MO Gunnedah, in north-western NSW. He played Rugby, lived with a couple of mates and had a good time. Prime Television was looking for a reporter, so Steve moved to Tamworth and a few months later, to Sydney, where he joined 2WS in the newsroom. They were looking for someone who could cover sport, so Steve worked a lot of weekends. It was a gradual learning process, but the big break came when he got a position with Channel Seven in their Sports Department. Steve recalls: 'I never really had any aspirations towards commentary but, when they offered me the chance to do some motor racing and tennis, I grabbed it.'

Steve worked with Channel Seven for six years, reporting for the news and 'Sportsworld'. As a young man just breaking into the heady world of television, he had an early taste of stage fright one morning on the set of 'Sportsworld' with the veteran Rex Mossop. Asked to introduce an AFL package, Steve suffered from a kind of dyslexia, perhaps brought on by nerves. Although he had the autocue to prompt him, Steve found he simply couldn't make sense of the script. What came out was something like this: 'In last night's game at

MCG, Collingwood … ummm … Carlton … ahh … seven goals … here are the highlights.'

Seeing his distress, Rex kindly said: 'Don't worry, son, it's happened to all of us.'

For Steve Robilliard, such moments have been rare, although he candidly admits to making plenty of mistakes. 'You just have to get over it and carry on. If you let it get to you, you're gone. I always think of Greg Norman when he suffered that humiliating meltdown at the US Masters and lost to Nick Faldo. He said something along the lines of "It's disappointing naturally, but the sun will still rise tomorrow. It's only a game." I try to remember that when I call sport — to err is human.'

This humanity comes through in Steve's commentary. He has a genuine interest in athletes as people, so he enjoys researching their backgrounds. This is especially obvious at one of his favourite events, the Hopman Cup, which I consider the best regular tennis event on Australian television. It shows players in a different light, men and women together in a more light-hearted, mixed format, and taking time off before the serious business of the forthcoming Australian Open. The players stay at the venue, the Burswood Resort in Perth, and enjoy seeing the sights of the city in between matches. When the ABC had the rights, all of this was covered by the ABC production team, with interesting features and player profiles, interspersed with the tennis. Another factor was the presence of Fred Stolle, simply the best tennis commentator in the game, from whom Steve has learned a lot about commentary.

Fred has a philosophy that some Australian sports commentators could do well to copy: 'You can't shine shit.' In other words, if you're watching a bad match, don't try to fool the audience into believing it's great. Steve agrees: 'If you're calling an AFL match and Hawthorn are leading the Kangaroos 3.11 to 2.14 you can't say it's great football, but you can say something like "The elements have had their say." Australians know their sport and don't like to be conned, so call it like it is.'

Steve also admits to learning a lot from former ABC colleagues Gordon Bray and Dennis Cometti, whom he regards as two of the best TV callers in Australia. 'I grew up watching Brian Moore's English soccer show "The Big Match" where the commentators always let the pictures tell the story. Martin Tyler is the best — every Australian commentator should be made to watch a few tapes of his commentary. Gordon and Dennis are out of the same mould — they let the game breathe.'

Like most of his generation, Steve grew up listening to Alan McGilvray on cricket, John O'Reilly on Rugby League and Norman May on the Olympics. They were his mentors, even though he hadn't met them. He also admires the best American commentators for their restraint and economy of words: 'A batter will make the winning hit in a World Series game and all the caller will say is "That's outta here." Then he'll let the crowd take over for as much as ten seconds before resuming his call — they let the viewer feel the moment.'

One of Steve's favourite calls was the final of the World Netball Championships in 1991 between traditional rivals

Australia and New Zealand. Before a capacity crowd at the Sydney Entertainment Centre, with Prime Minister Bob Hawke watching, Australia got home by a single goal. Calling the action with Anne Sargeant, Steve got tingles in his hands and arms: 'It was an extraordinary sensation. We were both struggling to get our words out. My heart was pumping and I had pins and needles in my hands. I've never felt such excitement.'

A different kind of enjoyment came in England that year when he accompanied Gordon Bray, 'Buddha' Handy and Gary Pearse on the Wallabies' victorious six-week tour to the Rugby World Cup finals. Steve had the unusual task at the final of interviewing upper-crust English fans in the Twickenham carpark before the game. 'They were so typical of the aristocracy — dressed in their tweed coats with leather elbow patches, sipping champagne and eating paté, mince pies and strawberries. I don't know what they made of me, this earnest young Aussie bloke trying to get some sensible comments from them, but I had a ball.'

In Dublin, Steve caught a cab from his hotel to Lansdowne Road for the quarter-final against Ireland. Most Irish cabbies are talkative but this fellow didn't say a word, despite Steve's friendly banter.

'Nice day, eh?' Nothing.

'How do you reckon Ireland will go?' Nothing.

'I'm from Australia, but my mother's family came from Ireland.' Still nothing.

'I've got accreditation, so we should be able to drive right through.'

Sure enough, the car park attendant waved Steve's cab through at the gate, without even checking his accreditation.

'There you go,' said Steve cheerily 'must be my good looks.'

'I don't tink so,' said the cabbie, finally breaking his silence.

One of the bonuses of travelling the world covering sport is the people you meet. Steve has covered five Summer and three Winter Olympics and four Commonwealth Games and has met all kinds of characters. Rubbing shoulders with the world media at big events has broadened his perspective and his network of friends. However, there is one country that he can't warm to: the United States.

'There are 15,000 media at the Olympics; it's like a big brotherhood. If you need to know the pronunciation of a Hungarian name, for example, you can pop into their compound at the International Broadcast Centre and they are only too happy to help you. It's the same with the Chinese or the Koreans, but the guys from NBC close themselves off and alienate people. It's the same at every Games.'

Steve's attitude wasn't helped at Atlanta, where he felt the Games were a disappointing shambles after the magnificent spectacle of Barcelona four years earlier. 'We even had a bomb go off — and I had walked through that park, Centennial Park, earlier in the day. Fortunately I was at the hotel watching a Rugby game with the guys from Channel Seven when the bomb went off.'

Steve likes to absorb the culture of countries in which he commentates and is a stickler for correct pronunciation.

Again, the Americans annoy him when it comes to Chinese and Korean names. 'We should respect their tradition of family name first and given name second, but the Americans disregard it. Take the Korean golfer Pak Se Ri — her surname is Pak — but the American commentators all call her Se Ri Pak. So omnipresent is the US media that she's now known around the world by that name, which is an insult to her country. American political commentators don't get the name of the Korean leader, Kim Jong Il, wrong — so why can't they get sports stars' names right?'

Another aspect of modern sport that gets under Steve's skin is the decline of sportsmanship. 'Ever since money came into sport, ethics have gone out the window. Cheating is rife, whether it's taking performance-enhancing drugs or bowling underarm — everything is results-driven. I was at a Rugby seminar the other day to explain the new experimental laws and one of the lecturers said that all props cheat, one way or another. We are all custodians of our sport, but the old traditions are slowly dying.'

Being a realist, Steve knows that you can't change human nature — when your livelihood is at stake, you're more likely to bend the rules. However, he still gets a frisson of pleasure, for example, when he sees Adam Gilchrist walk or Greg Norman declare a penalty on himself. 'That's what makes our job so great. Every now and then you see something that's out of the ordinary, a noble gesture that inspires us all, and we are there to communicate it to the public.'

At 54, Steve has no thoughts of retirement. He loves his work and has reached the stage where he wants to give something back. The specialist trainee system has been scrapped by the ABC, so nobody has been teaching the art of sports commentary. Steve wants to help budding young commentators out, if he can, with advice and guidance. Amanda Shalala is one young ABC sports caller who has benefitted from his mentoring. 'I've covered women's sport for twenty years and I know what a chauvinist country we are. Women get 10 per cent of the coverage and yet they make up 50 per cent of the participants. They need a voice, so perhaps Amanda can fill that role, and I'm happy to help her.'

Good on you, Steve — we need more like you.

THIRTY-TWO

Fred Stolle

MR NICE GUY

'We don't need the Nastase and McEnroe kind of histrionics to get people to watch tennis'

When it comes to Australian tennis commentary one man stands out as the most popular analyst: Fred Stolle. The amiable 'Fiery Fred' seems to be everybody's favourite. His nickname came about during his early playing days because of his fierce competitive streak but, in terms of personality, nothing could be

'Fiery Fred' Stolle was a three-time Wimbledon singles finalist, and is now a well-loved and respected member of the world tennis commentary fraternity

more inappropriate. I worked alongside Fred when I called tennis for the ABC and Channel Seven during the 1970s and 1980s, and you wouldn't find a nicer guy. I remember one night in Brisbane after Australia had beaten the USA in the 1986 Davis Cup semi-final having a few beers with Fred, who passed on some tips on the finer points of commentary. Having just joined Channel Seven, I was struggling with the demands of commercial breaks. Fred advised simply: 'Always leave 'em wanting more. When you throw to a break don't just say the score, give 'em something like 'And when we come back, Australia will be serving for the set with new balls.'

Born in Hornsby, on the north shore of Sydney, Fred was a late developer as a player. He left school at fifteen and joined a bank, playing tennis whenever he could. The top juniors in those days were snapped up by the sporting goods companies like Dunlop or Slazenger, where they would pack tennis balls or string racquets in the morning and practise all afternoon. Fred was told by Harry Hopman that he wasn't good enough, a stinging rebuke that may have accounted for Fred's trademark determination later on. So he spent five years working on mail transfers and currencies, something that came in handy when he travelled the world during his tennis career.

At the age of twenty, Fred and another youngster, John Pearce, made their first trip overseas. Fred's father and a supporter, Wally Boss, worked for nine months to raise the $3,000 needed to cover their expenses to tour Europe. They ran card parties, dances and barbecues and finally, Fred was on his way. They had mixed results, but qualified for the French Open and Fred did well on the unfamiliar, slow red clay. However, at this stage they were down to their last twenty pounds. So they went back to Italy and won some matches, which enabled them to go on to England and their first tilt at Wimbledon. Fred remembers: 'I lost in the first round of qualifying out on Court 5 but I just loved it — the grass, the atmosphere and everything. I couldn't wait to get back there.'

At 185 cm, the loose-limbed Stolle had a big serve and good volley, ideally suited to the fast grass courts at Wimbledon. Three times in a row he reached the final, but three times he lost — twice to his friend Roy Emerson, and once to American Chuck McKinley.

For a player who was supposedly 'not good enough' Fred excelled himself. From 1964 until 1966 he was ranked second only to Emerson in the world. He won the 1965 French Open, a feat which eludes even Roger Federer, and also the 1966 US Open, as an unseeded player. 'That fired me up a bit because I had just won the German Open and was number two in the world, but I'd lost second round at Wimbledon to my doubles partner, Bob Hewitt. They only seeded eight players in those days, compared to 32 nowadays, and the last three seedings went to Americans — Dennis Ralston, Cliff Richey and Clark Graebner. So it was pretty satisfying to knock off two of those on the way to the final, where I beat John Newcombe.'

A member of three victorious Davis Cup teams, Fred had a marvellous record, losing only three of sixteen matches in his career. His proudest moment came in Sydney, before his family and friends, where he came from two sets down to Manolo Santana of Spain to win, laying the foundation for an Australian victory. He also won 31 amateur singles titles.

Fred turned pro in 1967 and soon discovered how tough it was. Even Rod Laver, the world number one amateur in the early 1960s, struggled in his first year in the pro ranks. However, Fred won two singles and thirteen doubles titles in the pros, earning enough to set up a coaching business in Florida. He still runs the same club at North Beach in Miami, a kind of 'home away from home' for expatriate Australians. Although he and wife Pat have lived in Florida for 30 years, he still retains that distinctive Aussie accent.

Fred got his start in television commentary in 1977 when David Hill, the man who produced World Series Cricket for the Nine Network, called and asked if Fred would like to call Wimbledon. It was a tricky business, as Fred was based in Sydney, working from 10.00 pm until 4.00 am for two weeks, calling off the monitor and the BBC telecast. He had to insert his comments in between the BBC callers, Dan Maskell and John Barrett.

'I worked out that the only time I could get a word in was between serves, so I had about ten seconds to say something.' It must have worked because the next year Fred was sent to Wimbledon and he's been doing it ever since.

The great thing about Fred's commentary is his humanity. He's a down-to-earth bloke without a trace of ego and he has an empathy with players who battle, the way he did. He has a rapport with his fellow commentators, especially those who played top tennis. 'Cliff Drysdale and I played against each other and were good mates, so at ESPN we had a good working relationship. The same at Nine, where "Newc" and I have always taken the mickey out of each other.'

Fred, however, has no time for tantrums and poor sportsmanship on the court. 'We don't need the Nastase and McEnroe kind of histrionics to get people to watch tennis. Nice guys like Rosewall, Laver and Trabert didn't have to scream at umpires and throw racquets to pull crowds and Roger Federer is a perfect example these days.' Asked about the prospects of 18 year old Queensland prodigy, Bernard Tomic, Fred is blunt:

'He's certainly got the talent, but he's got to do the hard work. He's still got a long way to go.'

Australia is really struggling in men's tennis, with only one player, Lleyton Hewitt in the top 100 at the end of 2010. It's a far cry from the glory days of the Fifties and Sixties. At one stage Australia won the Davis Cup 15 times in 18 years.

Why was Australia was so good in the postwar years? Fred puts it down to the strong junior system in those days, added to the fact that there wasn't much else for youngsters to do. 'We would race home after school to get a court, usually in a mate's backyard and we'd play until dark. Then we would have to sweep the lines for the ladies next morning. On Saturdays we would have schools competition and it was really popular. I also played a bit of cricket and represented NSW Public Schools, but I had to make a decision and chose tennis. If you were any good in those days, you got a trip to the Australian Open (which used to rotate around the states) to play in the under-19 Linton Cup. Nowadays, as soon as they are any good, the kids get a trip overseas and, regardless of how they go, they get another trip the following year. It's all too easy — there's no incentive.'

As in any broadcaster's career, there have been blunders. Fred's pet hate is pronouncing Eastern European names. 'Back in the '80s we had this big guy from Yugoslavia called Slobodan Zivojinovic — I just called him "Bobo". Trouble is, there are more and more of them coming on tour — so I just leave it to Kerryn or Woodie to work out.'

Fred, however, is no dinosaur and loves the innovations which have made tennis more watchable on television. He considers Hawkeye, for example, as the best thing for tennis since yellow balls: 'Umpires generally don't like it but, when I point out that it's 98 per cent right and it takes the pressure off them, they tend to agree. It's a lot of fun for spectators, it adds a bit of suspense and leads to a closer rapport between player and umpire. The good umpires will nod if they agree with Hawkeye and the player won't challenge — but Roger didn't like it much at Wimbledon last year, did he? He kept saying: "This thing's killing me." He made four challenges in the final and they were all wrong. But I think it's great for the game.'

He's sad that tennis is losing popularity, in terms of playing numbers, in both Australia and America. 'With the rise of Eastern Europe, we don't dominate like we used to — and people love to watch a winner.'

Among the girls, Fred sees cause for Australian fans to be optimistic: 'Sam Stosur showed last year that she has the game to win a major title. Making the final of the French Open was a great effort and she beat all the top women last season. The former Russian girls, Rodianova and Rogowska are promising and former Slovakian Jarmila Gajdosora is another one to watch.'

At the age of 73, Fred is very fit and still hits a good ball. When I called he was about to travel up to New York with Pat for the Huggie Bear charity tournament, which leads into the US Open. Fred has won it three times, twice with his son Sandon, a Davis Cup player himself, and once with Wally Masur. The Huggie Bear Week has raised over US$25 million in the past twenty years.

These days Fred only covers the Grand Slams — his place with ESPN went to Patrick McEnroe, the younger brother of John. The powers-that-be wanted a balance between the accents and, with South African Cliff Drysdale as the play-by-play caller, they went for an American analyst. But Fred doesn't mind. He covers the US, French and Australian Opens working for the host broadcaster, usually Fox Sports in Australia. He likes them all but has a special love of Wimbledon, where he works for Fox Sports for the first ten days and for Channel Nine for the last four days. 'I'll keep doing it until they tell me they don't want me anymore. I love it and I just hope you folk back home love it as much as I do.'

We do, Fred, trust me.

THIRTY-THREE

Paul Vautin

NOT FAT, JUST FUNNY

It's not often that a commentator swears on debut – and is still working 23 years later – but Paul Vautin did. 'Fatty', as he's been known since he was a chubby red-headed kid with freckles, was sitting next to the ABC's David Morrow previewing the 1988 Rugby League Grand Final between St George and Canterbury-Bankstown. David asked a rather vague question: 'So, it seems every game in the finals has been stronger and stronger?'

And a nervous young Vautin, not really understanding the question, floundered a reply: 'Well, yes, the final four teams – Canterbury, St George and…err…ahh…f@*k!'

'It looks as though we're having communication problems here,' an ashen-faced Morrow said. 'Let's go down to Johnny Peard on the sideline.'

'Fatty' was never asked to work for the ABC again.

A born entertainer and an absolute natural broadcaster — Fatty, with his staunchest supporter, wife Kim

Brisbane born and bred, 51-year-old 'Fatty' is a survivor. In a tough TV industry where you're only as good as your ratings, he has been hosting *The Footy Show* for 18 years and calling the NRL for Channel Nine since 1992. He's had his ups and downs, but his happy-go-lucky nature has always seen him bounce back. In 2005, he literally bounced — cracking his head on concrete when a sumo suit stunt went wrong — suffering severe concussion. He pulled through, but it took 10 weeks before he was able to go back on air.

Beginning his Rugby League career at Wests-Mitchelton, 'Fatty' was hardly what would be described as a natural athlete. Short and stocky, he was slightly chubby as a youngster, but he had a temperament to match his fiery red hair. A tenacious tackler, he also had a good turn of speed and, moreover, a sharp football brain. Playing for Wests Panthers in the Brisbane Rugby League as a teenager in the late Seventies, he was spotted by a talent scout from Sydney and, at 18, joined Manly. He soon added 10 kilos to his 82-kilogram frame and the puppy fat turned to muscle. He was to play 193 A-Grade matches for the Sea Eagles in a decade with the club. Playing in losing Grand Final teams in 1982–83, he led them to the premiership in 1987 and was named 'Dally M Captain of the Year'. He played 13 Tests and 20 games for Queensland during their halcyon days under Wally Lewis in the Eighties. Fatty loved nothing more than pulling on the maroon jumper for Queensland against the old enemy, New South Wales:

'Whenever I feel a bit down I just think of those great times. Those guys I played with in the Eighties are still my best mates and we're pretty close. It was a special group of players with Wally, Mal Meninga and Gene Miles and the spirit was so good it was like having an extra player in your team. We were the Roadies against the Rockstars and throughout that decade I reckon we started as underdogs in every game, which made winning even sweeter.'

After retiring in 1991 'Fatty' had only one thought in mind – he wanted to become a Rugby League coach. He took the Brisbane Capitals to a premiership at his first attempt, a great start. But then came the phone call that changed his life. Channel Nine had won the rights to televise Rugby League and were looking for a couple of experts to sit alongside their chief caller, Ray Warren. They found them in Paul Vautin and Peter Sterling – 'Fatty and Sterlo'.

Sterling played halfback 18 times in Tests for Australia and 13 times for New South Wales in State of Origin games. He was regarded as a legend at Parramatta, for whom he played 227 games. What's more, he has a keen intelligence, which served him well as a slightly built halfback and even better as a Rugby League analyst. Although they only played together once, for the Kangaroos against Great Britain, 'Fatty' has the greatest admiration for 'Sterlo':

'I regard him as the best player of my era outside Wally Lewis. He's so smart, the way he reads the game. So, when I joined the commentary team, there was no point trying to match wits with him – you can't have three people in the box doing the same thing. 'Rabs' calls the action, 'Sterlo' analyses it and I make the jokes!'

He went to school at Padua College in Brisbane, where the discipline was strict, so the cheeky redhead was often in trouble. One time he was given six cuts by a priest and remarked that the last blow almost missed – so he got seven! It was a tough upbringing but Padua bred fine football players – among Vautin's classmates was Kangaroo forward, Paul McCabe, and a later product was Bronco Dane Carlaw.

'Fatty' undersells himself. He's actually an extremely astute man with a good football brain, shown by his success as coach of a young Queensland team during the Super League war in 1995. The Maroons had lost the previous three series against the Blues and it looked like nobody wanted the job. So 'Fatty' put his hand up. It was one thing being available for the job but another actually doing it.

'When we had our first training session at Lang Park I met the players for the first time. Without the Super League stars they were like a bunch of young kids and I honestly didn't recognise some of them. One young bloke came up to me and I told him that I wouldn't sign autographs until after training. He looked embarrassed and said: "I'm Ben Ikin – I'm in your team." Talk about being embarrassed!'

With such an inexperienced side, Queensland was given no chance by the pundits, but 'Fatty' proved them wrong, winning the series 3–0.

'I just went back to the old values we had in our side during the Eighties. I emphasised that it was to our advantage that we were the underdogs. The Blues' fame made them a bit complacent and we had no trouble building up a really strong team spirit.'

Always a good team player, 'Fatty' relishes his role in the Channel Nine commentary team.

'I think there's room for humour in almost any situation and we're in the entertainment business. I cop a bit of criticism for being pro-Queensland, but why wouldn't you be? I'm in the box with a bunch of NSW guys so, win or lose, I stick it up 'em. Seriously though, I love working with 'Rabs' – he's so professional and 'Sterlo' is fantastic with his analysis. What's more, they're great blokes who love golf and the punt, just like I do.'

Sometimes, though, 'Fatty' crosses the line, such as the time when he was calling the 1995 World Cup Final at Wembley saying: 'Tim Brasher actually fell over in front of Tony Smith. He's hit every limb, Rabs – all five of 'em – and he's brought Smith down.'

And another time, calling a Broncos try when the Walters brothers combined to send Allan Langer over, 'Rabs' enthused: 'A great try there by Brisbane, Fatty.'

' Yes, Rabs, the boys from Two-Head City really turned it on, didn't they!'

Next day the *Ipswich Times* headlined the remark: 'Two-Head Insult', so 'Fatty' rang the Mayor of Ipswich and apologised profusely. However, when the councillor kept on complaining, 'Fatty' couldn't resist. He asked the Mayor: 'And which head would you be talking with now, Mr Mayor?'

Such is his cheeky nature, though, 'Fatty' seems to get away with comments like that, for which other commentators might get a rap over the knuckles. It's why he's become a cult figure as host of *The Footy Show*, a position he's held since 1994. The grassroots fans love his down-to-earth knockabout style and the show's popularity has hinged on the earthy repartee and outrageous stunts of the presenters.

Like a lot of top sportsmen, 'Fatty' is an excellent golfer, playing off a handicap of 2. He's a member of working-class Monash in Sydney, where he rubs shoulders with carpenters, builders and plumbers, and also at the prestigious Gold Coast club, 'The Grand'. It sums up his personality; his ability to get on with anyone, rich or poor, male or female. And it seemed that he missed his true vocation when he took a brilliant one-handed running catch in the Allan Border testimonial cricket match at the Gabba in 1993. Running with his back to the ball, he dived headlong and caught Tim Horan just inside the boundary. The catch was so extraordinary it's still on YouTube.

When not watching Rugby League 'Fatty' is, surprisingly, a fan of Australian Rules.

'I really like the AFL – it's tough and skilful – and completely different to League. Imagine me trying to play it! I don't have a favourite team but I just sit back on a Saturday afternoon and enjoy the spectacle.'

'Fatty' was dropped from the Channel Nine commentary team for a couple of years following his sumo suit accident. He licked his wounds and moved to the Gold Coast, where his son Matt was hoping to crack the Titans NRL team. His wife Kim is a staunch supporter:

'She's my rock. When I'm down she keeps me positive and reminds me of what a great life I've got. We just celebrated our twenty-sixth wedding anniversary and our relationship is still the most important thing in my life.'

During his exile from the commentary box, he still hosted *The Footy Show* – he was disappointed but accepted his lot. He's back now, calling Broncos and Titans home games on Friday nights, and loving it:

'I'm really excited about being back calling *Friday Night Football*. I've been doing *The Footy Show* for 18 years and I still enjoy it, but I feel like a kid with a new toy doing the commentary again. And I won't change the way I am – I like to slip in a bit of a gee-up now and again.'

And we wouldn't have it any other way, 'Fatty'.

THIRTY-FOUR

Max Walker

COLOUR AND CHARACTER

'Well I wasn't great to look at, as a bowler. Right arm over left earhole, legs crossed at the point of delivery, bowling up the hill with an old ball on a flat wicket. But very difficult to be good looking and pretty on your feet!'

Typically self-deprecatory, Max 'Tangles' Walker is still the same cheerful, colourful character he was when he first came to the mainland from Tasmania in 1967. Looking back on a cricket playing and commentary career that led to fame and fortune, Max admits he was lucky:

'I was not even a bowler when I arrived in Melbourne, but the Melbourne Cricket Club was desperately short of fast bowlers

Twenty years before Kerry O'Keeffe, 'Tangles' brought humour to cricket broadcasting.

and I was given a chance with the new ball. Clive Fairbairn, the chairman of selectors, reckoned he saw some ability in my bowling, even though I thought I was a batsman. Well, he was right. I quickly captured a bagful of wickets in district cricket and was soon selected to play for Victoria. Yes my action was a bit, different but I could swing the ball in and cut it away!

I was picked to play for Australia against Pakistan in 1972 and was fortunate to have Dennis Lillee bowling at the other end. I took five wickets in my first Test in Melbourne. Then, on a greenish pitch in the Second Test in Sydney, I took 6 for 15 in the second innings, which set up a remarkable victory. That secured me a plane seat to the West Indies, and after the Caribbean, I never looked back.'

Max was also fortunate that his career coincided with a purple patch in Australian cricket. With the Chappell brothers, Lillee and Rod Marsh as spearheads, Australia dominated Test cricket for a decade.

Perhaps the highlight of a memorable tour of the Caribbean in 1973–74 in the Third Test. Australia had its back to the wall at lunch on the final day as the West Indies, with six wickets in hand, only needed 60 runs to win. Steel bands were belting out reggae tunes and Rastafarians were singing as they downed fiery Jamaican rum in anticipation of a home-side victory.

'In the break I was feeling pretty stuffed. Lillee and Massie had both broken down and a lot rested on my shoulders. I had a cool shower and Ian Chappell told me he wanted me to bowl the first over after lunch. Alvin Kalicharran was 91 not out, but he flashed at the first ball as it moved away, he got a thick edge and Marshie did the rest. It was a pivotal moment. They started to doubt themselves and 'Skull' O'Keeffe and I shared the wickets, as we went on to create an unlikely yet indelible win. I collected a record 26 wickets, at 20.7, in that series and we won 2–0.'

With his idiosyncratic bowling action, signature moustache and laconic manner, 'Tangles' became a popular figure, on and off the field. Articulate and intelligent, he was constantly in demand to speak at sportsmen's nights. So it was not surprising that, after an Achilles tendon injury cut short his career in 1980, ABC Radio called with an offer to commentate on a Sheffield Shield game.

'I'll never forget that first stint. Kardinia Park, Victoria, against South Australia, a handful of spectators, sitting next to Drew Morphett for six hours a day, no commercials – I loved it. I was a big, slow-talking Tasmanian who'd copped five broken noses playing VFL footy. Nevertheless I suppose I managed to give listeners an insight into the dressing-room, a mystery to many. Plus I was always full of mischief and humour – a trait I developed from my dad, Big Max, and his storytelling session across the bar of the Empire Hotel. The core of powerful communication is storytelling – whether it's over the radio, at a sportsmen's night 'live' or through Facebook and Twitter.'

Max recounts how he made a bad impression on his international commentary debut – a One Day International (ODI) against the West Indies at the Melbourne Cricket Ground (MCG):

'That ABC commentary box wasn't built for tall-legged ruckmen. I kneed Alan McGilvray in the back of the head trying to get to my seat; he nearly swallowed a lit cigarette. I had grown up listening to the great man's dulcet tones on my crystal set as a kid – Mac was simply the silky smooth voice of ABC cricket. When I put the headphones on, they reeked of sweat and cigarettes – Norman O'Neill had been in the chair before me. Then, at the end of my spell, as I tried to extricate myself from this constricting cocoon, I trod on one of Jack Cameron's shoeboxes, and stats cards went fluttering through the air around the MCG Member's area, like confetti at a wedding. (Jack was the doyen of statisticians in pre-internet days and kept voluminous records on cards in shoeboxes.) It wasn't a great start. But it was memorable!'

However, Max was a quick learner and soon settled in to the demands of cricket broadcasting on radio, ABC-style.

'Mac gave me plenty of sound advice, beginning with a simple rule – imagine you're speaking to a bunch of blind people. If you can satisfy their needs in word pictures, you've got it. Jack also gave me a gem of a tip – buy an exercise book and a pen. Your words need to be pertinent, relevant, concise and often at short notice, so make notes. I've still got those exercise books. That started a habit that led to 14 books, seven of them No. 1 best-sellers and over a million copies sold. It also contributed to me being noticed by Channel Nine, who headhunted me at the start of 1985.

Radio was a lot of fun, even though it didn't pay as much as television. I shared a microphone with Jim Maxwell at a lunch recently and he reminded me of the time we were handed a box of Mars Bars during a Test match. In those days the expert was normally required to comment only at the end of an over, so I tucked into a Mars Bar mid-over. Jim was describing the action of athletic fast bowler Michael Holding, on his first tour – the guy they called 'Whispering Death' because of his extreme pace and silky, lithe run-up. Jim asked me what I thought of Holding's future as a fast bowler.

"Tell us about this run-up, Max."

"Ooohagh…smooth as silk….oogh." CLICK, CLICK … (my tongue attempting to unstick the Mars Bar from the roof of my mouth).

He nailed me, fair and square, the mongrel.

However, there were also lessons about the discipline required to be an ABC cricket commentator. There were times when Max's fertile imagination and love of storytelling got him into trouble:

'I've been trying to tell listeners what Joel Garner looked like, effecting a run-out. I said, "He stuck his extension out like a giant stick of licorice and lasered the ball back over the stumps."

Producer Alan Marks had a word to me, explaining that those choice words may have been colourfully descriptive but were potentially offensive.

TV commentary didn't suit me as well as radio, but I enjoyed the challenge. The hard part for me was shutting up. Richie Benaud passed on the golden rule – don't say anything unless you can add to the picture. Think about economy of words. Plus there were the demands of the highlights reel, so you had to cease talking when the bowler got to the head of his run-up. So I was always fighting my verbose nature – I just loved telling stories.'

The Executive Producer of Channel Nine's cricket coverage, David Hill, told Max to smarten up his diction and spoke about elocution lessons, but they never happened. Australian cricket fans warmed to the big man's offbeat humour, in much the same way they do to Kerry O'Keeffe these days. His profile was boosted by the *Twelfth Man* tapes, lampooning members of the Channel Nine commentary team, and he was asked to host *The Footy Show* and *Wide World of Sport*.

'They wanted me to read scripts and speak with a refined accent, but it just wasn't me. No one could write like I spoke. So I decided to do what I had always done, tell stories in my own way, try and entertain. There must have been a point of difference, a unique turn of phrase, I suppose, because they stopped giving me scripts and just gave me my head. I went on to host *Wide World of Sport* for a record 16 years, think about it, spending five or six hours in someone's lounge room every Saturday afternoon – you become a member of the family. I just tried to do what I'd always done at sportsmen's nights.'

His profile grew to the extent that he was asked to front national TV commercials and one, for insect repellent Aerogard, won an award and made his name a household word, even to non-cricket viewers.

'Aveagoodweegend Mr Walker' was added to the Australian slang dictionary and no doubt boosted sales of books such as *Tangles*, *How to hypnotise chooks* and *How to kiss a crocodile*.

However, the axe fell on Max's commentary career in 1991, when Channel Nine management decided that they would go with former national captains, Ian Chappell, Bill Lawry, Tony Greig and added Greg Chappell. They explained to Max that they wanted his smiling face on their flagship sports programs as a host and he couldn't do both. Moreover, the commentary team was beginning to travel overseas for Test matches and that meant more time away from home.

'My work had already cost me a marriage and my first daughter, Alexandra, had been born earlier that year, so I was happy to be able to spend more time with the kids. So I stopped calling cricket on TV in '91. That's 20 years ago – can you believe it? Thanks to my PR man, Billy Birmingham, there are some people who think I'm still calling the game.

These days I'm communicating with people and storytelling in a much more modern way via Facebook, Twitter or YouTube. You can be looking at your mobile and here I am, the 'Silver Cyber Surfer', talking to you about Mercedes-Benz, for example, via streaming DVD on a secure mobile database. I'm involved with a website called Beehive which is cutting-edge. We did the first App in education in Australia and the first in the racing industry, the 150th VRC Melbourne Cup. I work with these smart young guys who look after the technology, while I just do the same old thing – I use my communication skills to tell a story in an entertaining and informative way.

Max has always been able to reinvent himself. An architect who became a Test cricketer, public speaker, author, commentator, TV host and, now, corporate mentor via new media platforms and portals.

Just keep telling those stories, Max – we love them.

THIRTY-FIVE

Ray Warren

THE VOICE OF RUGBY LEAGUE

'That's not a try, that's a miracle

Rugby League fans will instantly recall, on reading the above words, one of the greatest tries ever seen in State of Origin Rugby League, but how many remember who the commentator was?

So often we take commentators for granted and, like referees, if they do a competent job, we don't notice them. However, when you've been doing a good job for 45 years, people start to sit up and take notice.

This is the case with 'the voice of Rugby League', Ray Warren. Now a youthful 67, Ray still has the same zest he had when he started out calling the Maher Cup on station 2LF in south-western NSW at the age of 23. The hair is grey but he's in great shape for his age. His calls are now an integral part of the phenomenon of Origin, the best ratings-puller on Australian television every year. Even if you're not a

'No matter what you're doing, you've just got to watch — and that's great broadcasting' says Norman May of Ray Warren's Rugby League calls

died-in-the-wool League fan, Origin is like the Melbourne Cup, mandatory viewing.

Ray's deep and authoritative voice is part of the fabric of the game. This torrid and bloodthirsty spectacle is to modern sports fans what the gladiators were to ancient Rome — violent and bloody, but riveting theatre. Ray Warren has been there for the whole 31 years of Origin and then some, so he knows what he's talking about and his pitch is perfect.

Referring to the 'miracle' try, he immediately recalled it, as if his brain had clicked onto a video replay: 'It was Game One in 1994 in Sydney and there were only a few minutes left with the Blues leading 12–10. From inside their own half Queensland attacked; the ball passed through eleven sets of hands before Mark Coyne scored in the north-eastern corner of Aussie Stadium off the big fella — Queensland got up

14–12 and in the background "Fatty" was screaming his head off.' No need to elaborate — we all know that the 'big fella' was Mal Meninga, star player and now successful coach of the Maroons and there's only one 'Fatty' in Rugby League circles, proud Queenslander Paul Vautin. Was it the greatest try in Origin history?

Warren has seen so many matches and so many footballers that he's regarded as a guru on the game and yet he still finds it hard to judge true greatness. 'The Billy Slater try was special. I knew it immediately and, in retrospect, I'm proud of how I called it.'

Slater had run and chip-kicked, regathered and beaten the defence with speed and step — a marvellous piece of individual brilliance over half the length of the field. One was a team effort and the other individual, but both were truly memorable — and Ray called them exactly right. However, these things don't happen just by chance — it's the result of many years of hard work.

Ray Warren grew up in Junee, the son of a railway fettler and the youngest of seven children. From six years of age he wanted to be a race commentator. He used to listen to the great Ken Howard on the family radiogram, mesmerised by that gravelly voice and colourful turn of phrase. 'It's London to a brick on Tulloch winning this one …' and the inevitable ad-lib soft drink commercial: 'I tell you, Dad, you'd better shell out for Shelleys …'

As a boy, Ray used to stand outside the electrical store in Junee and call the races or whatever sport was shown on the television inside. He also listened to the Maher Cup Rugby

League with commentary by the late John O'Reilly, who later became the ABC's top radio caller in Sydney. Ray was a fan: 'O'Reilly was brilliant — he had this silky-smooth voice and he was so accurate. My love for racing and also for League were like parallel railway tracks, but I knew I'd come to a junction one day and have to make a decision.'

He got his first break on 2LF in 1967, calling the Maher Cup match between Barmedman and West Wyalong. He was so keen he drove from Young to Barmedman, over a hundred kilometres of dusty, corrugated road, just to watch training on Tuesday night. Then on Thursday he drove to West Wyalong and back to Barmedman for the game on Saturday. He was so nervous he took a milkshake container of Mylanta to the ground with him, taking sips to stop vomiting. His dedication paid off and he was invited to Sydney as an understudy to Ken Howard and Johnny Tapp. He played a tape of his race calls to the sports editor, Garth Cary, who listened and said: 'Why are you talking that way?'

'Back home in Junee the only race-caller I ever heard was Ken Howard, so I thought everyone called like him,' Ray replied.

'No way,' Garth said. 'You should never try to sound like someone else. Just be yourself.'

'Best advice I ever had,' says Ray. 'Whenever youngsters ask me for a tip I pass that on.'

After twelve months with 2GB Ray had a lucky break. Casual commentator Brian Surtees, took ill one weekend and Ray was asked to call the football for the first time. He must have gone well, because Surtees was told he was no longer required and Ray became a regular. Although still plagued by nerves, he loved it. He would sit on the sideline at suburban grounds, alongside famous callers like Frank Hyde, 'Tiger' Black and even his hero, John O'Reilly. There were no soundproof studios in those days, just a card table and a microphone on the sideline. He made a habit of going into each team's dressing-room before a game, sitting quietly in the corner, making mental notes. 'You'd check out things that might distinguish players to help your call, like a beard, a knee-guard or ginger hair. The players might have thought you were a bit of a perv, but I didn't care.'

Ray's career has been a roller-coaster ride. From 2GB he was signed by the Ten Network to head their Rugby League commentary team for the midweek night competition, the Amco Cup. It was an instant success and made Ray Warren a household name throughout NSW and Queensland. In 1984 Channel Ten won the rights to televise the Los Angeles Olympics and Ray was allotted one of the coveted presenters' spots. However, a deep-seated fear of flying caused him to withdraw from the team and colourful former dual international Rex Mossop took his place. By contrast to Warren, Mossop was a controversial, charismatic character with strong opinions on everything. He didn't even need an expert; he was judge and jury all in one. For Ray, it was back to his first love, calling the races. However, he struggled to get permanent work and, apart from calling country race meetings at $200 a day, he made ends meet mowing lawns.

In due course the Amco Cup folded and Channel Nine

bought the rights to televise the ARL in 1989. Ray was recalled from the wilderness as the chief caller and has never looked back. In 1992 he was joined by legendary players Peter Sterling and Paul Vautin and the trio developed cult status with league fans.

In his personal life, Ray has also made a comeback of sorts. He and his second wife, Cher, have a 12-year-old daughter, Holly, whose arrival changed Ray's perspective completely. 'I was just starting to wind down a bit I suppose and then she came along. It was the best surprise we could have had, but it gave me a shot in the arm. Far from wanting to give it away, I'm looking at working for the next ten years if I can.'

It's a far cry from the dusty roads of Junee to Castle Hill, a leafy suburb in the north-west of Sydney where Ray and his family live. One of his favourite relaxations is golf and the country club is just down the road. On the day of our interview the course was closed because of wind and rain, but Ray had still rugged up and hit some balls on the range. He's off eleven now and still loves the competition, but enjoys the camaraderie even more.

Far from resting on his laurels after so long at the top, Ray considers himself lucky and counts his blessings every day. He's modest but proud of his record and still works hard at every call. He's also generous with his time and advice. An example came just before our interview when Ray got a call from Brisbane sports poet Rupert McCall, whom he had met only briefly at a function, asking for advice on commentary. McCall had been chosen to front

Network Ten's call of the 2007 World Cup Rugby and he was blown away by Warren's kindness. 'I hardly knew him but Ray spoke to me for 40 minutes, it was so reassuring.'

'I don't mind helping youngsters along the way,' says Ray. 'If they end up better than me and take my job, so be it. But you know it helps me toe the line too.'

There are many funny moments in the commentary box that are not revealed to the public, but Ray shared one with me.

'I was doing an Amco Cup double-header with Frank Hyde as co-commentator and was busting for a piss. It was the fourth quarter of the second game, so I wrote Frank a note: "Can you fill in for me for five minutes?"'

'Frank's reply: "No thanks."'

So Ray did the only thing possible: he relieved himself into an empty soft-drink can, while keeping up a sparse call which sounded like this: 'Sterling ... shhh ... Vautin ... shhh.'

'Suddenly I felt a warm sensation down my leg and realised that I had missed the can by miles — lucky I was wearing black pants!'

As a commentator, Ray has his own self-imposed rules. He rarely ventures opinions. He leaves that to the former stars sitting next to him, nowadays Peter Sterling or Phil Gould. Ray concentrates on accuracy and reading the play. He has always used field glasses, even for television. Nowadays his research is confined to checking out the newcomers, finding out something interesting about them, rather than the statistics of the game. League statistician David Middleton sends out his figures each week but Ray will merely glance through them and never quotes them in a call. 'I leave that stuff to the other guys. I'm too busy making sure I call the right names and making the game more entertaining for the viewer.'

That's the key to 'Rabs', as Ray is generally known — his ability to make a game something special, to heighten the drama, without going 'over the top'. His passion for the game comes through and, with the credibility of thousands of calls, the result is a compelling mix. It's interesting that, although the ABC and the commercial stations are worlds apart, Ray considers the late John O'Reilly the best caller ever and, paradoxically, ABC legend Norman May, who's seen and heard the best over the past 50 years, says that Ray Warren is without peer. Norman observed: 'When we were in Auckland for the Commonwealth Games in 1990, Ray was doing the swimming on Nine for the first time. I helped him out with a few ideas but, basically, he taught himself. I was amazed how quickly he picked it up and how he used his horse-race commentary skills to cover swimming.'

Australia's prominence in swimming, allied to Channel Nine's innovative approach to technology, has enabled them to make their coverage of the sport a prime-time ratings-puller. And you can't exaggerate the contribution Ray Warren has made.

'His sense of theatre, combined with a great voice, enable him to capture the most exciting moments brilliantly,' says Norman May. 'He's a great commercial caller. Just as he lifts his excitement level for the last 25 metres of an Ian Thorpe swim, so the newsroom can replay the best 'grab' for their bulletin, he does the same in football when a try is on. No matter what you're doing, you've just got to watch — and that's great broadcasting.'

THIRTY-SIX

Peter Wilkins

ESCHEWING 'THE FAT'

'I can still feel the body contact — it was like cars colliding'

One of the prerequisites of being a sports commentator is to be a good actor. You have to 'sell' the broadcast and, sometimes, the game doesn't quite match the hype. In other cases, you might be calling a sport you don't particularly like, but you have to do it — it's all part of being a professional.

In Australia we have four major codes of football and, because of the vagaries of state bias, coverage differs from state to state. In winter, Victoria, South Australia, Western Australia and Tasmania have always had their fill of Australian Rules, while in NSW and Queensland, it's always been the two Rugby codes. Soccer, or football as it's become known, has struggled for recognition against the heavyweights, so Football Australia wisely decided to move their competition to summer.

For Peter Wilkins, this was a blessing, as he liked both soccer and Rugby League, and he could call both. For the past 30 years, he's been switching from one code to the other with aplomb, and he loves it. 'I still love the challenge. Every game is a contest in itself, it's theatre and each game is different. Not many people can say they love going to work, especially on a weekend, but I do.'

Peter grew up in Sydney and played soccer as a boy. He watched a lot of Rugby League and enjoyed it, but his heart was with the 'beautiful game'. 'I think the football you play as a boy stays in your blood and, while you can appreciate the other codes, you don't have the same gut feeling you have for your childhood game.'

Peter Wilkins catches up with Greg Norman at the NSW Open held at The Lakes. Why do they both look so young? Well, it was 27 years ago, in 1984

An example Peter recalls came in 1997 when he called the Super League Tests between Australia and Great Britain for ABC Radio. He was then required to call the World Cup soccer qualifier between Australia and the winner of the match between Japan and Iran. 'So there I was at Elland Road, trying to concentrate on the League Test, but also listening to the scores in my headphones from the soccer, which would determine whether I'd be travelling to Tokyo or Teheran the next day.'

As it turned out, Iran won, so Peter flew to Teheran and joined the throng of over 120 000 fans at the national stadium for the first leg qualifier. 'There was only a handful of media and I was the only radio caller, so I didn't know where to find the commentary box. I walked through this massive crowd up to the back of the stand but the commentary box was empty. Then I noticed that a microphone was standing on the sideline, near the benches. So I called the match standing up and, I must admit, I got a bit emotional. When Harry Kewell scored off a cross by Viduka, I went berserk — and then I realised that I was the only person in the stadium yelling. The crowd was absolutely silent — it was a mesmerising experience.'

When he interviewed Terry Venables, the Socceroos' coach, after the game the Englishman chuckled: 'You enjoyed that goal, didn't you!'

In November 2005, the situation was reversed when the Socceroos met Uruguay for the right to qualify for the FIFA World Cup finals. The Sydney Olympic stadium was packed with over 90 000 fans for the spine-tingling penalty shoot-out that decided which team would go to Germany.

'When the unthinkable happened and Mark Viduka missed,' recalls Peter, 'there was an audible groan from the crowd, but 30 seconds later, Mark Schwartzer made an incredible save, so Australia was back in it. There was no time to think — suddenly there's John Aloisi lining up the shot that decides the match. When it went in I don't really know what I said, the stadium just exploded with sound. Andy Harper and I were screaming, but the listeners probably couldn't hear it because of the background noise. They kept up the cheering for about three minutes, while Aloisi took off his shirt and ran deliriously over to his team-mates.'

It's moments like those that 'Wilko' cherishes. He feels privileged to be where he is, relaying the news to the nation via his radio broadcasts. It would be easy to lose control in situations like that — and plenty have. Queensland Rugby League commentator Kev Kelly is notorious for his call of an interstate game in 1970, before the days of State of Origin. An unsung young Queensland team upset NSW in a match at Lang Park and Kev got a wee bit too excited. Almost incoherent with excitement, he shrieked: 'They've done it! Queensland has won! They've humbled the mighty Blues! And I tell you what — it's great to be a Queenslander.' That call has gone down in the annals of radio broadcasting — how *not* to call football. You need excitement and involvement, not hysteria and blatant bias.

In 1991 Peter Wilkins began calling Rugby League for ABC Radio. At first, it was as a sideline commentator, with David Morrow and Warren Ryan in the box. Peter's first match was Origin II, at the Sydney Football Stadium, with the Maroons 1-up in the series. It was the match that provided that famous photo of Wally Lewis and Mark Geyer toe to toe, with referee David Manson trying to cool them down. Geyer had clipped tall Queensland full-back Paul Hauff with an elbow and Lewis had tried to get square. The situation was at flashpoint but the referee kept control. The tackling was ferocious and, on the sideline, the impact was frightening. 'I can still feel that body contact — it was like cars colliding. You're so close you can bring a different perspective from the commentators up in the box a hundred metres away.'

He will never forget that match. 'It was pouring rain in the second half and I had a coat over my head. Wally Lewis had a blinder in his last Origin match in Sydney but Mick O'Connor kicked a conversion from the sideline to win it 14–12, so the series was level.'

Peter maintains that, to really convey the nuances of a sport, you need to have played, at least at some level. Although no great player, Peter played League as well as soccer at school. When he began to call League, he sounded a bit like a soccer commentator, using terms like 'left side' and 'right side' instead of 'blind side' or 'open side'. However, his passion and accuracy shone through and he quickly formed a close-knit team with Warren Ryan and sideline caller Craig Hamilton. He immersed himself in the sport, going to training and watching players so he knew their idiosyncrasies as well as their appearance.

'If I made a mistake in a call I wouldn't be able to get to sleep that night, honestly. I prided myself on accuracy, probably because of my background in news and current affairs in the '80s, where you just couldn't afford mistakes of any kind.'

In the World Cup qualifier against Uruguay he missed the Marco Bresciano goal because he was unsighted, but got away with it. 'I saw Kewell bobble the ball into the path of Bresciano, but a couple of players were in the way and I wasn't expecting him to have a shot from that far out. But the crowd alerted me to it and I managed to call the right name instinctively.'

In calling League, if a player was obscured when he went over the line and Peter was undecided about the try scorer, Warren Ryan and Craig Hamilton would chip in with their opinions. In the 1990s the Bulldogs, for example, had several forwards who looked the same — short and stocky, with virtually no hair, a nightmare for callers. But the ABC team always helped each other out, and the result was compelling radio — some good-natured banter, lively debate and passionate commentary. 'It's like playing the game, it's a team effort and I got on well with those blokes, as well as Brian Smith, who did some commentary for us, and occasionally Greg Dowling.'

As a boy Peter's favourite sports program was the BBC's 'Match of the Day' with Brian Moore. The English Premier League was such a high standard and his favourite caller was the urbane Peter Jones. 'He had this mellifluous voice — it was beautiful — but he also had to ability the project you into the moment. He somehow captured, not just the play, but the whole ambient nature of the contest.'

Peter loves the lyrical style of English commentators such

as Henry Blofeld on cricket and Peter Alliss on golf. 'I could listen to Alliss all day. He makes it all so human and interesting, even if you're not particularly into the scoring and, of course, he too has a marvellous voice.'

'Wilko' has strong opinions on the technique of television commentary, believing that a good caller never states the obvious but always tries to add to the picture. Peter has called the Hopman Cup tennis for several years, always remembering to defer to his expert and keeping his commentary to a minimum. I happen to think that the ABC coverage of the Hopman Cup was simply the best tennis coverage on Australian television. Apart from being interesting in that it features international mixed doubles (the game we all tend to play in the backyard), it had a fine presenter in Karen Tighe, my favourite tennis caller in Fred Stolle and interesting player profiles, recorded away from the tennis court. The jury is still out on Ten's coverage after their first year.

Peter was also involved in another TV program that I consider to be the best of its kind, the satirical sports show 'The Fat'. Hosted by Tony Squires and including the hilarious Kerry O'Keeffe on the panel, the show was daringly different. It was the perfect blend of serious analysis and send-up, with 'Wilko' displaying his expertise in many lively discussions. It was a shame that it went the way of so many good ABC TV programs.

At the Sydney Olympics, Peter was called in at the last minute to cover the men's archery finals. Regular caller Drew Morphett was ill and there was only half an hour in which to prepare. Helped by producer Alan Marks with historical information and fellow caller Glenn Mitchell with the scoring details, Wilko went out and called Simon Fairweather's gold medal. Luckily he had seen coverage of one of the early elimination rounds, so he had the feel for how it was done. 'It's one of the things the ABC does so well. They train their people in technique so they can call pretty well anything, but I don't think I did an outstanding job that day. I just got by.'

Wilko 'got by' superbly when the Australian Rugby Championship was held in 2007 on ABC TV. Although a soccer and League devotee, Wilko turned his hand to Rugby with no problem at all. In fact, his unabashed passion and booming voice are perhaps something that has been missing in the culture of Rugby coverage.

He more than 'gets by' every weeknight when he presents a round-up of sport on ABC national television. It's a difficult job, covering the major international and domestic sporting events and at the same time keeping viewers in different states satisfied. There is a delicate balance required, as naturally Victorians would like more Australian Rules and Queenslanders want more Rugby League. Somehow 'Wilko' gets away with it, adding the odd witty one-liner or larrikin remark to remind everyone not to take it all too seriously. After all, it's just sport, isn't it?

Modest to a fault, 'Wilko' reminds me of Robert Plant, the lead singer of rock band Led Zeppelin, when asked by Parkinson how he managed to be so consistently brilliant: 'I'm not brilliant — I'm just happy not to make any mistakes on stage.'

THIRTY-SEVEN

Garry Wilkinson

SUMMERS IN THE SUN

'You've got the job, but first get rid of that awful Australian accent'

'I'll give you a three-month trial, but get rid of that bloody Pommy accent'

When it comes to tennis, nobody in Australia has called more matches than Garry Wilkinson. On a world scale, perhaps the globe-trotting Englishman John Barrett might surpass him, but Garry has seemingly been at it forever. In fact, he's in his fiftieth year of broadcasting and has now racked up 35 Australian Opens.

Garry and Peter Landy were as much a part of Australian tennis as Newcombe and Roche, fronting Channel Seven's coverage from the 1970s for 25 years. They would take it in turns to call matches, one doing the court introduction and post-match interview and the other calling the match from

Over 35 years Garry Wilkinson, seen here carrying the 2000 Olympic torch in Sydney, missed only one Australian Tennis Open

the box. Channel Seven in those days covered a lot of tennis and they were long days, but Garry never tired of it. 'I felt that it was a privilege. We were so lucky, travelling the country and staying in nice hotels. With the sun shining on a summer's day at Kooyong or Memorial Drive, it was glorious.'

Like a lot of journeyman commentators who have to describe sports at which they never actually excelled, Garry was no more than a social player. Like all good professionals though, he has always done his research and never stepped outside his role as an anchor, leaving the expert opinions to the commentators sitting beside him. Over the years, he's worked with the best of them: John Newcombe, Colin Long, Donald Dell, John Fitzgerald, Tony Roche, Wally Masur, Sue Barker, Pam Shriver, Ted Tingling and so on. Others come and go, but Garry has always been there, and is still doing it, albeit in a lower-profile role.

Actually Garry loved to play tennis but had to give up entirely when he injured his hip in a freak accident in 1986. He was calling the Australian Touring Car Championship at the remote Western Australian circuit of Waneroo, busy doing a last-minute edit for the telecast. Producer Mike Raymond realised that they needed an interview with Queensland driver Dick Johnson. It was urgent, so Garry volunteered and raced out the back of the huge broadcast van. There was a black curtain at the back and behind it, a steel tray that was normally down. However this time someone had pulled it up and Garry cartwheeled straight over the top, landing on his hip on a pile of TV cables. He was shaken but felt okay and considered himself lucky to have escaped relatively unscathed. However, next morning he couldn't get out of bed and his hip was one massive bruise. It took weeks of physiotherapy for him to walk properly and he still limped. As fate would have it, he had his fiftieth birthday just after the accident and his cheeky colleague, David Fordham, presented him with a handsome walking stick, suitably engraved: 'Just in case you go limp. Happy 50th birthday.'

Garry was born in Sydney but moved to Borneo with his parents at the age of nine. When he left school he applied for a job with Radio Brunei and, despite his tender age, he got it. The program manager got straight to the point: 'You will work two shifts of two hours a week but, first, get rid of that awful Australian accent.'

So for hours every day, Garry would practise the rounded vowel sounds and clipped consonants of the British colonial, and eventually was allowed to go on air. After eighteen months his parents returned to Sydney and Garry, now with a pronounced British accent, went with them. In those days, top Sydney disc jockeys like Ward 'Pally' Austin and John Laws were making what Garry thought was the princely sum of $300 a week, so he applied for a job. He tried all the commercial stations like 2UE and 2GB but, on hearing his audition, they all said the same thing: 'Why don't you try the ABC?'

Having worked in government or non-commercial radio in Asia, Garry was desperate for a shot at the money and glamour of the Sydney commercial scene, but eventually bowed to the seemingly inevitable and applied to the ABC. They said they would let him know but, in the meantime, he travelled to Port Macquarie where his father wanted to buy a dairy farm. Stopping at a café in Kempsey, he noticed the local radio station, 2KM, opposite. So he walked across the road, applied and got a position as a cadet journalist in the newsroom, earning $32 a week. Meanwhile, he was working on his voice 'to get rid of that bloody Pommy accent', as his boss put it.

Fate stepped in when a girlfriend's father, who worked for Cinesound News, tipped off Garry that 2UE were about to advertise a job in their newsroom. 'If you get in early before they place the ad in the paper, you might just get the job,' was the advice.

So Garry duly rang the general manager, Brian McLenehan, and was granted an interview. As he walked into the room, he sensed the disappointment on Brian's face, seeing one so young. 'I'm sorry but we're looking for an experienced journalist,' he said.

'Well, I may be young but I've got plenty of experience.' He began and went on to embellish his role as foreign correspondent in Brunei and chief newsreader in Kempsey. Brian took him around to the newsroom at 2UE and introduced him to the news director, one of the great men of Sydney radio, Don Angel. He once again launched into his spiel but Don stopped him and said: 'Son, we both know that's bullshit — but I'm willing to give you a three-month trial — and get rid of that bloody Pommy accent.' Garry stayed at 2UE for 13 years.

Eventually Channel Seven approached him as they were looking for a sports reporter for their news and Garry switched to television. He was told that he was free to apply for other positions in the network and, soon after starting out, saw that there was a job as a tennis commentator up for grabs. One of Channel Seven's veteran callers, Mike Williamson, had resigned after Mike Willesee was preferred for a prestigious role as host of a Davis Cup dinner. Garry ran into the ATN general manager, Ted Thomas, in the corridor. He asked about the job and Ted said: 'What are you like at calling tennis?'

'I'm a great tennis commentator,' said Garry cheekily. The fact that he had never called tennis didn't faze him a bit.

'Send me a memo,' said Thomas.

Garry went straight to his desk and typed up a memo, saying: 'Ted — this is to remind you that I'm a great tennis commentator — Garry Wilkinson.' Next morning he had the job.

Over the next 34 years, Garry only missed one Australian Open, in 1987. Garry was called on to host Channel Seven's coverage of the America's Cup defence in Perth. I remember it well, as I was called in to take his place for the final Open held on the grass at Kooyong. I joined John Alexander, Allan Stone, Peter Landy and English pair John Barrett and Sue Barker in the Channel Seven commentary team. On first impression Garry looked like someone out of 'Miami Vice', tanned and impeccably dressed, with so much gold jewellery he jangled when he walked. I dubbed him 'Garry Gucci', but over the next eight years, when I worked alongside him at the tennis, I was always impressed by his professionalism and poise. The bigger the occasion, the more he seemed to like it. He would swagger out onto centre court with his walking stick and host the presentations after finals as if he was on a Sunday morning walk with the dog. No wonder really, when you look at his experience: 30 Davis Cup ties, including five finals, seven Olympics, twenty Bathurst 1000 motor races, America's Cups — it was like brushing his teeth.

It wasn't always like that, though. Early in his tennis commentary career he had to do a post-match interview on court with the irascible Jimmy Connors, who had just lost. Garry rarely ventured into the realm of technique, but he had picked up on a comment by Allan Stone during the match about Connors' problem with his backhand. 'Bad luck, Jimmy, but do you think you might have done better if you had got a bit more topspin on your backhand?'

Connors' face was a mask of frustration and rage. He simply turned the racquet towards Garry and offered it to him.

'Oh no, Jimmy, I didn't mean that ... I wouldn't presume to tell you how to play.'

'You just did,' the grumpy American barked and walked off the court.

Fortunately for Garry there weren't many moments like that, and he learned from his mistakes. So well, in fact, that the Women's Tennis Association once voted him 'best commentator in the world'. Not a bad wrap. Some might say over the top, but the fact was that Garry did his homework and worked hard at his craft. He had a habit of mixing socially with players to find out more about them as people, invaluable scraps of information that meant all the difference to his commentary. 'Every viewer can tell a good forehand from a bad one, but not everyone knows where this kid went to school, who his first coach was, and what he eats for breakfast.'

It might have helped that, in the late 1970s and early 1980s, Garry had a relationship with American player Sharon Walsh. He learnt more about the game and the tour from Sharon than anyone else. In a funny way, it also caused him to give up smoking. Once an 80-a-day man, Garry was talked into playing socially with Sharon, which revealed his lack of fitness. One stifling day in Palm Springs, California, Garry played a match with Sharon against US Davis Cup captain Denis Ralston and local pro Tommy Tucker. In oppressive heat, Garry played until he dropped, literally. Helped to his hotel room, he sat under a cold shower for twenty minutes. He then settled in with a bottle of bourbon and smoked the remainder of his last packet of cigarettes that night. To this day he has never had another cigarette.

There were plenty of light-hearted moments too in those long summer days at the tennis. One time at Kooyong he was calling a match with Allan Stone while Peter Landy sat in the box, idly watching the match. Landy borrowed Garry's binoculars and, during the ad break, said: 'Hey Garry, you should see the stunner in the pink bikini in the back row!' So intent was he on the girl that he didn't notice Jenny, his second wife, standing at the open door of the box. She attempted to wrest the binoculars from Landy, who refused to let them go. So the commentary continued, to the groan and grunt of their domestic altercation, with Garry and Allan trying to suppress their laughter.

On a serious note, Garry feels that his dedication to the job cost him his first marriage. Away from home every weekend and most public holidays, he hardly ever saw his eldest son play school sport. Now, happily married the second time to Kerrie, he has twin boys and rarely misses their soccer matches on weekends.

As a freelancer these days, Garry is a sometime newsreader with Sky News, still commentates at the Australian Open tennis, the Olympics and has also evolved into something of a specialist commentator on equestrian events. The opportunity to call this rather esoteric sport first came about in 1992 when Channel Seven was looking for an offsider for British commentator Lucinda Prior-Palmer. Strangely enough, because of his love of punting, it was thought that Garry might fill the bill, so he was given a trial at the Werribee Three-Day event. The telecast was a success and his role was confirmed for the Olympics. However, when he got to Barcelona, it was discovered that the venue was too far from the studios for Garry to fulfil his other roles as host and commentator for the Opening and Closing Ceremonies. So Cameron Williams was thrown into the role, and Australia won both the team and individual gold medals.

In 1996 at Atlanta the same thing happened. Garry was chosen to call the equestrian events but, as he had to host the nightly news report as well as the daytime coverage, Stan Grant got the job. Eventually in Sydney at the 2000 Olympics, Garry got his chance. Australia duly won another equestrian gold medal and Garry has been covering the sport ever since. Nowadays, he does more public address commentary than TV, but still gets a kick out of it. 'I just love what I do. Whether its tennis, motor racing or equestrian, it doesn't matter which sport, I just consider myself lucky. It's been a privilege — and I'll keep doing it as long as they want me.'

Well, they still want you Garry. It's like the French Open — a baseline battle, you're into the fifth set, but it could go on for years yet.

THIRTY-EIGHT

Roger Wills

A LABOUR OF LOVE

'Imagine being asked to interview Seb Coe, Steve Ovett, Steve Cram and Daley Thompson all in one afternoon. Then in walks legendary New Zealand miler, John Walker'

ABC commentators are a breed apart. In these days of shock jocks and egomaniacs, it's refreshing to come across humility, and you won't find a more modest man than Roger Wills. Although he's been calling sport for 40 years he is just grateful for what he calls 'the best job in the world', sitting at the beautiful Adelaide Oval in summer calling cricket or Football Park doing the footy in winter. 'I specially love

The thoroughly professional, undemonstrative Roger Wills is grateful for 'the best job in the world'

calling sport to the country because you know how much they appreciate it. Although I prefer radio to TV, I did call Test cricket on television to the bush for four years and loved it.'

There have been many people like Roger in the 75-year history of ABC Sport. They are knowledgeable, undemonstrative and thoroughly professional. We tend to take them for granted because they do such a consistently good job, bringing us 'around the grounds' reports during the football season, score updates from the cricket during summer and a comprehensive summary of sport from home and abroad every night. 'I learned by watching people like John O'Reilly record "Sportsman's Parade" and Geoff Mahoney do "Ringside News" in my days as a trainee in Sydney,' Roger recalls. They were different in style but equally professional in technique, so you were able to pick up the little things, the tricks of the trade. For example, I recall John teaching me not to ask a question that could be answered in one word — and never the old cliché: "How do you feel?"'

Roger is a wanderer. Born in Brisbane, his parents moved to Sydney when he was five and he grew up listening to Alan McGilvray at the cricket, Norman May at the Rugby and Doug Heywood at the Davis Cup. 'I was mesmerized by their sense of theatre and wonderful voices. I'll never forget listening to the drama of the Davis Cup in 1953 when the Sydney teenagers, Hoad and Rosewall, upset the Americans, Seixas and Trabert.'

After boarding at Tudor House in Moss Vale, Roger was sent to Geelong Grammar and discovered a wonderful new game: Australian Rules.

'Geelong had "Polly" Farmer, Billy Goggin and Doug Wade — it was wonderful to see the way they handled the ball — and I became an instant convert. Forty-four years later they finally won the flag and where was I? Sitting on a beach in the Bosphorous in Turkey!' After completing an Arts degree at ANU in Canberra, Roger went into National Service for two years and, on returning to civilian life, applied for a job as a Specialist Trainee in the ABC Sports Department.

Roger has worked in Sydney, Melbourne, Hobart and Adelaide and is one of the few commentators to have called four codes of football. League and Union in Sydney, Rules in Adelaide and soccer all over. 'I called the NSL on television — I've not got the face for TV — but I really enjoyed it. I've also done a fair bit on radio — the Maradona match in Sydney, the World Cup qualifier against Uruguay and the Australia vs. Greece game in 2006, with 95,000 people, it was electric.'

At Moss Vale, Roger played Rugby and he's loved the sport all his life. 'One of the regrets of my career is that I haven't been able to call more Rugby. I'm patron of my local club here in Adelaide and, when I get the chance, I love to follow the Wallabies overseas. Going to Cardiff Arms Park for the Test against Wales in 1975 was one of the great sporting experiences of my life. Apart from the match, the singing by the Welsh fans was absolutely superb.'

In Rugby League, Roger used to be an 'around the grounds' reporter in the 1970s in Sydney at grounds like Henson Park and the newly opened Penrith Park. This broad knowledge of football gives him a sense of perspective in his commentary. Rational and reasonable, he's never one to indulge in a string of superlatives. 'I really believe in using the expert. He's the one who has played the game at the highest level and the listener wants to hear from him, not me, so I try to lead to the expert as much as possible.'

Roger has worked with some good ones — like Les Favell, Eric Freeman, Terry Jenner and Bob Massie at the cricket. 'Les could say more in 60 seconds than others in five minutes and hearing Jenner on spin or Massie on swing bowling was fabulous.'

His respect for Freeman, who was a big-hitting all-rounder and a Port Adelaide footballer, comes through their years of working together. They are good mates, which adds an intangible bonus to a broadcast.

In football season, he enjoyed the ABC's Ken Dakin, Dick Mason and Doug Heywood (all great voices) Doug Bigelow for his wit and an Adelaide favourite, Jimmy Deane, whose summaries were superb. Without going into too many statistics, he could point to the spark that turned a game.

Like most ABC cricket commentators of his era, Roger was influenced by the great Alan McGilvray, who told him to imagine he was talking to a blind man.

One of the greatest thrills of Roger's broadcasting career came in 1982 when he and producer Robbie Weekes travelled to Europe and Africa for five weeks, recording radio and TV profiles for the upcoming Brisbane Commonwealth Games. 'It was a fabulous experience. Imagine being asked to interview Seb Coe, Steve Ovett, Steve Cram and Daley Thompson, all in the one afternoon. Then in walked John Walker, the legendary New Zealand miler — I did fifteen minutes with him.'

These brief profiles were, in my opinion, one of the main reasons why the 1982 Games were the best with which I have ever been associated. Two crews, the second led by Drew Morphett, combed the world and profiled 50 of the leading gold medal contenders. For example, we had 60-second cameos of Daley Thompson, training in the rain in Manchester and sprinter Don Quarrie, running along the beach in Jamaica. If there was a delay at the event, say a false start, I would throw to a profile (I was the ABC anchorman for those Games). The viewer would then have a deeper knowledge of them as people and feel a greater empathy when they competed. So, when we came back to the race, there was Thompson or Quarrie, standing behind the blocks and suddenly, we cared whether they won or lost. It was brilliant pre-production from the man who was responsible for the ABC's rock music phenomenon 'Countdown'.

Roger has travelled a lot, is genuinely interested in people and it comes through in his commentary. He loves two things in particular about his job — there's no script and you meet fascinating people every day. 'The other day, for example, I had to interview William Henzell, a silver medallist in table tennis from the Melbourne Commonwealth Games. At his home in the Adelaide Hills, he taught me all about the finer points of his sport — and what a lovely fellow.'

Pressed on his favourite commentators, Roger opts for Scotsman Bill McLaren on Rugby and his Dream Team at the cricket would be Alan McGilvray, John Arlott, Freddie

Trueman, Tony Cozier ('that wonderful West Indian accent') and Johnny Moyes. 'Anyone who heard that 1960–61 series against Frank Worrell's West Indies team that summer would never forget it. I think that was a major turning-point for Test cricket — they brought entertainment to the game — and Johnny summed it up perfectly.'

On TV one commentator stands head and shoulders above the rest, according to Roger: Richie Benaud. 'It's a long while since I've sat on the edge of my seat, hanging on every ball, but Richie had me doing that in that fantastic Ashes series in 2005.' His Aussie Rules football calling team would be Ken Dakin, Dick Mason, Dennis Cometti, Malcolm McDonald, Doug Bigelow and Jimmy Deane. Although he's not really into motor sport, he loves listening to Will Hagon and, when it comes to cycling, he picks Phil Liggett.

Roger is married to Sue, whom he credits for his sanity: 'When I come home we talk about theatre, books, cooking — anything but sport. We went to the new Tom Stoppard play last night, so I was a bit bleary-eyed at my early morning swim today.'

A keen tennis player and jogger, Roger keeps superbly fit and looks much younger than his 64 years. He is a passionate reader and enjoys having a beer with friends. 'Adelaide is a wonderful place to live and I never want to go anywhere else. As long as the ABC wants me, I'll keep going. It's getting harder to keep up with the pace of football these days, but the young blokes like Peter Walsh keep me on the ball.'

Good on you, Roger — and we'll keep listening.

THIRTY-NINE

A tough gig for a lady

'It was the proudest moment in my life calling Wimbledon. Having been there as a player, calling a final was a dream come true'
                                                                Kerryn Pratt

There have been very few female sports commentators of note in Australia, which is strange, because our sportswomen are extraordinarily good. In fact, while women comprise only 20 per cent of the make-up of our Olympic teams since 1896, they have won over 40 per cent of our medals. Australian women are traditionally among the best in the world in sports like netball, basketball, surfing, water polo, swimming, athletics, cycling, squash, gymnastics and rowing, just to name a few.

It was a hard country when the first settlers arrived and it took tough, resilient women to survive. The temperate climate and abundant healthy food lent themselves to an outdoor lifestyle and sport became a unifying force in this huge, diverse land. Girls ran, jumped and swam alongside their brothers and the government soon realised that excellence in sport gave the fledgling nation a standing in the world.

Unfortunately, female broadcasters were not given the same support. Indeed ABC Head of Sport, Bernard Kerr, when asked about this apparent discrimination in the 1960s, stated: 'Women do not have the depth or authority in their voices that men do. They sound too shrill when they get excited.'

So there were very few female broadcasters employed in the early days of radio and television in Australia. June Ferguson, an Olympic athlete and coach, was an exception, working as an expert radio commentator on athletics from the early 1960s. Debbie Spillane came from commercial radio to become the ABC's first female Specialist Trainee in the Sports Department. At the instigation of ABC Board member Wendy McCarthy, Spillane was sent to the 1984

Debbie Spillane was the ABC Sports Department's first female specialist trainee. She has called Rugby League, and sport later met comedy when she appeared as Sportsbitch on ABC-TV's iconic 'Live and Sweaty'

Los Angeles Olympics as part of the affirmative action policy, to redress the imbalance. However, she had precious little experience in commentary and was soon relegated to studio presentation. She returned to commercial radio, where she found her niche as a reporter on Rugby League. She then made her way in a distinctly man's world, being at various times Media Manager for the Canterbury Bulldogs and a board member of the NSW Greyhound Racing authority. Sport then met comedy when she appeared as Sportsbitch on the quirky and iconic ABC-TV show 'Live and Sweaty'. She now presents authoritative sports reports on Breakfast, ABC News Radio.

Another short-lived experiment involved actress Kate Fitzpatrick, who was tried out as a commentator in the early 1980s by Channel Nine. However, she was like a square peg in a round hole and quit after just one season. For some reason, Australian sports fans, women included, seem to prefer male commentators. Women are regarded favourably as presenters or reporters, but you can count on one hand the number of regular female sports commentators.

As recently as December 2009, Channel Nine axed their sports presenter and interviewer Stephanie Brantz, who had been signed with much fanfare from SBS the previous summer. The face of the 2006 FIFA World Cup on SBS, she was recruited by the then-CEO Eddie Maguire as a high-profile reporter and presenter, with a lucrative contract. Told she would be employed as an analyst, interviewer and roving reporter at the cricket, Stephanie was virtually kept in cotton wool. She interviewed just one Australian player, Shane

Watson, in the whole Ashes series in 2006 and was upset to be given only trivial reports on the Barmy Army and model Lara Bingle. Nine management was reported to have said: 'Australian players preferred to speak to Ian Healy or Mark Taylor.' It's a shame, as she made impressive strides at SBS and appeared to have a big future. After a spell as a reporter on Fox Sports, she signed with ABCTV in October 2010 as a News sport presenter and reporter and is a sideline commentator on the W-League.

Kerryn Pratt, a former tennis pro, has made a good fist of TV commentary after starting out as a reporter with Channel Seven. She now works regularly alongside the likes of Fred Stolle and John Newcombe for Australia's Channel Nine and Channel Seven or Sky Channel in England. Her experience as a player shines through and she makes it her business to get close to the players and find out the personal details that humanise the commentary. Moreover, she is just as comfortable as the play-by-play caller as she is being the expert. Most former players in the past, such as Sue Barker, Pam Shriver or Virginia Wade, have been used exclusively as analysts, so Kerryn has been something of a pioneer.

Melbourne-born, Kerryn was a talented tennis player who rose to professional standard in the 1980s. No relation to Queenslander Nicole Pratt, she represented Australia at Junior Wimbledon and toured overseas with six Australian underage teams. She won a scholarship to the Australian Institute of Sport in 1981–82 and then embarked on a professional career. She had a degree of success in Australia, winning the national Hardcourt Doubles. She was a finalist in the Queensland and Western Australian Open Singles and reached the last sixteen at the Australian Open. She was a good doubles player, winning a British Satellite Masters title and reaching the semi-finals at Beckenham and the Australian Open. She had a lot of fun, even if she didn't make huge amounts of money. 'I used to play doubles with a girl called Elizabeth Little and I wondered why some of the crowd at Wimbledon were laughing at odd times. Of course the scoreboard read "Little Pratt", which was very amusing to the English fans.'

She reached a career-high ranking of number 140 in the world. She fell in love, married and had children, retiring from the arduous life of a touring professional and got a BA

A rose surrounded by thorns. Kerryn Pratt, a former tennis professional, with her Channel Nine Wimbledon tennis commentary team colleagues. From left, Fred Stolle, John Newcombe, Tim Sheridan and Mark Woodforde

in sports studies and journalism. She got a job as a sports journalist with Channel Seven and worked on the news, 'Sportsworld' and the tennis as a reporter.

I worked alongside her at various tennis tournaments and was impressed with her knowledge of the game and empathy with players. She had always nursed an ambition to do some commentary and, when pay TV came along, she got her chance. Starting on C7, she began calling tennis, sometimes as the play-by-play commentator, and sometimes as the analyst. With her journalistic knowledge, she could handle the former, and with her playing background, she had the credibility for the latter. Channel Nine liked what they saw and snapped her up for Wimbledon. 'That was the proudest moment of my life — calling Wimbledon. Having been there as a player, I knew and loved the tradition and, to sit next to someone like Tony Trabert, calling a final, was a dream come true.'

Kerryn is now a regular member of the Nine commentary team for Wimbledon and calls the other Grand Slams for the host broadcaster. Channel Seven producer Andy Kay offered her the chance to call other sports, as well as tennis, at the Athens Olympics. So she became a softball and badminton commentator, again as the describer, not the expert.

At the Melbourne Commonwealth Games in 2006 Kerryn called table tennis, a sport she had never played, which was a challenge: 'We called an enormous number of matches, so many that I began seeing ping pong balls in my sleep! However, I grew to understand the nuances of the sport and really enjoyed the experience.'

Her favourite experts in the tennis commentary box have been John Newcombe and Martina Navratilova. 'That was really a thrill — to sit beside one of my heroes and call tennis. I played doubles against Martina and she was really intimidating but, in the box, I loved working with her. She has very strong opinions — I call her the ultimate expert.'

Kerryn's commentary is well researched and lively. She gets very excited at Grand Slams, particularly before calling a final. 'The boys think it's a bit of a joke but I can't help it. I just love the atmosphere of the Grand Slams and I must get as nervous as the players.' She has also been a sports administrator, being a board member of the Australian Sports Commission and has been a Fed Cup selector, all of which helps in her commentary. 'We have been struggling a bit in the past few years in the Fed Cup. It's just so much tougher now, with the emergence of so many good players from Eastern Europe. They seem to have the fire in their bellies, they see tennis as a way out of poverty and misery, so they're just a lot tougher mentally than our girls. I love the rags to riches stories of Sharapova and many of the other Eastern Europeans. It makes you appreciate their play all the more.'

Another outstanding caller has been Anne Sargeant. She became so synonymous with netball on television that she was known simply as 'the voice of netball'. A brilliant player, she represented Australia for a decade from 1978 and was captain from 1983 onwards. An articulate and passionate ambassador for her sport, Anne called the national league, the Commonwealth Bank Trophy, from 1989 until 2006, when she was suddenly and inexplicably axed. Apparently the move came, not from the ABC, but from the sport itself, which was seeking a new, younger image. I will never forget the ABC's coverage of the final of the 1991 World Championships between Australia and their arch rivals, New Zealand. Watched by Prime Minister Bob Hawke and a national TV audience, Australia won a cliff-hanger. The ABC even held back the 6.00 pm news bulletin to cover the finish of the match.

History repeated itself in 1999 when Australia did it again in Christchurch, Sharelle McMahon making the clutch shot, like a female John Eales. On both occasions it was the commentary of Anne Sargeant and Steve Robilliard that kept us riveted to the edge of our seats.

One sport that has emerged in the past 15 years, in terms of winning over viewers, is gymnastics. The main reason is the commentary of Liz Chetkovich. An outstanding coach from

A brilliant netballer, and captain of the successful Australian team for many years, Anne Sargeant later became known simply as 'the voice of netball'

Perth, Liz has brought gymnastics into our loungerooms with such passion and knowledge that we've all become armchair experts. The courage and skill of the elf-like gymnasts is marvellous enough, but Liz adds the esoteric knowledge of a coach, with just a dash of humanity, so that we all agonise with every performance. Of course, gymnastics only gets a run every four years when the Olympics come around, but it gets more exposure every time. Sandy Roberts, a newcomer to gymnastics, worked with Liz on the Channel Seven commentary team at the Barcelona Games in 1992 and soon became as enthusiastic and involved as she was.

Equestrian events get little exposure outside the Olympics, but Lucinda Prior-Palmer has made it quite popular. English-born, Lucinda has a wonderful voice that seems perfectly suited to the elegance of dressage. Of course, it helps that Australia has emerged as a world force in the sport and won gold medals at Barcelona, Atlanta and Sydney.

Former swimming stars, Lisa Forrest (ABC) and Nicole Livingstone (Channel Nine), have done a fine job in making their sport the most popular amongst Australian viewers at the Olympics, but both work as analysts rather than callers.

Also in this category are athletics commentators Raelene

Lisa Forrest is multi-talented: a dual Commonwealth Games swimming gold medallist, author, TV and radio personality, and actor

Boyle and Jane Flemming. Working at major events like the Olympics or World Championships, they have added credibility in their role as the expert.

While Bernie Kerr's chauvinistic attitude may have held back female commentators at the ABC, it hasn't stopped them becoming household names as presenters on radio and television. Karen Tighe and Simone Thurtell and Tracey Holmes have all became popular hosts of the ABC weekend radio program 'Grandstand'. Karen blazed the trail when she started hosting the show every Saturday and Sunday afternoon from 1997. As befits one who has a degree in communications and psychology from Macquarie University, she is a tremendous interviewer and she has great all-round knowledge of sport. To make it in a man's world, women need to be just that bit better and she was. Whether it was hosting the ABC's radio coverage of the 1998 Commonwealth Games in Kuala Lumpur, the Hopman Cup tennis from Perth, the Paralympics from Sydney 2000 or just a normal winter

Karen Tighe's all-round knowledge and human touch made her a great favourite on ABC Radio's 'Grandstand'. She's pictured here with husband Glenn Mitchell who is an intregral part of ABC cricket's commentary team

Saturday afternoon's sporting coverage, Karen has it all under control, with a nice human touch.

Married to ABC cricket commentator Glenn Mitchell, Karen has cut back on her 'Grandstand' role for 2 years to concentrate on raising their first child, but still read the ABC sports news on weeknights in Perth.

The most recent addition to the elite club of female sports commentators has been Kelli Underwood. Born in Adelaide, Kelli attended Mercedes College and gained a Bachelor of Arts degree at the University of South Australia. She played basketball and was good enough to be part of a national underage title-winning team. But she always had a passion for broadcasting and got her first job at radio station 5MU at Murray Bridge. Kelli worked her way up steadily, moving to K-Rock in Geelong, then 3AW, before starting at Network Ten in October 2005.

In 2006, she started working on radio for the ABC's iconic 'Grandstand' programme, as boundary rider and commentator on AFL games. She also covers the Australian Open tennis for ABC Radio.

But Australian Rules is her passion and she really made the headlines when she was appointed to call the AFL in

The only female ball-by-ball football commentator in Australia, Kelli Underwood has a huge future.

season 2009. Working in such a male-dominated sport, she was under a lot of pressure, but soon showed her knowledge and enthusiasm. Opinions were divided on her success — some thought she did an admirable job while others vehemently demanded her sacking.

Ten's management showed their satisfaction by reappointing her for season 2010 and although she only got to call an average of one game a month, she grew in confidence. However, at the end of the season, the axe fell. Naturally she was devastated but accepted the umpire's verdict.

'I still have a lot to learn. But I'm as keen as ever and looking forward to calling the AFL in 2011 on ABC Radio and the national Netball League on Ten.'

She's now notched up 12 AFL grand finals as a commentator, as well as the World Swimming Championships, motor racing grand prix and the World Surfing Tour in Hawaii, in her 14 years as a broadcaster. As recently as last October in Delhi, she was part of the Ten Network athletics coverage which was nominated for a Logie Award. Kelli played a significant role, interviewing sprinter Sally Pearson several times in the process of her controversial disqualification after winning the 100 metres. Just 33 at the time of writing, Kelli has a long and promising career ahead of her.

It's a tough gig for a lady, Kelli, but you, and all the other excellent women commentators, have done us proud.

FORTY

So, you want to be a sports commentator?

> *Let's face it, people will always watch and enjoy sport!*
>
> Peter Meares

I worry about the future of sports commentary in Australia. Perhaps I'm getting more finicky as I grow older, but I think standards are falling. With the advent of pay TV, there are more and more commentators bursting onto our screens but, for the most part, I'd prefer to turn the sound down. All too often, producers are grabbing players as soon as they retire and putting them into a commentary box with a mic and headphones. Most of the time they have no idea.

ABC Sport no longer has its specialist trainee program,

which produced dozens of commentators over the past 50 years. So, where is a keen youngster to go to learn the art of sports commentary? The best way these days is to simply watch and listen to the experts, and try to do your best. I always advise budding young broadcasters to get a tape recorder and listen to their own voice. You are your own best critic and you know immediately when you've made a mistake.

A good way to start is to read stories from the sports pages of the newspaper onto the recorder, then listen to them, time and again. You need to follow the old edict: 'If you sound interested, then you'll be interesting.'

Above all, try to be natural, to be yourself, but remember to stress the important words in each sentence. It takes lots of practice, so be prepared to work hard. Then, when you're satisfied it's okay, play it back to someone whose opinion you respect. Ideally, try to speak to someone with broadcasting experience and get their opinion.

Once your diction is okay, the next step is to try some commentary. Again, use your trusty recorder to call something from television, pretending you're on radio. These tips will help you out:

1. Write out the teams (and numbers, if it's football).
2. Jot down a few brief notes on the players, so you can embellish your comments on them.
3. Remember to repeat the score at every stoppage.
4. Describe the scene as if the listener is blind — weather, ground, crowd, etc.

5. Do your homework — have plenty of facts and figures to fall back on when nothing is happening.
6. Use your voice to make it exciting — a higher pitch, for example, when a team is close to scoring, or for a boundary in cricket.
7. Copy technique — not style. Be yourself, not a poor imitation of some famous commentator.
8. Don't be afraid to entertain. In between the action, reminisce about former games or players, discuss topical issues and ponder about the outcome of the game you're watching. Involve your listener.
9. Vary your language. Try very hard not to fall into the habit of using stock phrases — use your imagination.
10. Don't worry about minor mistakes, be confident and end on a definite note.

Take your recording along to an expert when you are satisfied and ask for critical comments. Then, go back and try again, and again. I remember when I started out as a fledgling Rugby League caller with ABC Radio in Brisbane in 1971. My boss, Arthur Denovan, told me not to worry about how badly I went in my early calls, as it would take me at least two years to become a half-decent commentator. And he was right. I called every match at Lang Park or suburban grounds each weekend in winter for fifteen seasons and was still learning when I changed networks and gave it away.

Ask any sports commentator and he'll tell you he has the best job in the world. Imagine being paid for doing what you love! If you're enthusiastic enough, you will make it, but it's harder these days for a journeyman to become a commentator. Most callers are former internationals, which is a shame in my opinion. I still think the best balance is to have a professional describer sit next to a former player, so the former can ask the same naïve questions a listener would ask. Former Test players have seen it all and don't ask each other dumb questions. That's why I prefer Harsha Bhogle with Kerry O'Keeffe to Tony Greig with Bill Lawry — but it's a matter of taste.

Who are the stars of the future? Again, this is purely subjective, but there are some talented young callers around. In cricket, I think Ian Healy, Shane Warne, Mark Nicholas and Michael Slater are doing a fine job and will head the Nine team in a few years. I like the enthusiasm of ABC cricket callers Peter Walsh in Adelaide and Quentin Hull in Brisbane. When it comes to League, Andy Raymond on Fox Sports has a big future, in my opinion. ABC still do a mighty job on Rugby, with Tim Gavel in Canberra and Toby Lawson in Sydney two shining lights. I'm no expert on Australian Rules, but I enjoy the calling of James Brayshaw, Dan Lonergan and Anthony Hudson. I love Olympic sports, so I must mention the work of David Basheer, calling athletics, and Duncan Armstrong on swimming. I have already mentioned Kerryn Pratt's work calling tennis and she has an enormous future as does Kelli Underwood.

Sports commentary is not something you can pick up overnight — it takes years to perfect. One of the most extraordinary examples of commentators being thrown to the wolves came at the 2007 Rugby World Cup, where

Network Ten chose three callers with absolutely no commentary experience to cover the tournament. Through no fault of their own, sports poet Rupert McCall was teamed with former Wallabies Ben Tune and Ben Darwin, and they received torrents of criticism. The viewing audience, accustomed to a diet of Gordon Bray, Chris Handy, Greg Clark, Greg Martin and other veteran callers, was dissatisfied with the commentary, describing it in terms ranging from 'excruciating' to 'uninformed'. It was like a maiden horse having its first start in a Melbourne Cup.

Sport is big business for TV networks, so commentators will have plenty to do in the years to come. With all the gimmicks and graphics at a producer's disposal these days, the commentator has often become secondary to the pictures, simply supplementing the on-screen information. There is less time to talk and, when you do, you need to be quick. There's still room for the old-fashioned wordsmith on radio though and, I must admit, I enjoy cricket now more on radio than on television.

I always think a commentator is a bit like a referee or umpire. If he does a good job, the game will be the main focus — you won't even notice him. If, on the other hand, he does a bad job, then he'll be about as popular as Steve Bucknor in Bombay.

But let's face it — no matter what we say as commentators, people will always watch sport and enjoy it.

PHOTO CREDITS

The photos in this book have been obtained through the generosity of the commentators and the radio and television networks. I would like to thank the following:

Paul Smith (Ian Healy)
Michelle Pownell, ABC Brisbane (Warren Boland, Gerry Collins and Quentin Hull)
Lester Townsend Publishing (Warren Boland)
Jenny Sherland, ABC Sport (Kerry O'Keeffe)
Susan Robinson and Belinda Lee, ABC Melbourne (Drew Morphett, David Morrow, Debbie Spillane)
Liz Ransom, ABC Adelaide (Roger Wills)
Ann Yardley, ABC Perth (Karen Tighe)
Penelope Cross, Channel Seven (Dennis Cometti, Sandy Roberts, Bruce McAvaney, Jack Newton)
Anne Johnson (Bruce McAvaney)
Kate Amphlett, Channel Seven (Gordon Bray)
Cathrine Mahony, Channel 9 (Ian Chappell, Richie Benaud)
Nicholas Wilson (Richie Benaud)
Bayview Tennis Club (Ian Chappell)
Heidi Packer, SBS (Les Murray)
Ludvik Dabrowski (Lisa Forrest)
Tim Lane
Darrell Eastlake
Phil Liggett
Peter Donegan
Steve Robilliard
John McCoy
Chris Handy

Elaine Dixon (Max Walker)
Catherine Donovan, Network Ten (Kelli Underwood)
Ian Baker-Finch (IBF family collection)
Wayne Grady (Grady family collection)
Paul Vautin (Vautin family collection)
Tony Greig
Ray Warren
Garry Wilkinson
Peter Wilkins
Judy Grljusich
Peter FitzSimons
The rest are from the author's collection.

INDEX

Ablett, Gary 279
Agassi, Andre 197
Aggiss, Richard 202
Agnew, Jonathon 2-3, 219
Alderson, Colin 245
Alexander, John 334
Ali, Inshan 70
Ali, Muhammad 205
Allan, Peter 242
Allan, Rod 122
Allan, Trevor 13, 32, 63
Allenby, Robert 38, 135
Alliss, Peter 39, 125, 130-1, 263, 266, 280, 327
Aloisi, John 324
Alston, Rex 25
Angel, Don 333
Appleby, Stuart 38-40, 135
Arlott, John 19, 25-7, 46, 183, 231, 342
Armstrong, Duncan 85, 359
Armstrong, Lance 191
Arok, Frank 261
Ashes 10, 20-2, 25, 45, 51, 70, 72, 173, 176, 239, 272, 343, 347
Athletics 16, 102, 152, 170, 180-1, 197-200, 204, 252, 344-5, 352, 355, 359
Austin, Tracey 164

Austin, Ward 'Pally' 109, 332
Ayers, 'Nunky' 14

Bailey, Michael 12
Bailey, Trevor 218
Baker-Finch, Ian 34-42, 130, 164, 263, 265, 269
Ballesteros, Seve 264
Banks, Norman 28
Barber, John 212
Barker, Sue 330, 334, 347
Barrett, John 294, 329, 334
Baseball 76, 242
Basheer, David 262, 359
Bassey, 'Ironbar' 112
Basketball 182, 242, 344, 354
Beale, David 153
Beckham, David 252
Bedser, Alec 16
Beetson, Artie 59, 210
Benaud, Richie 2, 43-51, 72-4, 121, 126, 141, 143, 162-4, 166, 178, 186, 194, 231, 233, 309, 343
Bennett, Chester 71
Bennett, Gordon 102
Bennett, Wayne 6
Bertrand, John 233
Bhogle, Harsha 219, 272, 359
Bichel, Andy 90
Bigelow, Doug 341, 343

Bingle, Lara 347
Biondi, Matt 85
Birmingham, Billy 49, 73, 143, 202, 205, 222, 311
Bishop, A.N. 8
Black ,'Tiger' 31
Blagojevic, Milan 260
Bland, John 265
Blight, Malcolm 279
Blofeld, Henry 327
Boland, Warren 52-9
Bonner, Tony 13
Booth, Peter 181, 246
Border, Allan 221, 303
Boss, Wally 292
Botham, Sir Ian 51
Boustead, Kerry 211
Boxing 58, 146-50, 153, 208, 221, 237
Boycott, Geoff 27, 217, 232
Boyle, Raelene 181, 196, 200, 353
Bradman, Sir Donald 22, 45, 68
Brantz, Stephanie 346
Brasher, Tim 302
Bray, Gordon 2, 19, 21, 40, 68-74, 135, 165, 189, 235, 294-5, 368
Brayshaw, James 359
Brennan, John 55, 124
Bresciano, Marco 326
Bright, Ray 27
Broadcast training 11-3, 45, 186, 188, 243, 277-9
Brooks, Neil 230
Brown, Bill 16

Brown, Ken 130
Brundage, Avery 228
Bryant, Bert 79, 100
Bucknor, Steve 360
Budd, Zola 199
Burgess, 'Baby John' 109
Burgess, Mark 218
Burke, Jimmy 216
Burns, Gary 116
Burns, Lauren 89
Burton, Mike 195
Burton, Richard 156
Butler, Terry 57

Cable, Barry 94
Calcavecchia, Mark 132
Campese, David 62
Carlaw, Dane 301
Carter, Jimmy 229
Cary, Garth 315
Casey, Ron (Melb) 29, 278
Casey ,Ron (Syd) 31
Catchpole, Ken 13, 227
Chappell, Greg 69-71, 140, 271, 306, 311
Chappell, Ian 2, 50, 67-77, 111, 140-1, 146, 271, 306, 311
Chappell, Martin 71
Charlton, Michael 25, 92, 273
Charlton, Tony 29
Chave, Alf 9
Chetkovich, Liz 281, 351, 352
Christie, Linford 152
Christison, David 202
Churchill, Clive 121

Clark, Greg 78-84, 360
Clark, Tim 135
Clayton, Derek 64-5
Clews, Gaylene 203
Clinch, Lindsay 45
Close, Chris 210
Closs, Don 14, 64
Coates, John 86
Coe, Sebastian 341
Collins, Bill 100, 197, 278
Collins, Gerry 85-91, 170, 172, 225
Cometti, Dennis 2, 11, 92-8, 122, 286, 343
Commonwealth Games 54, 75, 102, 105, 107-8, 111, 147, 153, 180, 187-8, 194, 203, 209, 224, 249, 252, 288, 319, 341-2, 349, 352-3
Compton, Dennis 22
Coney, Jeremy 218
Connell, Cyril 6, 56
Connors, Jimmy 334
Cook, Natalie 126
Cornelson, Greg 250
Cornish, Hugh 212
Couples, Fred 133, 265
Courier, Jim 164, 281
Coyne, Mark 313
Cozier, Tony 48, 141
Cram, Steve 341
Craven, Dr Danie 124
Cricket 8-11, 13, 19-21, 23-7, 43-4, 46-51, 58, 67, 69-71, 73-4, 76, 90, 93-4, 96-7, 111, 122, 124, 127, 137, 139-45, 148, 159-65, 168, 170-3, 176-8, 180, 183-6, 194, 214-7, 219-22, 225, 231-2, 237-8, 242, 245, 252-3, 270-3, 286, 294-5, 303, 305-11, 327, 338, 341-3, 346, 354, 358, 360
Critchley, Bruce 125, 135
Crowley, Dan 63, 161
Csortan, Laura 264
Currey, Vince 79, 208
Cutler, Steve 61
Cycling 116, 186-7, 190-1, 243-4, 343-4

Dahlberg, E.H. 28
Dakin, Ken 29, 341, 343
Darwin, Ben 360
Davidson, Alan 46
Davis, Ian 271
Davis, Reg 110-11, 123
Day, Jason 38, 135
Dawes-Smith, Peter 216
De Castella, Rob 180, 203
Deane, Jimmy 341
Decker, Mary 199
Delgado, Pedro 190
Dell, Donald 330
Denovan, Arthur 104, 358
Devers, Gail 102
Dexter, Ted 121
Dick, Leanne 277
Didak, Alan 95
Didham, Midge 106

Dimitric, Sacha 126
Dipierdomenico, Robert 126
Donald, Allan 168
Donegan, Peter 99-106
Doohan, Mick 114
Dooley, Dr Tom 212
Doubell, Ralph 16
Dowling, Greg 57, 326
Drysdale, Cliff 294, 297
Duckmanton, Sir Talbot 33
Dunning, Jack 71
Dunworth, David 156
Durack, Fanny 20
Dyer, Jack 279

Eales, John 351
Eastlake, Darrell 107-18
Edmond, Bob 112
Edmondson, Mark 172
Edwards, Ross 69
Egerzecki, Kristina 195
El Guerrouj, Hicham 201
Ella, Mark 63
Elliott, Doug 29, 278
Elliott, Herb 180
Els, Ernie 41, 135
Emerson, Roy 293
Equestrian 152, 336-7, 352
Evans, Peter 230
Evert, Chrissie 280
Expert analysis 300, 308, 316, 327, 330, 341, 345, 347, 349-50, 352-3, 357-9

Faine, Jon 185
Fairbairn, Clive 306

Fairweather, Simon 328
Faldo, Sir Nick 37, 285
Farmer, Graham 'Polly' 93, 340
Farr-Jones, Nick 63, 126
Farrelly, Midge 108
Farrington, John 64
Favell, Les 341
Federer, Roger 197, 281, 293, 295
Feherty, David 37
Fenton, Gary 243
Ferguson, June 345
Ferguson, Roy 88
Fernando, Dilhara 273
Fignon, Laurent 189
Fitzgerald, John 172, 330
Fitzgerald, Sarah 54
Fitzmaurice, Jim 12, 240
Fitzpatrick, Kate 346
Flack, Edwin 20, 234
Fleming, Damien 165, 238
Flemming, Jane 353
Flintoff, Andrew 51
Foley, Steve 245
Football (Aussie Rules) 8, 14, 28-9, 64, 88, 126, 171, 235, 240, 256, 303, 321, 328, 339, 354, 359
Fordham, David 110, 119-28, 159, 331
Foreman, Wally 11, 94
Forrest, Lisa 352
Fortune, Charles 231
Foster, Craig 262
Francis, Bruce 139
Fraser, Dawn 126, 150, 195, 233

Frazier, Joe 205
Freeman, Cathy 182, 196
Freeman, Eric 341
Freney, Mick 156
Fuad, Gordon 'Sheik' 165
Fuller, Lyn 71
Furber, Barry 109

Gajdasova, Jarmila 297
Galati, Dominic 261
Gale, Butch 279
Gallagher, Peter 109
Gardner, Wayne 114
Garner, Joel 309
Gasnier, Reg 121
Gavaskar, Sunil 74
Gavel, Tim 359
Gee, Peter 11, 102, 181
Geyer, Mark 325
Gibbs, Lance 70
Gibson, Mike 111
Gilchrist, Adam 166, 219, 289
Gildermeister, Hans 172
Gilligan, Arthur 23
Giltinan, James 20
Goggin, Billy 340
Golf 34-5, 37, 39-42, 44, 49, 64, 66, 80, 84, 102, 105, 125-131, 133, 147, 193, 200, 206, 213, 233, 263-269, 276, 279-80, 302, 317, 327
Gonzales, Francisco 281
Goosen, Retief 135
Gould, Phil 318
Grabham, Dave 133

Graddy, Sam 198
Grady, Wayne 42, 129-36, 164, 269
Graebner, Clark 293
Graf, Steffi 197
Graham, Jack 36
Graham, Mark 211
Grant, Hugh 221
Gray, Reg 29
Greedy, Terry 261
Gregory, Dave 20
Greig, Sandy 138
Greig, Tony 48, 71-3, 75, 126, 137-46, 311, 359
Grenda, Michael 244
Griffith-Joyner, Florence 'Flo-Jo' 199
Griffiths, Robbie 245
Grljusich, George 94, 146-54
Gross, Michael 85
Grosso, Fabio 262
Gymnastics 227, 276, 281, 344, 351-2

Hackett, Grant 195
Hadlee, Sir Richard 69
Hagon, Will 343
Hall, Gary Jnr 87
Hall, Wesley 46
Hamilton, Craig 251-2, 326
Hamilton, Gordon 63
Hammond, Jeff 70
Handball (team) 126
Handy, Chris 'Buddha' 63, 66, 120, 127, 155, 161, 287, 360

Harper, Andy 324
Hart, Vern 251
Harvey, Neil 218
Hassett, Lindsay 24
Hatton, Ricky 153
Hauff, Paul 325
Havers, Nigel 221
Hawke, Bob 287, 351
Hawksworth, Ron 101
Hay, Alex 130-1
Hayden, Matthew 167
Hayes-Bell, John 102
Healey, Dick 226
Healy, Ian 126, 162-9, 347, 359
Henzell, William 342
Hewitt, Bob 293
Hewitt, Lleyton 295
Heywood, Doug 9, 339, 341
Hill, David 48, 72, 75, 111-12, 294, 310
Hill, David (ABC and Soccer) 259
Hill, Mike 260
Hill, Simon 262
Hinault, Bernard 191
Hoad, Lew 339
Hockey 53-4, 66, 84, 202, 234
Hogg, Brad 237
Hohns, Trevor 166
Holding, Michael 69, 218, 309
Holmes, Tracey 353
Hooker, Hal 9, 22
Hopman, Harry 292
Horan, Michael 247

Horan, Tim 63, 161, 303
Horse Racing 17, 44, 101-2, 105, 151, 174, 189, 197-8, 251, 254
Hose, Ken 126
Howard, Ken 79, 314-5
Hoy, Andrew 153
Hristov, Alexander 148
Hudson, Anthony 359
Hudson, Nikki 126
Hughes, Graeme 81, 92
Hughes, Merv 53, 238
Hull, Alan 171
Hull, Quentin 17, 121, 170-6, 359
Hume, Ray 252
Humphries, Alan 13
Hunt, Geoff 15
Hunt, Rex 184, 279
Hurst, Keith 'Spaz' 114
Hutton, Sir Len 45
Hyde, Frank 2, 19, 30-2, 316, 318

Ikangaa, Juma 180-1
Ireland, Andrew 126
Ishikawa, Rio 135

Jack, Garry 253
Jackson, Grace 200
Jacobs, Tom 30
Jagger, Mick 274
Jardine, Douglas 21
Jayasuriya, Sanath 73-4
Jenner, Terry 341
Jesaulenko, Alex 126

Johansson, Kjell 'The Hammer' 15
John, Elton 221
Johnson, Ben 152, 198, 205
Johnson, Michael 204
Johnston, Dick 331
Johnston, Ian 30
Johnston, Brian 25, 27, 46, 217
Jones, Alan (Rugby coach) 66
Jones, Alan (Motor Racing) 114
Jones, Dean 127
Jones, Mat 38
Jones, Peter 326
Jones, Roy Jnr 149
Jong-Il, Byun 148
Jordan, Michael 197
Judo 53-4, 171, 174
Julian, Brendan 173

Kabbas, Robert 112
Kafer, Rod 82-3
Kallicharran, Alvin 70, 306
Kaluwitharana, Romesh 73
Kane, Justin 153
Kanhai, Rohan 46, 139
Kasprowicz, Michael 274
Kay, Andy 349
Kearns, Phil 82-3
Kelly, Ned 27
Kelly, Kev 324
Kelly, Sean 191
Kelly, Shane 244
Kenny, Grant 225
Kenny, Jim 155
Kerr, Bernie 10, 31, 232, 353

Kerry, Mark 230
Kewell, Harry 323
Khan, Imran 69
Kidman, Nicole 35
Kim, Jong-Il 289
Klusener, Lance 168
Knott, Alan 26
Kopliakov, Sergei 230
Kostis, Peter 37, 39
Komissaroff, Irina 104
Konrads, John 195
Korfball 177
Kosmina, John 260

Laidlaw, Renton 125
Laird, Ray 210
Landy, Peter 101, 334, 336
Lane, Samantha 185
Lane, Tim 2, 11, 177-85
Langer, Allan 302
Laver, Rod 294-5
Lawn Bowls 64, 239
Lawrence, Charles 19
Lawry, Bill 44, 69, 72-3, 141, 144, 242, 311, 359
Laws, John 332
Lawson, Geoff 73, 127, 219, 272
Lawson, Ross 32
Lawson, Toby 359
Leckie, David 108, 112, 144, 164
Lemond, Greg 189
Lewis, Carl 152, 198, 205
Lewis, Wally 56-7, 206, 211, 300-1, 325

Liberatore, Tony 96
Liggett, Phil 186-92, 343
Lillee, Dennis 27, 51, 69-70, 138, 217, 232, 237
Lindwall, Ray 24
Little, Elizabeth 348
Livingstone, Nicole 352
Lloyd, Clive 71
Lonergan, Dan 247, 359
Long, Colin 330
Longhurst, Henry 44, 266
Longman, Peter 181
Longo, Dominic 260
Lovejoy, George 32, 211
Lovely, Deborah 108
Lowe, Graham 81
Lowe, Ted 112
Loxton, Sam 29
Luge 187, 200
Lukin, Dean 108, 112
Lush, Ginty 44
Lynagh, Michael 62
Lyons, Joseph 8

Macatee, Bill 37
McAvaney, Bruce 96, 102, 122, 193-205
McCabe, Paul 301
McCall, Rupert 169, 317, 360
McCann, Heather 116
McCann, Kerryn 102, 249
McCarthy, Wendy 345
McCord, Gary 37, 40
McCormack, Mark 280
McCosker, Rick 271
McCoy, John 32, 206-13

McDonald, John 'Cracker' 210
McDonald, Malcolm 343
McEnroe, John 195, 197, 281, 291, 295
McEnroe, Patrick 297
McEwen, Robbie 188-9
McFarlane, Peter 220
Macgill, Stuart 237
McGilvray, Alan 1, 9, 13, 22-6, 88, 92, 94, 122, 183, 214-22, 231-2, 238, 240, 273, 286, 339-41
McGrath, Glen 165
McGrath, John 150
McGregor, Rod 8, 28
McGregor, Tom 208
McIntyre, Doug 32
McKenna, Peter 279
McKinley, Chuck 293
McLaren, Bill 62-3, 125, 342
McLenehan, Brian 332
McMahon, Sharelle 351
McMaster, Danny 210
McMullen, Geoff 13
Madden, Simon 279
Maguire, Eddie 184, 198, 346
Mahoney, Geoff 13, 251, 339
Major, Ian 94
Mandela, Nelson 124
Manjrekar, Sanjay 167
Manson, David 325
Maradona, Diego 340
Markovski, John 260
Marks, Alan 11, 13, 88, 148, 152, 327
Marquis, Peter 14

Marsh, Rod 51, 141, 306-7
Martin, Brian 103
Martin, Greg 81-4, 360
Maskell, Dan 44, 294
Mason, Dick 178, 241-2, 341, 343
Massie, Bob 69, 306, 341
Masters, Roy 55
Masur, Wally 330
Matthews, Leigh 279
Maurice, Ian 113
Maxwell, Jim 11, 13, 73, 183, 214-23, 250, 254, 273
May, Norman 'Nugget' 2, 11, 12, 32, 40, 69, 93, 96, 130-1, 224-235, 238, 240, 246, 286, 319, 339
May, Peter 231
Mayes, Jack 'Bluey' 114
Maynard, Bob 12-3
Meares, Peter 127, 207, 356
Melbourne Cup 99, 101-2, 106, 154, 193, 197-8, 204-5, 254, 311, 313, 360
Meninga, Mal 250, 300, 314
Merchant, Gordon 109
Merckx, Eddie 190
Messenger, Dally 20
Metassa, Fonda 32
Mickelson, Phil 134
Middleton, David 318
Miles, Gene 57, 300
Miles, Greg 91
Miller, Keith 44-5, 68, 77, 232
Miller, Johnny 132
Miller, Paul 153

Mitchell, Glenn 219, 273-4, 328, 353-4
Mohammed, Sadiq 69
Moneghetti, Steve 202
Moody, Peter 245
Moore, Brian 286, 326
More, Ivan 29
Mori, Damian 260
Morelli, Brian C 113
Morgan, Cliff 62
Morphett, Drew 11, 13, 105, 236-47, 327, 342
Morris, Mel 8, 28
Morrow, David 91, 248-54, 298, 324
Moses, Sir Charles 9, 21-2, 33, 226
Mossop, Rex 284, 316
Motor Racing 114, 193, 200, 284, 337, 355
Motorbike Racing 114
Mottram, Craig 195
Moulds, Laurie 253
Moyes, Johnnie 24, 44, 272, 343
Moyle, Roger 128
Muir, Barry 210
Mullinar, Rod 13
Mullineux, Rev Matthew 20
Murdoch, Rupert 113
Murphy, Paul 12, 15
Murray, Deryck 139
Murray, Les 146, 194, 255-62

Nantz, Jim 37, 39
Nastase, Ilie 202, 295

Navratilova, Martina 350
Neill, Lucas 262
Nelson, H.G. 146
Netball 283-4, 286, 344, 350-1, 355
Newcombe, John 329-30, 347-48, 350
Newman, Sam 184
Newton, Jack 39, 42, 49, 130, 263-69
Ngeny, Noah 201
Nicholas, Mark 162, 359
Nichols, Kevin 244
Nicholson, Andrew 152
Nicklaus, Jack 41, 197, 280
Noble, Monty 9, 21-2, 231, 240
Norman, Greg 41, 132, 280, 283, 285, 289, 322

O'Brien, Aiden 106
O'Callaghan, Gary 240
O'Connor, Michael 325
O'Donnell, Simon 77
Ogilvy, Geoff 38
O'Keeffe, Kerry 2-3, 73, 159, 214, 217-8, 223, 237, 270-75, 305, 307, 310, 327, 359
Oliver, Bert 11
Oliver, Damien 97
Olle, Andrew 12
Olympic Games 13, 20, 53-4, 84-5, 87, 89, 96, 102, 105, 114, 126, 147-8, 150, 152, 174-5, 182-3, 187-8, 191, 193, 195, 198-200, 205, 224-5, 228, 234-5, 243-4, 251, 260, 278-9, 281, 286, 288, 316, 327, 334, 336-7, 346, 349, 352-3
O'Neill John 91
O'Neill, Norman 46, 231-2, 245-6, 308
Oosterhuis, Peter 37
O'Reilly, Bill 'Tiger' 75
O'Reilly, John 11, 122, 250, 286, 315-6, 319, 339
O'Sullivan, Peter 44
Ovett, Steve 341

Packer, Kerry 48, 71, 111, 115, 117, 139-41
Pak, Se Ri 289
Pamensky, Joe 124
Papworth, Brett 33
Parkinson, Sir Michael 328
Parry, Craig 132
Patterson, Ric 14
Pay TV 28, 81, 105, 188, 206, 349, 356
Pearce, John 292
Pearce, Wayne 124
Pearse, Gary 63
Pearson, Sally 355
Pereira, Reds 219
Perkins, Kieren 87, 96, 195
Phillips, Bill 227
Pienaar, Francois 124
Pike, Benny 146-54
Plant, Robert 328

Platz, Greg 210
Player, Gary 41
Poidevin, Simon 63
Poll, Graham 262
Ponting, Ricky 222
Powell, Asafa 102
Power, Dave 180
Pratt, Kerryn 347-50, 359
Pratt, Larry 91, 104
Pratt, Nicole 347
Prenzler, Mike 210
Price, Nick 41
Prior-Palmer, Lucinda 336, 352
Pritchard, Bill 264
Prenzler, Mike 210

Quarrie, Don 342
Quinn, Keith 62-3, 125
Quinn, Paul 89

Radford, Bob 220
Rae, Vern 14
Rafter, Pat 126
Ralston, Dennis 293
Raymond, Andy 359
Raymond, Mike 331
Rebelledo, Pedro 172
Reardon, Jack 211
Renfry, Ern 241
Research 12, 61, 81, 90, 105-6, 123, 150, 188, 200-1, 227, 318, 330
Reynolds, Alan 225
Rhodes, 'Dusty' 138
Richards, Barry 219

Richards, Lou 29, 278-9
Richards, Sir Viv 219
Richardson, Bob 226
Richardson, Vic 9, 22-3, 71, 272
Richey, Cliff 293
Roberts, Tom 122
Roberts, Sandy 39, 101, 122, 276-82, 352
Robilliard, Steve 33, 283-90, 351
Robinson, Susie 105
Roche, Stephen 190
Roche, Tony 329-30
Rodd, Michael 99
Rodianova, Anastasia 297
Roebuck, Peter 219, 237, 272
Rogowska, Olivia 297
Rolton, Gill 153
Rose, Lionel 233
Rose, Murray 195
Rosewall, Ken 9, 295, 339
Royal, Martin 259
Roycroft, Bill 153
Roycroft, Wayne 153
Rugby League 5-6, 13, 20, 30-2, 52, 54-9, 78, 80-2, 88-90, 109-10, 113, 122, 124-7, 171, 206-11, 248-52, 256-7, 267, 269, 286, 298-301, 303, 312-4, 316, 322, 324, 328, 340, 345-6, 358
Rugby Union 13, 32, 60-1, 78, 81, 90, 175, 225-6, 232, 235, 250, 284

Ryan, Matt 152-3
Ryan, Warren 251-2, 325-6

Salnikov, Vladimir 195
Santana, Manolo 294
Sargeant, Anne 287, 350-1
Saunders, David 189
Schwartzer, Mark 324
Scott, Bob 110
Scott, Gordon 11
Scott-Young, Sam 81
Senior, Peter 133
Seixas, Vic 17, 339
Sexton, John 12
Shalala, Amanda 290
Shahanga, Gidamas 177, 180-1
Sharapova, Maria 350
Sharland, Wally 'Jumbo' 8, 28
Sharpe, Nathan 83
Sheahan, Paul 27
Sheene, Barry 114, 116
Sheepdog Trials 107, 117
Sheridan, Tim 348
Sherwin, Paul 189
Shew, Georgie 264
Shriver, Pam 330, 347
Si-Hun, Park 149
Sieben, Jon 244
Sim, Michael 38, 135
Simpson, Bob 231
Sitch, Rob 205
Skase, Christopher 242, 266
Speed Skating 187
Ski-jumping 187
Slater, Billy 314
Slater, Michael 359

Slaven, Roy 146
Smallicombe, Bill 7
Smith, Billy J. 32, 208
Smith, Brian 81, 326
Smith, Calvin 152
Smith, Paul 133
Smith, Terry 66
Smith, Tony 302
Snow, John 69
Sobers, Sir Garfield 46, 139
Soccer (Football) 84, 121, 171, 194, 204, 241, 252, 255-60, 286, 321-3, 325, 328, 336, 340
Spillane, Debbie 345
Squash 15, 53-4, 344
Squires, Tony 327
Stackpole, Keith 141
Starmer-Smith, Nigel 125
Startin, Andrew 205
Statham, Brian 138
Sterling, Peter 127, 300, 317-8
Stevens, Max 101
Stolle, Fred 291-7, 327, 347-8
Stone, Allan 334, 336
Stosur, Sam 296
Stuart, Ricky 250
Surtees, Brian 315
Sutcliffe, Ken 111
Swimming 85, 87, 90, 96, 185, 228, 230, 319, 344, 352, 359
Symond, John 61
Symonds, Andrew 90
'Synthetic' broadcasts 21-2

Table Tennis 15, 84, 105, 342, 349
Tae Kwon Do 89, 102
Tapp, Johnny 194, 315
Taylor, Mark 126, 166, 347
Tennis 13, 44, 54, 64, 66, 76-7, 80, 84, 105, 145, 164, 170-2, 193, 197, 200-1, 208, 213, 254, 279-80, 284-5, 291-2, 294-6, 327, 329-31, 333-7, 342-3, 337, 342-3, 347-50, 353-4, 359, 361
Thevener, Barnard 189
Thomas, Ted 333
Thompson, Daley 204, 341-2
Thomson, Eddie 260
Thomson, Jeff 138, 220
Thomson, Peter 39
Thornett, Dick 13, 233
Thorpe, Ian 87, 319
Throsby, Margaret 13, 64
Thurtell, Simone 353
Tighe, Karen 327, 353
Tilghman, Kelly 37, 40
Tinling, Ted 330
Tipper, Trish 187
Titus, Ray 220
Tonelli, Mark 230
Torrance, Sam 130
Towers, Cyril 13, 32
Trabert, Tony 9, 295, 349
Trevino, Lee 76
Triathlon 187
Trueman, Freddie 48-9, 218, 245, 343

Tucker, Tommy 335
Tune, Ben 360
Tuqiri, Lote 82
Turtur, Michael 244
Tyler, Martin 262, 286
Tyson, Frank 141
Tzu, Kostya 153

Underwood, Kelli 17, 354-5
Urban, Keith 35
Urge, Laszlo – see Murray, Les 255

Van Der Haar, Paul 279
Vaughan, Michael 51
Vautin, Paul 'Fatty' 298-304, 314, 317-8
Vegas, Jhonattan 135
Venables, Terry 323
Verockin, Michelle 221
Viduka, Mark 323
Vine, David 111-2
Viren, Lasse 243
Vogels, Henk 188
Voice 15, 24-26, 30-1, 34, 39, 43, 49-50, 60, 73, 86-7, 89, 92, 103, 108, 129-30, 159, 161, 164, 178, 183, 186-7, 207, 209, 213-5, 218, 238, 246, 250, 252-3, 256, 290, 308, 312-5, 319, 326-8, 352, 357-8
Volleyball 54, 106
Voukelatis, Nick 112

Wade, Doug 340

Wade, Virginia 347
Walker, Billy 94
Walker, John 202, 342
Walker, Keith 148
Walker, Max 48, 69-70, 141, 305-11
Walsh, Peter 222, 343, 359
Walsh, Sharon 335
Walters, Doug 27, 219, 232, 302
Warne, Shane 163, 359
Warren, Johnny 146, 256-7, 259-60
Warren, Ray 2, 81, 300, 312-20
Water Polo 83, 344
Water Skiing 102
Watkins, John 69
Watson, Shane 346-7
Watson, Tom 264
Watt, Len 21
Waugh, Bob 109
Weekes, Robbie 341
Weightlifting 107-8, 111-2
West, Peter 46
Westwood, Lee 136
Whately, Gerard 105, 247
White, Derek 251
White, Johnny 7
Whitington, Dick 44
Whitten, Ted 279
Wilkins, Peter 321-8
Wilkins, Phil 220
Wilkinson, Garry 329-37
Wilkinson, Johnny 62
Willesee, Mike 333
Willey, Peter 218

Williams, Cameron 337
Williams, Steve 131
Williamson, Mike 279, 333
Willis, Bob 271
Wills, Roger 11, 338-43
Wills, Tom 98
Wilson, Vicki 126
Wodjat, Arthur 85
Woodley, Bruce 223
Woods, Dean 244
Woods, Tiger 40, 131, 197
Woodforde, Mark 348
Woodward, Jim 220
Worrell, Sir Frank 46, 343
Wright, David 52, 127
Wyndham, Arthur 10

Yachting 15, 80
Young, Nat 108

Zelic, Ned 260
Zivojinovic, Slobodan 'Bobo' 296

www.ingramcontent.com/pod-product-compliance
Lightning Source LLC
Chambersburg PA
CBHW022026290426
44109CB00014B/762